THE EYE OF THE STORM

THE EYE OF THE STORM

Living Spiritually in the Real World

Kenneth Leech

HarperSanFrancisco
A Division of HarperCollins*Publishers*

THE EYE OF THE STORM: *Living Spiritually in the Real World*.
Copyright © 1992 by Kenneth Leech. All rights reserved. No part of
this book may be used or reproduced in any in any manner whatsoever
without written permission except in the case of brief quotations embodied in critical articles and reviews. For information address
HarperCollins Publishers, 10 East 53rd Street, New York, NY 10022.
FIRST EDITION

Library of Congress Cataloging-in-Publication Data

Leech, Kenneth.
   The eye of the storm : living spiritually in the real world / Kenneth
Leech — 1st ed.
      p.   cm.
   Includes bibliographical references.
   ISBN 0–06–065208–X (alk. paper)
   1. Spirituality. 2. Church and social problems. I. Title.
BV4501.2.L42575   1991
248.4'83—dc20
                                                                  90–56453
                                                                     CIP

92 93 94 95 96 ❖ HCMG 10 9 8 7 6 5 4 3 2 1

Manufactured in the United Kingdom by HarperCollins.

This edition is printed on acid-free paper that meets the American
National Standards Institute Z39.48 Standard.

CONTENTS

We theorise and construct in the eye of the storm.
ERNST TROELTSCH, 1922

There is a bird called the stormy petrel, and that is what I am.
When in a generation storms begin to gather,
individuals of my type appear.
SØREN KIERKEGAARD, 1845

Behold, the storm of the Lord! . . .
In the latter days you will understand it clearly.
JEREMIAH 23:19, 20

PREFACE

A central theme in my writing over the years has been the essential unity of Christian spirituality and Christian social and political commitment. I am, frankly, appalled at the way in which "spirituality" is being promoted as a way of avoiding and evading the demands of justice and of struggle for a more equal world. Nor do I find the interminable discussions about the need to "unite spirituality and social action" very hopeful. Indeed I find the very debate about "bringing together" these two "dimensions" an increasingly unreal one, since it seems to presuppose the very fragmentation that I reject. I believe in fact that the whole notion of something called "spirituality" and something else called "the social gospel" has done very great damage to Christian consciousness. The recovery of theological wholeness is necessary if we are to avoid these false polarities. That is what this book is about.

There are several aspects of the book that call for explanation. First, I have deliberately drawn on experience within the British scene, and specifically within London, particularly in chapters 3 and 4. Though some of this material may be unfamiliar to the American audience, I believe it is important to begin from one's own context. Almost all of my ministry, and much of my adult life, has been spent in the East End of London: that is my context, theologically and pastorally. It is there that I have learned to pray, and there that my theology has been put to the test. I have therefore located the discussion of social and political issues within this context, and I invite my American readers to make the connections. It seems better always to write from the situation one knows best, and it is often when one speaks most personally and concretely that one finds connections being forged with people from very different backgrounds. In any case all theological work is contextual, and I believe it to be necessary to make this context clear.

In chapter 4 I have drawn on the insights of a number of writers and thinkers who helped to shape my understanding. All of us are, to a great extent, the products of such influences, and it is important to identify them and to be grateful for them. I therefore invite my readers to reflect on the influences on their own lives and their own understandings of these matters. It is also important to say that I write as an Anglican, a member of that small Christian tradition whose origins lie in England and that has stressed strongly the incarnational and sacramental roots of both spiritual and social life. I have no wish to present Anglicanism as the way for all people, or as a model for the Christian world, but I do believe it has insights that are urgently needed in the present crisis of spirituality in all Christian churches.

Some of the material in chapter 3 was given at seminars in the Universities of Essex and Edinburgh. The material on "Thatcherism" and Christian theology appears in a more developed form in a collection on fundamentalism and tolerance published in 1991 for the Centre for the Study of Theology at the University of Essex; that on Anglo-Catholic socialism is more fully developed in many of my articles for the Jubilee Group in Britain, especially in a pamphlet, "The Catholic Social Conscience: Two Critical Essays" (London, Jubilee Group, 1991).

I am grateful to the Archivist of the University of Hull for the use of material on Canon Stanley Evans, some of which is referred to in chapter 4; to Carl Leech and Emmett Jarrett for comments on chapter 1; to Janet Batsleer, Sara Maitland, and David Randall for reading and commenting on chapter 2; and to members of the "Launde Abbey cell" of the Jubilee Group—Jenny Barrett, Janet Batsleer, Sabine Butzlaff, Alan Green, Ros Hunt, and Sara Maitland—with whom I was able to share many of the ideas in this book over several years in our times together. Most of all, I thank Rheta and Carl for their support and their patience while it was all being completed.

Kenneth Leech
Saint Botolph's Church, Aldgate, London
The Birthday of Saint John the Baptist, 1991

1

THE SOUL AND THE SOCIAL ORDER
The Crisis of Modern Spirituality

Talking to young people about their interest in the occult and science fiction, and the success of films like *Alien* and *The Omen*, it appears that a whole generation has been delivered to private enterprise for their most exalted spiritual experiences. The material obsessions of the world in which they have grown failed to extinguish their spiritual needs; these are being met, not by religion, but by the artifacts of the same world, the film and junk fiction industries.

JEREMY SEABROOK

A certain zaddick died, and soon after appeared in a dream to Rabbi Pinhas who had been his friend. Rabbi Pinhas asked him: "What is the attitude toward the sins of youth?" "They are not taken seriously," said the dead man, "not if a man has atoned. But false piety—that is punished with great severity."

HASIDIC TALE

The term "spirituality" is experiencing a comeback. The phenomenon of prayer and interest in adult spirituality is clearly at the forefront of American culture today.

MATTHEW FOX

Almost seventy years ago G. A. Studdert Kennedy ("Woodbine Willie"), probably at the time the best-known clergyman in Britain, told a church congress,

> A very large number of the people who attend our services and partake of the sacraments are disassociated personalities. They are one person on Sunday and another on Monday. They have one mind for the sanctuary and another for the street. They have one conscience for the church and another for the cotton factory. Their worship conflicts with their work, but they will not acknowledge the conflict. I want to press home what seems to me to be obvious, that while this unfaced conflict exists, the soul is not on the road to salvation.[1]

His words have a depressingly familiar ring in the climate of the 1990s. In a recent study Langdon Gilkey has claimed that there seems to be "the same deep split in our day as there was half a century ago between an individual and a social interpretation of the Christian religion." Gilkey goes on to argue that "the deepest substantive question of current theology is . . . the mediation of this false opposition, an opposition untrue both to scripture and to an adequate theological interpretation of history and of human destiny."[2] Midway between these two writers stands the major watershed of the Second World War. Since the end of that war, and the collapse or eclipse of earlier Christian social movements, there has been a return to individualistic and private understandings, followed since the 1960s and 1970s by a renewal of concern, in a variety of Christian traditions, for a reintegration of soul and society, prayer and politics, mystical and prophetic dimensions of Christian life. It is with this renewal that I shall be concerned in this book.

"Spirituality" and "the Inner Life"

It is not difficult to be cynical about the current vogue of "spirituality." Undoubtedly it is a fashionable concern, certainly a growth area for the religious book trade. Spirituality is "in" again; there is a lot of it about. But what is it? What do people mean when they speak of "spirituality"? Certainly today, in contrast to the atmosphere of the early 1960s when the word "spiritual" was identified with escapist pietism and with a retreat from the needs and demands of the world, there is a resurgence of interest in prayer, devotion, techniques of meditation, ascetical practices, and the "inner life" in most sections of the church. When Christians speak of spirituality, it is this inward quest to which they usually refer.

However, the word has come to be used in so general and vague a way that its continued usefulness needs to be questioned. William Stringfellow indicated something of the conceptual sloppiness and confusion surrounding it:

> "Spirituality" may indicate stoic attitudes, occult phenomena, the practice of so-called mind control, yoga discipline, escapist fantasies, interior journeys, an appreciation of Eastern religions, multifarious pious exercises, superstitious imaginations, intensive journals, dynamic muscle tension, assorted dietary regimens, meditation, jogging cults, monastic rigors, mortification of the flesh, wilderness sojourns, political resistance, contemplation, abstinence, hospitality, a vocation of poverty, non-violence, silence, the efforts of prayer, obedience, generosity, exhibiting stigmata, entering solitude, or, I suppose, among these and many other things, squatting on top of a pillar.[3]

It is therefore necessary to sound a warning. Much of the current interest in the realm of the spirit is of a superficial and bizarre kind, and there seems little reason to welcome it. The spiritual world is not universally benign. Without careful cultivation and discipline, it can be extremely dangerous. Those who are tempted to shout, "Hooray! Spirituality is in again!" need to realize that "spirituality" can be a dangerous diversion from the living God, from the demands of justice, from the engagement with reality. It can be a form of illusion.

Today "spirituality" is marketed as a product, in competition with others, on the book stalls. It belongs to the area of "private life." And it would be foolish to deny that this "private" approach to religion has roots within Western Christianity. For within Western societies religion itself has come to be seen as an option, one of the wide range of choices that consumerism offers. Spirituality is widely seen not as a way of living in every sphere but as a sphere in its own right: "the spiritual dimension." The action of God is thus confined within extremely narrow limits. It is not surprising that in much of the popular literature that has emerged from the spiritual revival of recent years, prayer and meditation are offered as ways of coping with existing reality, not as ways to change it.

> With some notable exceptions . . . books of popular spirituality treat prayer and spiritual exercises as personal and private, having to do with the relationship between the individual and God. By this privatization of spirituality the relationship between prayer and social and political activity is not addressed. The net result, whatever the intention of the authors or compilers, is the reinforcement of the status quo, as religious energy is poured into personal holiness rather than social justice.[4]

One common way of describing the fate of spirituality is by use of the concept of dualism: the dualism of soul and body, of public and private, of sacred and secular. If we consider the history of the Christian tradition we will recognize a persistent element within it that is dualist, locating the spiritual realm in a dimension separate from, and superior to, the world of flesh and matter. Margaret Miles has shown how such distorted ideas influenced, and at times dominated, the manuals of Christian devotion.[5] Thus Thomas à Kempis's *Imitation of Christ,* for centuries more popular than the Bible itself among Roman Catholics, offers an understanding of the Christian life that despises passion, emotion, desire, and the body itself, and regards human beings as hindrances to the encounter with God that occurs within the soul.

But in Western culture it is not only dualism but also pluralism that presents the problem. Within a plural society, spirituality has become simply one option among many, and increasingly a marginal option. It belongs within the realm of individual choices, not within the realm of public activity. Of all the distortions of Christian faith and discipleship, it is individualism that has most deeply penetrated the American spiritual consciousness. Even within the Catholic tradition, in which the ideas of the Mystical Body of Christ and the solidarity of the eucharistic sacrifice have been such important features, the sense of the sacred has increasingly shifted from the community to the self.

The church becomes simply an association of individuals. Even redemption is described by one Roman Catholic writer as "just another name for learning the lessons of intimacy."[6] Individualism goes very deep in American history and constantly assumes new forms. Thomas Merton described it as "an economic concept with a pseudo-spiritual and moral facade,"[7] and though historians differ on the details, it is clear that religious individualism and the growth of capitalism are related.[8] Individualist ideology is so central in American religious life that it has become virtually impossible to disentangle its assumptions from the language of Christianity itself. Yet it really does represent a cleavage with the worldview of traditional Christianity.

In fact it is essential to emphasize that, in traditional Christian understanding, there can be no "private" spirituality. The word *private*, with its origins in *privatio*, "robbery," is not a Christian word at all. Nor does individualism find any place within the spiritual climate of the Scriptures. The repudiation of individualism and of a spirituality deriving from it was a central feature of Michael Ramsey's seminal study *The Gospel and the Catholic Church*, published in 1936. "Individualism," wrote Ramsey, "has no place in Christianity, and Christianity verily means its extinction."[9] A recent writer has made the same point with equal force:

> Individualism is incompatible with Christian spirituality.
> None can possess the Spirit as an individual but only as a
> member of the community. When the Spirit blows, the result
> is never to create good individual Christians but members of
> a community. This became fundamental for Christian spiri-
> tuality in the New Testament and was in direct line with the
> Old Testament mentality.[10]

To be a Christian at all is to be incorporated into this body which is Christ. At its very heart the Christian life and identity is a process of incorporation into a new social organism, a new community. Spirituality cannot exist apart from this social context.

Linked with the individualistic ethos is the notion of a spiritual realm that is unconnected with the spheres of politics and economics, a pure world of the spirit that exists in its own right. On this understanding, "spirituality" and "politics" do not relate. This view too is extremely modern and highly suspect. It would, for example, have astounded Christians in the Middle Ages.

> If you had told any typical Christian thinker in any century from the twelfth to the sixteenth that religion had nothing to do with economics and that bishops must not intrude in these matters upon the deliberations of laymen—propositions which to many of the correspondents to our newspapers appear to be axiomatic—he would either have trembled for your faith or feared for your reason. He would have regarded you, in short, as either a heretic or a lunatic.[11]

To remind ourselves of this is not in any way to suggest a return to medieval approaches, but it is to insist on the very modern character of the individualism that we take so easily for granted.

In fact the notion of an "inner life" that exists as an entity in its own right is a modern one. The idea of a segment of religious life labeled "spirituality" or "the inner life" that was somehow different from, or to be added to, the life of the Christian or any other person would have been unthinkable in the early centuries of the Christian movement. Only after the thirteenth century did "spirituality" become divorced from the Christian life as a whole. From the thirteenth century the distinction between natural and supernatural had encouraged a dualism of a kind unknown to the early church. The concern with "the inner life" as a developed and specialized compartment of Christian study probably dates from the Renaissance, though there are elements of such ideas in early Gnostic thought and in some of the medieval movements. It is clear that such notions affected Catholic spirituality in the post-Tridentine period.

Indeed the very use of the word *spirituality* is modern, and "the confident modern use of the word is . . . *very* modern."[12] The origins of the word lie in seventeenth-century France, and it was taken up by the English writer F. P. Harton in his study *The Elements of the Spiritual Life* in 1932. By this time the notion of a "spiritual life" as a world apart was firmly established, at least within the Western Catholic tradition.

Long before the age of liberal pluralism, mainstream spiritual theology had been influenced, and damaged, by the dualism of soul and body that we have come to associate with the Gnostic and Manichaean heresies. Thus in the literature of the inner life within the Catholic tradition since the sixteenth century we find that most of the discussion is about "the soul" as if this were somehow different from the human person. "The soul" is seen as the site of the divine action. As we read this literature what strikes us is the loss of historical substance and the "spiritualizing" of the language of grace. It is the inner life, the life of the soul, that really matters, and it is here, rather than in the rough-and-tumble of social life, that grace is seen to operate. Often linked with this inward focus is an elitism of the kind that we see in writers such as William James and Baron von Hügel where direct experience of God ("mysticism") seems to be reserved for a small segment of humanity. Spirituality more and more came to be seen as an occupation for the leisured middle class and for those with a special vocation to climb the higher steps of the spiritual ladder. For the "ordinary Christian" it was not seen as relevant. Within Catholicism, contemplative prayer, spiritual direction, and the writings of the mystics were seen as belonging to an "advanced" stage of Christian life, while the poor and ordinary Christian was encouraged to hear Mass, say the Rosary, and be content with the little manuals of devotion. Within other parts of the Christian community the dominance of liberalism and the rational spirit led to the location of "spirituality" on the margins of the church; among both evangelicals and liberals any reference to "mysticism" was likely to lead to suspicions of the esoteric, the occult, and an ethos at odds with the gospel.

The Importance of the Counterculture

The contemporary revolt against an excessively cerebral and activist understanding of religion came initially from outside the Christian community. The revived thirst for the mystical in the later years of the nineteenth century was manifested in the work of H. P. Blavatsky and the growth of theosophy, and there was a revival of many esoteric cults in Britain during the early years of the twentieth century. Reaction against rational and scientific reductionism had set in by the 1940s, when Aldous Huxley was complaining that mysticism was dying and that Western society was "dangerously far advanced into the

darkness."[13] Huxley in a number of ways anticipated the counterculture of the 1960s, not least in his quest for "the chemical conditions
of transcendental experience."[14] Yet during these years mainstream
Christian thought paid little attention to the need for spiritual resources. Of course, there were exceptions. In 1948 Thomas Merton
was insisting that mysticism was part of the "normal" Christian life.[15]
But these were words uttered in a religious wilderness, and they were
not heard until the spiritual revival of the late 1960s forced the issue
upon the Christian community.

In 1966 Ken Kesey and his Merry Pranksters took the drug LSD,
got hold of some electronic equipment, and moved into the Haight-
Ashbury district of San Francisco.[16] The result was a record album
called *The Acid Test*, and it heralded the public beginning of the
psychedelic culture that quickly transformed whole areas of Western
society. Out of the Haight-Ashbury came the San Francisco sound,
acid rock music, developed by groups such as Jefferson Airplane and
the Grateful Dead. A whole new language was born, and terms like
hippie, turn on, psychedelic, and *drop out* entered the popular vocabulary.
Around the Haight-Ashbury grew a peaceful community of "flower
children." Haight Means Love was painted on walls. Soon the use of
psychedelic and other drugs spread throughout Europe as well as the
United States, and "dropping out" became a widespread social phenomenon. The quest for alternative lifestyles led to the growth of a
complex structure known as "the underground" or "the alternative society" with its own methods of communication and its own literature.
Out of the original hippie culture emerged a series of spiritual movements that are of tremendous importance for understanding the contemporary search for faith and spirituality among young people.

It would be wrong to see the psychedelic drug culture simply as a
revolt against technocratic society. In one sense the chemical approach
to consciousness is a mainstream Western phenomenon, a by-product
of a revolution in pharmacology. Timothy Leary and Alan Watts, who
promoted the use of psychedelic drugs for spiritual development, represented a particular form of the "better living through chemistry" thesis that is so inseparable from mainstream Western society. Our
drug-oriented culture has assumed that there is a chemical solution to
all human problems. Between 1965 and 1970 in Britain, the same

period that saw the emergence of the counterculture, there was a 220 percent increase in medical prescribing of the minor tranquilizers, described by one physician as "a pharmacological [lobotomy] on a large section of contemporary society." By 1970, 47.2 million prescriptions for psychotropic or mood-altering drugs were issued in England and Wales alone, amounting to some three billion pills.[17] Far from being a straightforward radical rejection of the dominant culture, in some respects the psychedelic drug cult represented the development of one aspect of this culture, its reliance on chemical solutions. As the American writer Theodore Roszak wrote in 1968, "The gadget-happy American has always been a figure of fun because of his facile assumption that there exists a technological solution to every human problem. It took only the great psychedelic crusade to perfect the absurdity by proclaiming that personal salvation and the social revolution can be packed into a capsule."[18]

However, while it is wrong to see the use of LSD as an alien growth against the dominant culture—it was, after all, introduced into psychiatric medicine at Powick Hospital in Worcestershire some thirteen years before the hippies in San Francisco discovered it![19]—there is no doubt that it did provide a bridge from this culture to a new position that has attracted increasing numbers of people. As one Indian guru told Richard Alpert, the materialistic country of America wanted its avatar in the form of a material, and so they got LSD.[20]

In a detailed study of spirituality in the counterculture published almost twenty years ago, I attempted to describe the shape of the emerging spirituality under four main headings.

1. The resurgence of Eastern mystical traditions: Zen, Hindu Yoga, Sufism, as well as Westernized movements and Westernized gurus—Maharishi Mahesh Yogi and Transcendental Meditation, Krishna Consciousness, Meher Baba, guru Maharaj Ji, and so on. Recent years have seen the continued growth of most of these movements.

2. The resurgence of the occult and magical movements: astrology, witchcraft, various occult sciences, the ancient British myths around Glastonbury, and a very wide range of "new age" cults.

3. The quest for new forms of community, alternative lifestyles, and earth-based spirituality: communes; the beginnings of the ecological movement; women's liberation; alternative newspapers, bookstores, and networks of information.

4. The renewal of various contemporary forms of Christianity, including both a new fundamentalism (the Jesus movements) and a new radicalism (the "underground church").[21]

As I look back over the spiritual currents of the last twenty years, it becomes clear that the significant movements have occurred in precisely these four areas that were central to the counterculture of the 1960s.

One of the most important intellectual influences on the alternative spiritual quest was the psychiatrist (or "anti-psychiatrist," as he at one stage preferred to be called) R. D. Laing. For Laing, who had devoted many years to the study of schizophrenia, Western materialism and technocracy represented the death of the soul. Our culture was dying because of its lack of access to experiences of the transcendent. Laing believed that true sanity must involve the dissolution of the normal ego. In his best-selling work *The Politics of Experience*, published as the hippie culture of the Haight-Ashbury was exploding upon the world, he pointed to the spiritual deprivation of the age: "We live in a secular world. To adapt to this world the child abdicates its ecstasy. Having lost our experience of the spirit, we are expected to have faith. But this faith comes to be a belief in a reality which is not evident. There is a prophecy in Amos that there will be a time when there will be a famine in the land, 'not a famine for bread, nor a thirst for water, but of hearing the words of the Lord ' (Amos 8:11). That time has now come to pass. It is the present age."[22] Laing saw that, in a culture as deprived and undernourished as ours, transcendental experience sometimes breaks through in the experiences that are termed *psychosis* or *madness,* and he sought to relate the journey of madness to the experiences of the divine in all living faiths. The heart of his work was a questioning of conventional interpretations of psychosis. Madness, he claimed, was a journey and an experience, not a sickness. Moreover, the experience of madness might be closer to the mystical quest than the experience of the "sane." The transcendence of the ego was the aim of the great world religions, and it was the loss of a spiritual framework that was central to the human crisis.[23]

In the years after Laing's book, others pursued these themes. Theodore Roszak, who had made his name with a critical account of the counterculture, followed it with a prophetic, but neglected, study entitled *Where the Wasteland Ends*, in which he argued that the religious dimension had been exiled from Western culture and that technocracy and scientific materialism had led to the starvation of the human spirit. "The expertise we bow before derives from a diminished mode of consciousness." Yet, Roszak suggested, "We have arrived, after long journeying, at an historical vantage point from which we can at last see where the wasteland ends and where a culture of human wholeness and fulfillment begins. We can now recognize that the fate of the soul is the fate of the social order; that if the spirit within us withers, so too will all the world we build about us. . . . It is the energy of religious renewal that will generate the next politics, and perhaps the final radicalism of our society."[24] So, as the communications theorist Marshall McLuhan was telling us that we were "heading into a profoundly religious age"[25] and the Viennese psychiatrist Viktor Frankl was warning that "the spiritual dimension cannot be ignored, for it is what makes us human,"[26] the economist E. F. Schumacher attacked the autonomy of the economists, the high priests of materialism, and called for a renewal of spirituality. In a book that was to become the bible of the green movement, he wrote, "The guidance we need for this work cannot be found in science or technology, the value of which utterly depends on the ends they serve, but it can still be found in the traditional wisdom of mankind."[27] In writings such as these can be found the early indications of an emerging politics of identity and a spirituality that took ecological and related issues on board.

Of course, there was, and still is, a great deal of overstatement and exaggeration of the impact of the counterculture. Data that relate to a small minority of people in certain locations are applied to whole cultures and social groups. Charles Reich's important study *The Greening of America* was an extreme example of the naïveté with which many adults viewed the emerging counterculture: "Whatever it touches, it beautifies and renews," he claimed, and went on to say that "in time it will include not only youth but all people in America."[28] A few years later Joseph Needleman claimed that the contemporary disillusionment with religion had revealed itself to be a religious disillusionment.[29] However, to claim that there was a concern with religion and spirituality among the young is quite different from claiming that the entire "youth culture" (itself a questionable concept) was involved in an explicitly spiritual quest. Data from California or Central London are not a reliable guide to what is happening elsewhere. As a critic of my own early work observed, "Life in Burslem, Tadcaster and Crewe was remarkably unaffected."[30]

Moreover, the growth of counterculture spirituality did not basically alter the dualistic framework of Western thought in this area. Much of it was a return to ancient Gnosticism, with the classic concern with techniques. Christopher Lasch was soon to speak of a "culture of narcissism" in which people lived for self and for the moment. There was a loss of any sense of historical continuity, any sense of belonging. It was this loss, Lasch claimed, that was central to "the spiritual crisis of the seventies."[31]

Yet the years of the counterculture saw also a profound quest for community and for a visionary politics. This was an era of communes, of utopian dreams, of cooperation and solidarity. Reich wrote of the movement as "the greening of America" and claimed that the new spirituality had "emerged out of the wasteland of the corporate state, like flowers pushing up through the concrete pavement."[32] Roszak saw the possibility of a religious renewal that would provide the basis for a new politics that could move beyond the wasteland of the present.[33] Of course, much of this hopefulness and vision has turned to disillusionment and despair. Yet it is quite wrong to dismiss the counterculture as a cul-de-sac, a road that led nowhere. At its heart was "an entire culture of disaffiliation,"[34] a cultural constellation that broke with the dominant values and assumptions that had governed Western society since the seventeenth century. The processes of disaffiliation from, and cynicism about, mainstream politics and the dominant culture have now become more pervasive and form the basis for many present critiques and developments.

Inevitably much has been trivialized. It is ironic that many of the texts, and much of the thinking, of counterculture spirituality have now been absorbed into the new capitalism, into management training, and into the enterprise culture. It would be a serious mistake, however, to blame "the sixties," or even the twentieth century, for the debasement of spirituality, its reduction to technology and method. The process of marginalization and trivialization has taken place over centuries. There has been the phenomenon of minimalism, with its concern about how much is needed in order to be saved, or, in secular terms, to survive. A French tract of the late eighteenth century entitled *Comment éviter le Purgatoire (How to Avoid Purgatory)* recommended that Christian people should perform an act of charity at least once every five years![35] It was to a large extent the trivial nature of spirituality of this type that led to the revolt against it in the first place.

By the early 1970s the renewal of concern with spirituality had spread to the church and to some of its most politically active members. In 1973 a conference took place in Huddersfield, England, entitled Seeds of Liberation. It attracted nearly four hundred people, mainly young Christians who were concerned with the recovery of spiritual resources for political struggle. The tradition of American Christian radicalism was present in the persons of Daniel Berrigan and Jim Forrest; the communities of resistance in southern Africa were represented by Colin Winter, the exiled Anglican bishop from Namibia; the Benedictine monk Thomas Cullinan reflected the unity of solitude and solidarity. Throughout the conference, as throughout the movement as a whole, the figure of Thomas Merton (who had died in 1968) was a source of inspiration and influence. Prayer was seen as a way of renewing strength, a neglected resource for struggle. As one of those present explained, "The reexamination required was not so much a cerebral critique of theology or politics but a flesh and blood discovery of spiritual roots."[36] Another participant, an academic theologian, noted, "A new term has entered the vocabulary of politically radical Christians in Britain—spirituality. Willingness to look again at this area, an area previously regarded as alien to activism, reflects the mood of the moment."[37]

Christopher Lasch was one of those who claimed that the rebirth of "spirituality" was directly related to the superficial character of the radicalism of the preceding years. "It is essential to realize that the 'inner revolution of the Seventies' . . . grew in part out of an awareness that the radicalism of the Sixties had failed to address itself to the quality of personal life or to cultural questions in the mistaken belief that questions of 'personal growth' . . . could wait until 'after the revolution.' "[38] Lasch here falls into the modern trap of identifying spirituality with "personal growth." Yet he is surely correct in recognizing that much of the radicalism of the 1960s was superficial, rootless, naively optimistic, and gradualist and had little sense of the importance of fundamental beliefs and of spiritual roots. In this it was perpetuating a tradition that went back some considerable time. In spite of this, it was part of the achievement of the 1960s to begin the process of reintegration of these wrongly separated areas.

The Culture of False Inwardness

Today among Christians in the West there is a rebirth of self-styled "traditionalism," a movement that is deeply individualistic and regards any connection between spirituality and politics with suspicion. Such suspicion is, of course, not new. In 1896 Kaiser Wilhelm II stressed that "pastors should concern themselves with the souls of their parishioners, should promote charity, and should keep out of politics";[39] a few years later a correspondent to the London *Church Times* wrote, "Political churchmen have been the bane of our church. . . . The political spirit is always fatal to spirituality."[40]

Such attempts to polarize spirituality and politics were not without their critics in these years. Bishop Charles Gore, writing in the early years of the twentieth century, had commented that there was "a tendency in Protestantism . . . toward a conception of spirituality which is certainly not completely Christian,"[41] one that dissociated the material and social dimensions of life from the realm of spirit. Today many Christians seem to have regressed to that crude polarization. We find one English bishop lamenting that he sees "a seeming unwillingness to present spirituality as the central message" and complaining that clergy see themselves as no more than social workers.[42] In the United States a survey of Episcopalians suggested that 75 percent of the laity wanted the focus of the church to be on worship and spirituality. The implication was that concern with social justice and political issues was somehow hostile to such a focus.[43] (However, in the same year, it was claimed that two-thirds of those working for social change in the United States were doing so from a religious motivation.)[44] And we find wardens of retreat centers complaining that courses on the "inner life" attract large numbers in contrast to those that deal with issues of social justice, peace, or the environment.[45]

The false inwardness that is common in many current spiritual movements represents a serious danger to the church. Lacking any roots in life, it encloses the self within a pseudo-identity, within "the false sweetness of a narcissistic seclusion."[46] Such a narrowing of the realm of the spiritual is popular with both the otherworldly and the this-worldly. And, of course, the otherworldly and the this-worldly often turn out to be the same people. Otherworldliness in theology often manifests itself as extreme worldliness in practice, because it encourages a sharp division between the realms of spirit and matter, between religion and world affairs. Since the former cannot influence, question, or shape the latter, they end up coexisting peacefully.

Yet though individualism and otherworldliness have flourished in the current climate, many Christians have become more "political" in recent years. Politicization has been most marked among neoconservatives in the mainstream churches, the evangelical and fundamentalist "moral right," and the Christian Reconstructionists, based in California and Texas. Again, at one level, this is not new. Christians who used to deny that they were political had a selective view of what constituted the political arena; they were deeply concerned about, for example, pornography, the teaching of the theory of evolution, communism, and so on. However, it is now obvious that fundamentalists and others have learned about political method from the successes of the civil rights campaigns. But this revived political action has not really altered the understanding of "spirituality," which is still seen as belonging to the world of the inward. Though the number of church leaders who urge their flocks to avoid the political realm altogether is diminishing, it is still believed that the more spiritual ones must be less involved. The fear of contamination remains. In other sections of the Christian tradition there is much talk about "faith and justice" and "spirituality for justice," but much of it remains at the level of rhetoric—genteel, disconnected.

In the face of all this fragmentation and distortion, it must be emphasized that a deep reflective and critical spirituality is a necessary element in the renewal of politics, that "any spirituality which does not incorporate social involvement is to that extent false. Similarly social action which lacks a solid theoretical base and persistent reflective dimension is not only phony but also dangerous."[47] Such a "spirituality" will not be comfortable. It will be unpopular among both the otherworldly and the this-worldly. The otherworldly will fear the contamination of the spiritual realm through its entanglement with politics; the this-worldly will fear the potentially subversive effects of an awakened critical consciousness upon the social order.

What of the future? Can we continue to use this word *spirituality?* I believe that any further use will be highly precarious and fraught with danger. Its recent history has been so allied with the cult of the inward and the retreat from politics that for the foreseeable future both the concept and the practice of "the spiritual life" must be subjected to the most rigorous scrutiny. Many of those who now are proud to proclaim that they are "getting into spirituality" are in fact moving away from any serious social and political commitment, although such moves need not be seen as signs of moral failure so much as of a general loss of any coherent sense of the political. Others have made the shift into therapy. And yet it is still possible to speak of "the spirit of the people" and "the spirit of freedom" and to give "a spirited defense." I believe that we can speak of spirituality as a necessary bedrock and foundation of our lives, provided we understand that we are speaking of the foundation and not of a compartment. To speak of spirituality in this sense is to speak of the whole life of the human person and human community in their relationship with the divine. It is to insist that, in speaking of spirituality, we are speaking of that which lies at the very heart of the Christian faith. The Roman Catholic theologian Karl Rahner claimed that the devout Christian of the future would either be a mystic or nothing;[48] the Protestant theologian Paul Tillich believed that all faith and all experience of the divine was mystical, and that the mystical tradition must be restored to Protestant religion.[49] Others have noted the "alienation of theology from religion."[50] The recovery of unity in these areas is a vital task for the Christian future. There should be no future for spirituality as a marginal realm, a private zone on the edge of the Christian and human community.

Most of all we need to reassert the corporate character of spiritual life. Spirituality is not a subdivision of Christian discipleship. It is the root, the source, the life. The Spirit gives life and nourishes the whole. Spirituality is a corporate discipline, a corporate experience. A collective of North American women, visiting some of their fellow Christians in Nicaragua, brought out the contrast in terms of the clash between an individualist ethos and a corporate and cooperative one.

> The revolutionary love practiced by Jesus that we saw practiced by the people of Nicaragua made us realize how corrupt the concept and practice of love have become in the United States. Like the notion of forgiveness widely pedaled in the United States, the notion of love is individualized—it is a love confined to one's spouse, children, family, lover. It is a love for those who are like ourselves. Ultimately it is a love that excludes social responsibility and reaps benefits primarily for the propertied, Anglo-individualistic males who dominate the United States. It is a love that suits their needs and desires. It is not the love practiced by Jesus or the people of Nicaragua—a love of neighbor, a love especially of those who are poor and marginalized. The love we saw impracticed in Nicaragua is practiced in community and it benefits individuals. It is a love for the poor and marginalized and for friends, children, spouses, lovers. It is a love that reflects spirituality because it emphasizes social responsibility. The love being practiced in Nicaragua means that the hungry are fed, the prisoners are treated humanely, the sick are cared for, human life is cherished.
>
> Against the backdrop of Nicaragua, we saw that the love, forgiveness and Christianity that predominate in the United States are incomplete. They have been corrupted by individualism.[51]

If we are to rescue Christian spirituality from its captivity to individualism and the culture of false inwardness, we will need to recover the sense of its social character, indeed, the sense of the social character of the gospel itself. And this means an examination of the strengths and weaknesses of the "Social Gospel" tradition and of the ways in which our perception of that tradition has colored and distorted our understanding.

The Social Gospel and Liberal Optimism

The current sense of a cleavage between "spirituality" and "social action" is most evident in the United States, and this is not at all surprising. For it was here that the movement that was to become known as the Social Gospel began in the final years of the nineteenth and the early years of the twentieth century. The Social Gospel movement was a tradition, strongest within liberal Protestantism, that emphasized the responsibility of the church to work for social transformation. In this concern it was profoundly influenced by theological liberalism with its commitment to biblical criticism, its tendency to stress action more than dogma, and its openness to scientific and political movements. Indeed the origins of what we now call fundamentalism lie in a response to this movement. To understand its significance we need to go back to the middle years of the nineteenth century, when there developed a kind of liberal Protestantism that emphasized the coming of the Kingdom of God as the culmination and completion of existing tendencies in accord with a broadly liberal doctrine of progress.[52] Associated with such names as Walter Rauschenbusch, Josiah Strong, Washington Gladden, and Robert Archey Woods, the "Social Gospel" movement was rooted in a form of gradualism that was highly suited to the American political mainstream. Its leading exponent, Walter Rauschenbusch, appealed to the sense of middle-class moderation combined with a social conscience: indeed, he saw the comfortable middle-class neighborhood as the best base for the expression of Christian social responsibility.[53] The appeal was extremely popular, and his book *Christianity and the Social Crisis*, published in 1907, sold over fifty thousand copies. Of all the individuals within the movement, Rauschenbusch was the only one to describe himself as a Christian socialist,[54] yet his ideas show a close affinity with movements in Europe of a right-wing and authoritarian complexion.

Rauschenbusch wished to "Christianize the social order." "Under the warm breath of religious faith," he claimed, "all social institutions become plastic."[55] Indeed he believed that much of this process had already occurred in the United States, and that the "fundamental redemption of the state" had taken place when special privileges were removed from the Constitution and personal liberty and equal rights were established.[56] His optimism about the possibilities of such "Christianization" went hand in hand with his commitment to the American way of life as a close approximation to the Kingdom of God. There was nothing revolutionary about this movement, and its approach to Christianity as an active crusade rather than a dogmatic system appealed to the pragmatic elements within American culture. Thus Washington Gladden wrote in 1909, "Philanthropy, the principle of compassion and kindness, has been largely organized into the social life of the nation. The defective and dependent classes are now wards of the state. A considerable part of the life of civilized society is now controlled by the Christian principle, and we have come to a day when it does not seem quixotic to believe that all social relations are to be Christianized."[57]

Nevertheless, it is not correct to see the Social Gospel as a movement without theological foundations or to dismiss it as wholly naive and idealist. Indeed, Rauschenbusch was concerned to develop a theology for the Social Gospel. "We have a social gospel. We need a systematic theology large enough to match it and vital enough to back it."[58] Rauschenbusch himself was a deeply spiritual figure who wished to recover lost and neglected truths from the Christian tradition. A Baptist minister with a background in pastoral work in New York's Hell's Kitchen district, he saw the Social Gospel as a bridge between revivalism and the renewal of the social order. In much of his thinking he was way ahead of his time. In his first book, *The Righteousness of the Kingdom*, written in the 1890s but not published until the 1960s, he rejected individualism and the adequacy of "a world of regenerated individuals." It was necessary to deal with the laws, customs, and institutions of corporate life. It was necessary, he claimed, to recover "the forgotten ideas of the Christian evangel," and in particular to restore the centrality of the theme of the "divine transformation of all human life." The Kingdom of God was "a social conception" and represented the perfect society of the future.[59] His spirituality was a spirituality of transformation. "Ascetic Christianity called the world evil and left it. Humanity is waiting for a revolutionary Christianity which will call the world evil and change it."[60] Gladden, too, attacked those Christians "whose chief concern is their own spiritual condition" and called them to self-forgetful service and ministry to others.[61]

The leaders of the movement certainly did not, as is sometimes claimed, see Jesus as a modern type of social reformer. Nor did they ignore sin. Rauschenbusch stressed both the reality of sin and the demand for righteousness. The prophetic concern with social righteousness and the hope of a Messianic reign on earth in a religion devoted to the present life needed to be revived. There was an urgent need, claimed Rauschenbusch, to revive the "millennial hope" of a just social order.[62] These are important truths that need restating in every generation.

Yet what is remembered of the movement is the optimism of its assessment both of human nature and of the possibilities of social reform within existing political and economic structures. The movement moreover was associated in the minds of many Christians with a loss of any firm hold on Christian dogma and with a neglect of the "spiritual dimension." There seems little doubt that these partial images of this movement have helped to distort the understanding of Christian social theology and action in the minds of many Christians and to encourage the view that spirituality has no concern with such matters.

The Social Gospel movement was not peculiarly American. The British theological scene before the First World War was also dominated by liberal optimism. Some writers went so far as to identify Christianity with social welfare. "Christian belief and the welfare of society are one," said F. W. Bushell in 1907.[63] There was much talk among the British political group known as the "new Liberals" of the early years of the twentieth century about "practical Christianity." The climate of Christian thought in Britain after the Second World War was very different. Many believed that the experience of the war years had undermined the social optimism of the earlier thinkers, while the coming of the "welfare state," itself the result of the thought and work of Christian social activists like William Temple and R. H. Tawney, seemed to have undermined the basis of Christian social criticism and action. In a memorable lecture of 1955, Michael Ramsey, later to be archbishop of Canterbury, claimed that "Christian sociology" (the old term for Christian social criticism) was now dead, but he related this not only to the factors mentioned above but also to the fact that the preaching of the gospel had "gone awry" under the corrupting influence of individualism.[64] In the same period there was talk of a "crisis of Christian thought" involving the abandonment of any real belief in social transformation.[65] As late as 1965 the Methodist leader Donald Soper said in a parliamentary debate that many believed the "nonconformist conscience" had "gone into liquidation and . . . become almost vacuous."[66]

The Critique of the Social Gospel: Niebuhr, Barth, and Beyond

There were a number of reactions to the Social Gospel movement. New Testament scholars called into question its understanding of the Kingdom of God. The notion of the Kingdom as a commonwealth to be created gradually within the framework of the existing structures seemed to give inadequate attention to the apocalyptic element in the gospel teaching, with its stress on crisis and judgment rather than continuity and growth. The rediscovery of the apocalyptic, and the emphasis on the origins of the Christian proclamation in eschatology, led many to a kind of "theology of crisis" that located "crisis" outside history altogether and removed Kingdom theology from any social or political context. Yet critics from a more radical political tradition also stressed that the Social Gospel, with its implicit approval of the dominant structures, left little room for a radical critique of those structures, for the possibility of revolutionary change, or for the element of upheaval that is so central to the teaching of the Gospels.

One of the leading critics of the Social Gospel was Reinhold Niebuhr. Niebuhr was opposed to what he saw as "utopian" religion. Human communities, in his view, were inevitably selfish. There was simply not enough imagination in any social group to make it open to the possibility of love. Niebuhr therefore made a sharp distinction between social and individual behavior and potential. Love and justice belonged to different realms. In his major work *Moral Man and Immoral Society* (1932) he argued that both the secular liberals and the proponents of the Social Gospel had failed to understand the brutal character of all collectives, the sheer power of self-interest and of group egoism. His critique was also a critique of his own earlier liberal optimist position. Yet he remained in a deep sense a liberal, and his theological work occurred within the accepted framework of Western liberalism, both theological and political.

Niebuhr was the last American theologian to play any significant role in the public arena, though ironically he believed that the private and public realms were separate and that the visions of the social utopians could not be made effective. He believed strongly in original sin, though he seemed to confine this belief to individuals and not to apply it to governments or institutions.[67] He was a Christian pragmatist who was suspicious of all grand schemes of social change and in many ways would have been happy among the protagonists of "postmodernism" in theology today. At the same time he maintained a curious devotion to the millenarian and visionary elements within Christianity. They were important, in his view, so that radical forces did not degenerate into relativism. So while the vision of a just society was impossible of realization, it was necessary to have people who believed that it was possible! Martin Luther King, who was much influenced by both Rauschenbusch and Niebuhr, believed that Niebuhr neglected the transforming power of grace. "The truest visions of religion," he claimed, "are illusions which may be partially realized by being resolutely believed."[68] Niebuhr's "Christian realism," though it showed a perceptive awareness of the ambiguities and compromises in social and political life, was weak in its understanding of the work of grace in transforming individuals and structures.

However by 1934 Niebuhr had come to the view that the most hopeful way forward was through a synthesis of traditional religion and radical politics, and for a brief period he sought to combine a traditional theology with a radical political stance. In a most interesting and suggestive passage he argued that

> the liberal culture of modernity is quite unable to give adequate guidance and direction to a confused generation which faces the disintegration of a social system and the task of building a new one. In my opinion adequate spiritual guidance can only come through a more radical political orientation and more conservative religious convictions than are

comprehended in the culture of our era. The effort to combine political radicalism with a more classical and historical interpretation of religion will strike the modern mind as bizarre and capricious. It will satisfy neither the liberals in politics and religion, nor the political radicals, nor the devotees of traditional Christianity. These reflections are therefore presented without much hope that they will elicit any general concurrence.[69]

Niebuhr was a perceptive observer and commentator on world events. In 1946 he wrote the book *Discerning the Signs of the Times,* a phrase that was to become profoundly significant in the spirituality that emerged from the Second Vatican Council. And there are many abiding aspects of his teaching that are central to any renewal of Christian social thought and action. More than any other American theologian of his day, he stressed the importance of social structures. The health of the social organism depends on the adequacy of the structure, just as the human body depends on its biochemical processes. Goodwill cannot cure deficiencies in glandular secretions. In his writing, justice is stressed more than benevolence; he held that growth in reason should lead toward justice in society. But his thinking lacked the element of gospel conflict, and Niebuhrian realism was soon to become a sanctification of the middle ground of liberal democracy. His theology eventually became a cold war instrument, and on 8 March 1948 *Time* described him as "the official establishment theologian."

The other major theological figure who dominated these years was Karl Barth, the theologian of transcendence and the grace of God. For Barth, all theology and all Christian preaching began with God's revelation in Christ, not with human striving or human experience. Grace and truth came through Jesus Christ. He saw "natural theology," with its claim that there was some other source of knowledge and revelation apart from that in the Scriptures, as the main enemy of faith. His commentary on Romans, first published in 1919, represented a major break with theological liberalism. In his "dialectical" period (1921–28) he stressed the distance between humanity and God, the otherness of the divine. He rejected attempts to make Jesus into an activist or a reformer and his message into a welfare program. In the second edition of his book on Romans, every existing order was seen as evil, and there was a discernible trend toward a kind of theological anarchism.

Because of this, many saw Barth as an enemy of the Social Gospel, of social theology, and of any real involvement of Christians in the social and political arena. To this day Christian theologians are divided about the relevance of Barth's work for social ethics.[70] But to portray Barth as an opponent of Christian social action and political struggle is to ignore both his thinking and his historical record. He was a socialist. He wrote that he had turned to theology in order to find "a better basis for my social action."[71] It has been said that his quest was for "the organic connection between the Bible and the newspaper, the new world and the collapsing bourgeois order."[72] His "crisis theology" was born out of an acute sense of the inadequacy of the existing spiritual resources for action and resistance to evil. His stress on grace did not lead to quietism but to impatience and discontent. He sought to express a unity between justification and justice. He looked for "the Archimedean point from which the soul, and with the soul, society are moved."[73] He laid great emphasis on the two natures of Christ as the basis for a theological critique of the social order. Because Christ was human, there was a gospel imperative to respect, revere, and defend the dignity of every living person. Because Christ was divine, standing over and against all human earthly endeavor, no human project or initiative could be given unqualified approval. Barth was one of the earliest exponents of what has recently become known as the "preferential option for the poor." God, he insisted, was always on the side of the weak and lowly.[74]

Both Niebuhr and Barth were important in their critical responses to the liberal Social Gospel. But they had little time for each other. Niebuhr saw Barth as a pessimist and his theology as "irrelevant to all Christians in the Western world who believe in accepting common and collective responsibilities without illusion and without despair."[75] If Barth was relevant to the political realm, he was only relevant at the point of crisis. Such a crisis came in Nazism, and Barth became the theologian of resistance. Niebuhr recognized the importance of a theology of transcendence in the context of the resistance to Nazism, as did Paul Tillich. But Tillich warned that "an instrument that is a mighty weapon in warfare may be an inconvenient tool for use in the building trade."[76] Niebuhr claimed, with some justification, that Barth's system of thought had "helped at an earlier date to vitiate the forces which contended against the rising Nazi tyranny."[77] Today it is significant that the relevance of Barth's theology is being rediscovered by anti-apartheid Christians in South Africa in the context of a resistance movement comparable to that in the Nazi period.[78]

It was the other Niebuhr, Reinhold's brother Richard, who was to make the memorable comment in 1959 that the earlier liberal optimism was an unsatisfactory basis for Christian theology. "In its one-sided view of progress which saw the growth of the wheat but not that of the tares, the gathering of the grain but not the burning of the chaff, this liberalism was indeed naively optimistic. A God without wrath brought men without sin into a Kingdom without judgment through the ministrations of a Christ without the Cross."[79] Yet to draw from this critique the conclusion that the struggle for social justice is not central to the Christian task is unjustified. The attack on the Social Gospel is an attack on its theological and moral inadequacy, not on its aims and objectives.

Niebuhr and Barth were theologians who reflected, and interpreted in Christian terms, what had happened as social and political fact: the disillusionment with, and rejection of, the earlier liberal optimism. The death of liberal optimism, however, was not the result of the work of intellectuals, whether theologians or others, but of concrete experience, in particular the experience of the devastation and horror of world war. As the British sociologist A. H. Halsey has said, this tradition was "maimed in Flanders in the First World War and finally destroyed in Belsen in the Second."[80] For, as Churchill observed, "War is always bad for liberals."

Yet in spite of the mistrust of such liberal reforming movements, during the 1960s there was a renewal of the Social Gospel tradition. Many commentators have claimed that the present resurgence both of fundamentalism, on the one hand, and of interest in spirituality, on the other, is a direct result of the perceived inadequacy of the 1960s activism. There has been much talk about exhaustion, disillusionment, and "burnout." However, it seems likely that the activism of the 1960s has been exaggerated. Most Christians, lay and clerical, were not particularly activist in this decade, and many of those whose consciences were awakened continued their work along fairly conventional lines.

However, it does seem to be broadly true that during the 1960s, and perhaps earlier, there was a neglect of the life of prayer and of personal piety and devotion. Such exercises were seen as escapist and perhaps harmful. An important result of waves of activism and the responses to them has been the growth of a sharp polarization between "spirituality" and "social concern" in many parts of the church. Exponents of the essential unity between these dimensions of Christian life have come to be seen as odd and noteworthy.

The weaknesses of the Social Gospel movement are clear. Recent years have seen the decline of the "liberal" churches and increasing dissatisfaction with both liberal individualism and a social reform tradition with inadequate theological and spiritual roots. Yet for all its weaknesses, its cultural captivity, its limitations, this movement does hold a permanent place in Christian consciousness. Truths and priorities were proclaimed here that we must not lose. Today what needs asserting strongly is that the gospel is social at its very heart. There is no "social gospel" apart from the gospel itself.

And there are encouraging signs that people in widely differing Christian traditions now accept the need for a recognition of the social character of the gospel and the importance of a unity between spirituality and social and political action. This acceptance is no simplistic capitulation to a passing trend, to "the spirit of the age," or to secular pressure; it is a significant maturing of Christian consciousness, a real movement of spiritual renewal. Christians from confessional traditions with major theological differences, rooted in extremely diverse historical conditions, have found common ground in recent years, often as a by-product of work in common. It is worth examining some examples of this convergence.

Resources for a New Synthesis

In the period since 1945 old confessional divisions have broken down, and both new unities and new conflicts have emerged across the Christian world. One fundamental area of convergence as well as conflict is that of spirituality and its relationship to the structures of the world. In the concluding pages of this chapter I want to identify some of the key elements that have contributed to the renewal of Christian spirituality and Christian social commitment and their potential for future change.

A major feature of all these developments has been the increased sense of the need for a living tradition and for roots of social commitment that go deep. It has been recognized more and more that the quest for truth does not, and cannot, occur in a vacuum but requires some kind of community, some sense of solidarity in quest and struggle. The revived concern for tradition has not been uncritical. Traditions themselves embody dimensions of conflict and ambiguity, and a quest for tradition should never be confused with a return to past conventions of a straightforward kind. Tradition is rather a quest for rich and fertile soil, for grounding, for a profound basis for discipleship, for something that is more adequate and abiding than the shifting sands of fashion. To be outside all traditions is, as Alasdair MacIntyre has argued, to be intellectually and morally destitute.[81]

What are the elements within Christian tradition that have contributed (and could contribute more) to the renewal of that tradition and its spiritual and social consciousness?

"Scriptural Holiness": The Heritage of Wesley

The tradition of corporate holiness, associated particularly with Wesley and the Methodist movement, may seem an odd place to start. For Methodism is a modern movement that grew out of an already fragmented post-Reformation European Christian culture. Moreover, John Wesley was both an individualist in theology and a conservative in politics, probably a supporter of Adam Smith, and by no means a radical social thinker. Some of the more extreme claims made for the Methodist movement do not bear sustained examination; unlike the earlier movement of John Bunyan, Wesleyanism was never truly a religion of the poor. If "British socialism owed more to Methodism than to Marxism," it is not clear that this was altogether to its benefit.

Yet paradoxically it is precisely the origins of Methodism in the culture of modernity that makes its future so crucial for Christianity as a whole. It became a vigorous church in the United States, and its division into black and white segments has mirrored the divisions within American society. Perhaps more than any other Protestant tradition, Methodism manifests the strengths and the conflicts of the liberal era, as it manifests also the possibilities for a social conscience rooted in evangelical fervor and social holiness.

In particular, there are aspects of Wesley's movement that have important implications for the renewal of spirituality. The Methodist tradition remains an abiding witness to the integration of spiritual and social commitment as well as to the potential for change and engagement within the Christian church. Much of the strength of Methodism goes back to the origins of the movement. Wesley was a kind of latter-day Ignatius Loyola, with his insistence on personal holiness, on discipline and "method," the origin of the movement's name, and on meditation on the Scriptures. There was also an emphasis on the social character of holiness. There could be, Wesley insisted, "no holiness but social holiness."[82] His aim was to extend the Reformation into the area of righteousness, and this was bound to have social effects. This social emphasis was expressed in practical terms in the band meetings, those early intensive groups in which something of the apostolic concept of *koinonia* was restored.

The social effects of the Wesleyan movement are well documented. The holiness churches, which grew out of the work of revivalists such as C. G. Finney and provided a link between evangelism and social reform, were an outgrowth of Wesley's revival, and the contribution of the holiness tradition to the ending of slavery is clear. Because of the holiness tradition's insistence on Christian perfection, and its rejection both of Calvinistic fatalism and of a minimalist view of Christian behavior, this movement became known as "perfectionism." In the United States, Wheaton College in Illinois was founded by the Wesleyans as a "center of perfectionist reform." Though it later became more Calvinist and premillennialist (believing that the Second Coming of Christ must precede any significant improvement in earthly conditions) and its commitment to social concern consequently declined, its recent history has been marked by a return to the vision of its founders.

The potential of, and the problem for, the Wesleyan tradition lies in the link between personal sanctification and the transformation of society. Does sanctification lead to dissatisfaction with the prevailing order? Can the stress on "scriptural holiness" lead to an examination of what this means for communities that seek to embody holiness and justice? Whatever happens to world Methodism, it is clear that the Wesleyan tradition, with its concern for perfection, its insistence on social holiness, and its roots among the common people, could make a major contribution to the renewal of spirituality in the last part of the twentieth century.

"A New Pentecost": The Second Vatican Council and the Renewed Catholic World

The face of the Roman Catholic communion has changed beyond recognition since the Second Vatican Council (though research in Britain has shown that most younger Catholics had never heard of the Council![83] Nevertheless they have been affected by its work). Before the Council the Catholic community was dominated and shaped by the highly personal atmosphere of the Tridentine liturgy, an atmosphere that was not conducive to social action except insofar as it preserved and protected the "realm of the sacred." The preservation of this sacred realm, embodied in the shrines that were the foci of devotion, was the purpose of the church.

Of course, there was the tradition of the "social encyclicals," which began with Leo XIII in 1891. But these documents, though they condemned liberal capitalism and became increasingly obsessed with "bolshevism" did not really engage with the modern world or modern culture at all. *Quadragesimo Anno* of 1931 did lay stress on social justice, the social characteristics of property, and the common good, so much so that Mussolini regarded it as a manifesto for his fascist movement. Throughout these years the Roman curia's primary concern was with the preservation of its power and status, and its spirituality was one that reinforced this preservative tradition.

The Roman communion was not without its alternative voices and its rebels, however. In seeking to understand the origins of Catholic radicalism in America, the spiritual witness of Dorothy Day and the Catholic Worker movement is of major importance. Today, wrote the evangelical Jim Wallis, "the faithful persistence of Christians like Dorothy Day and the Catholic Worker is bearing much fruit."[84] Some even see recent statements by the American Catholic bishops on peace and the economy as the fruit of Dorothy Day's work over many years.[85] Established on May Day 1933, *The Catholic Worker* aimed "to make known the encyclicals of the popes in regard to social justice and the program put forth by the Church for the 'reconstruction of the social order.'" Over many years the Catholic Worker movement pioneered the road of radical Catholic witness, insisting on the priority of liturgical worship and of solidarity with the poorest sections of society.

If we are to look to the Roman communion as a source of renewal, we need to understand the theology of the Second Vatican Council. The most important theological shift brought about by Vatican II was its doctrine of grace. In this it was anticipated by Karl Rahner, who broke with the dualism of "nature" and "supernature" and began the shift toward a more unified and whole understanding. In the thinking of the Council, grace is part of the whole of human life. There is only one history. Grace is social and operates in history. The break with supernaturalism was crucial. The concept of "supernatural" was unknown in the early Christian writers like Augustine; the term came into use in the ninth century, after which it fell out of use until the thirteenth. Moreover, whereas in Augustine grace restored nature to its true condition, in later theology grace came to be seen as the giving of a new nature. The supernatural was seen as something added to nature. Such a view of grace came increasingly to be seen as mechanical and abstract, not rooted in human experience, so grace and the human experience came to be seen as separate realms. In the documents of Vatican II the supernatural language almost disappears. The word is used fourteen times in all the documents. In the document *Gaudium et Spes* (1965) the word *supernatural* is not used at all.

Another major contribution of Vatican II was its stress on the need for "a theology of the signs of the times" involving discernment and spiritual vision. Pope John XXIII believed that such discernment was a necessary spur to Christian action. Work for peace was particularly emphasized and was the theme of the major encyclical *Pacem in Terris* of 1963.

The Third Synod of Bishops in 1971 was another landmark. This synod issued the document *Justice in the World,* with its emphasis on social sin, on the need to address injustice within the church itself, and on the struggle against injustice as a constituent part of the proclamation of the gospel. This document was a major turning point in Catholic consciousness. Pope Paul's letter *Octogesima Adveniens* of the same year emphasized the need for reflection on the concrete realities of the local situation.

The message of the era of Pope John Paul II has been ambivalent. Many of the positive features of the Council have been reinforced; thus human dignity was stressed in *Redemptor* Hominis (1979), and the social tradition was stressed in *Laborem Exercens* (1981). Later documents, such as the American Bishops' letter *Catholic Social Teaching and the U.S. Economy,* have been significant. The encyclical *Sollicitudo Rei Socialis* (1988) emphasized "the church's . . . critical attitude toward both liberal capitalism and Marxist collectivism" (par. 21).

Within Catholic spirituality, questions of discernment and the "signs of the times" have led to a renewed social consciousness among many individuals and parish communities. Within the Jesuit tradition, the Ignatian Exercises have assumed a new significance, and there has been much emphasis on the politics of discernment. The transitional figure of Thomas Merton will be considered later, but his importance in shaping a theology of social involvement, as well as helping people to discover the spiritual resources for resistance to injustice, is difficult to exaggerate. Recent Roman Catholic writing has stressed the "need for a social spirituality and particularly for a link between discipleship and social compassion."[86] In contrast to the "privatizing" of religion in many areas of American Christianity, the Roman communion seems to stand firm on social responsibility and commitment to the public realm. It has even been suggested that in their approach to social ethics Roman Catholics and many evangelicals in the United States may be "on a collision course."[87] However, what is not at all clear is the extent to which the social teaching expressed in documents from the hierarchy is reflected among lay Catholics at the parish level. Here what data exist do not suggest an entirely hopeful picture. For thousands the social teaching of the church is well described as its "best kept secret."[88] It has been claimed by one leading theologian that American Catholics are deeply individualistic and "less sensitive than ever before in their history to the interests of the poor and the socially marginal"[89]—whatever the bishops may say. There are undoubtedly signs of hope and resources for struggle, but there is a long way to go before Catholic social teaching is "earthed" and takes root in the back streets.

"The Spiritual Journey of a People": Liberation Theology

Liberation theology is a spiritual tradition that has grown up in various parts of the world. In its literary form it is particularly associated with Latin America. Gustavo Gutierrez, who first coined the term, saw that such a theology could only have arisen out of the unified view of history that was central to Vatican II. Liberation theology is concerned with the spiritual experience of communities and even of whole nations and peoples. Gutierrez's book *We Drink from Our Own Wells* (1984) is subtitled *The Spiritual Journey of a People*. Within this movement of struggle and reflection there is a search for "political holiness." The shift toward a deeper spiritual basis for struggle was marked in the seventies and has continued and been strengthened since then. The Chilean pastor Segundo Galilea is the best known of a number of Latin American theologians who have written of the coming together of the contemplative and the militant in a quest for "integral liberation."[90] The fact that liberation theologians are so concerned to hold together the spiritual and the social dimensions of the Christian tradition is confirmation of their insistence that, far from being fashionable innovators, they are "shameless conservatives . . . looking for the literal gospel."[91]

"Let My People Go": The Place of Black Spirituality

I will discuss the importance of the black liberation movement and the theology that has grown from it in chapter 2. Here it is necessary to stress that this is a tradition that from its earliest days has emphasized the unity of spirituality and concrete struggle. Such an emphasis has been "an integral part of the black religious tradition from its beginning."[92] The tradition of evangelical and pietistic Christianity has been the "most influential and enduring intellectual tradition"[93] in black religious experience. In particular, Pentecostalism has been extremely important, and it is the only kind of Christianity formed and shaped by black people.[94] In Britain the black Pentecostal churches are the largest and fastest-growing Christian groups in the inner urban areas; here, in the most deprived districts of the city, pietism and radical politics fuse in a precarious and potentially explosive communion.

"Radical Discipleship": The New Evangelical Consciousness

There was a time when evangelical religion and social commitment went together, though the commitment was of a reformist kind and did not involve real social analysis. What has been called "the great reversal"[95] in evangelical thought and practice took place at the end of the nineteenth century. One of the main influences on the withdrawal from social commitment was the dominance of "premillennialism," the belief in the imminent return of Christ, a belief supported by a detailed eschatology. This theology, reinforced by individualism, was particularly influential in the United States. As Paul Henry wrote in 1974, "American political culture is based upon a highly individualistic concept of man and society. Evangelicals have generally tended to be part of that individualistic culture rather than to stand against it."[96] Such complaints were common as late as 1979, when Richard Lovelace claimed that "most of those who pray are not praying about social issues and most of those who are active in social issues are not praying very much."[97]

By the middle of the twentieth century, changes were occurring. In 1966 a congress took place at Wheaton, Illinois. The Wheaton Declaration, which emerged from the congress, attacked what it called the "unscriptural isolation" of evangelicals from the life of society, involving a failure to deal with racism, poverty, and other areas of social injustice. Wheaton marked an important turning point in evangelical social awareness within the Western churches. It was followed by the Keele Conference in Britain in 1967. Several years later the Chicago

Declaration of 1973 was hailed as "the awakening of a slumbering evangelical social conscience."[98] Since these events, there have been the Lausanne Congress of 1974, a further Wheaton Declaration in 1983, and a range of evangelical documents relating to of social justice. Central to these documents is the belief that "vigorous and systematic social involvement requires not that Christians weaken the structure of their piety but rather that they carry it through to its natural social consequences."[99]

Typical of one direction taken by the new breed of evangelical radical is the thinking of the Sojourners Community in Washington, D.C. Described by its critics as "a fundamentalist social gospel"[100] and by its supporters as "the modern-day bible for the radical Christian community movement in America,"[101] their journal, *Sojourners,* stands in an ambiguous relationship to the Christian community in the United States. Originating as *The Post American* in 1971, the journal is now one of the most widely read evangelical journals in the Western world. Its principal thinker, Jim Wallis, has expressed the theology of the community and movement in a number of books, particularly *Agenda for Biblical People* and *The Call to Conversion.*

Wallis sees the war in Vietnam and the civil rights movement as the context for the new evangelicalism, "the historic occasion for a revival of biblical faith."[102] A new movement was appearing; old divisions were breaking down. The journal aims to unite social justice and spiritual transformation. It seeks to rediscover the meaning of discipleship and attacks the "heresy of grace without discipleship" (p. 47). Wallis believes that there is a deeply subversive quality about the radical evangelical faith: "an independent biblical vision is what the present U.S. government and its religious apologists are most afraid of."[103] In *The Post American* in 1974 he wrote, "The new evangelical consciousness is most characterized by a return to biblical Christianity and the desire to apply biblical insights to the need for new forms of sociopolitical engagement."[104]

In *Agenda for Biblical People* Wallis stresses the need to link analysis of social systems with the Bible, prayer, and worship. Resistance to injustice and oppression lies at the heart of Christian discipleship in the present climate. Churches need to disentangle themselves from the dominant value system, and need to be transformed biblically. Wallis sees the Christian community as a countersign within the structures of the fallen world order. Here "the Fall" is applied structurally. Indeed, this stress on the social character of fallenness lies at the heart of the new evangelical radicalism. It rejects "the theological naïveté of failing to take the fall seriously."[105] The whole of Christian witness is a renunciation of the fallen world order and its values. The very heart of Christian worship lies in this radical act of disaffiliation from the idolatrous demands of the culture. Here, in the worshiping community, we cry, "Jesus is Lord"—and by that act repudiate all earthly claims to domination and lordship.

Christians of the Sojourners tradition hold strongly to the view that a deep inner life is vital to prophetic witness. "Only those who have a deep spiritual base and active political sensitivities can be prophetic in the biblical sense"(p. 130). In the movement for such a prophetic church, the Bible is of fundamental importance as "a vehicle for personal transformation and the emergence of new people who embody the basis for social liberation." Through this movement, a "new biblical radicalism" is emerging, along with a new "loosely connected cross-confessional consciousness"(pp. 8, 10). Wallis is very emphatic that the radicalism he offers is rooted in a deeply traditional theology:

> This process of radicalization does not require the creation of a new theology or value system. It involves rather a return to biblical Christianity. However strong the opposition to the established order, however revolutionary the vision, the basic values and commitments are familiar to those acquainted with the biblical and historic traditions of the church. The startling thing about the insurgents is their affirmation of biblical faith, their sense of continuity with the radical Christian heritage of times past. (pp. 11–12)

Any other way is seen as barren and futile. Wallis is forceful in his rejection of revisionism and of any watering down of the faith:

> The hope of meaningful countercultural resistance to any social or political consensus is not to be found in depreciating transcendence or moving in secular directions. That practice

has in fact become a formula for conformity. On the contrary, the church's proper role as an alternative corporate reality and prophetic presence in any social order will be recovered only as the people of God return to their biblical roots and stand firmly on the ground of revelation. (p. 53)

The Sojourners Community is but one example of the renewed social consciousness in the evangelical world, and it would be naive and foolish to exaggerate its influence. Statistically evangelicalism remains individualist, affluent, and deeply conservative. At the same time it is impossible to deny that a real process of radicalization has been under way. The movement has been aided by a number of writers. In the United States, Robert Webber, Donald Dayton, and Ronald Sider have been important. In Britain, David Sheppard, Jim Punton, John Gladwyn, and Chris Sugden come to mind. But the movement is international. One of the most exciting and important contributions in recent years, for example, has been the way in which evangelicals in South Africa have, in the name of the gospel, attacked the pietism that has justified oppression.

One major influence on the renewed social conscience of evangelicals has been that of the radical Anabaptist or Mennonite tradition. A central emphasis here is on the fact that the church itself is an integral part of the gospel and must therefore manifest gospel values in its own structures and lifestyle. In the words of John Howard Yoder, "The primary social structure through which the gospel works to change other structures is that of the Christian community."[106] Yoder's book *The Politics of Jesus* (1972) has played a crucial role in forcing many Christians to reconsider the conventional assumption that Jesus' ministry was "apolitical" and addressed only to individuals. Mennonites lay great emphasis on the corporate nature of the faith, on the church as the Body of Christ, on simplicity of life and economic sharing, and on nonviolence and love of enemies. Stanley Hauerwas is one theologian who, though himself a Methodist, has been profoundly influenced by the Mennonite tradition, seeing it as "the most nearly faithful form of Christian witness."[107] Again, we are speaking of a very small community in relation to the total Christian movement in the West, but the Mennonite contribution is a vital resource for the maturing Christian social consciousness.

Via Media: The Anglican Social and Spiritual Tradition

The Anglican churches have always claimed to stand for a Catholicism linked with a deeply biblical and intellectual tradition. The centrality of social witness is basic to Anglican theology and pastoral practice, and even its politically conservative members from time to time testify to it. Thus the British politician Enoch Powell: "The Gospel is indeed a social gospel. . . . The good news of the Gospel is imparted to the individual only as a member of a society. . . . The most fundamental heresy of all is to imagine that the Gospel is given to individuals or received by individuals or apprehended by individuals."[108] Of course this is not to say that most Anglicans take seriously this central emphasis of their tradition: like Christians of other traditions, many of them take their theology more from the pages of the secular newspapers than from the teaching documents of their own church.

Nevertheless there is within Anglicanism a long tradition of social theology. Michael Ramsey has shown how the emphasis on the doctrine of the incarnation helped to create the theological framework of Anglican social thinking. Charles Gore's 1891 lecture "The Incarnation of the Son of God" opened up an era of both theology and pastoral strategy motivated by this strongly incarnational tradition. Modern Anglicanism owes many of its characteristics to the central place of the incarnation. Though Ramsey admitted that there was a certain amount of "naive optimism" associated with this tradition, he himself stood firmly within it and, as archbishop of Canterbury during the 1960s, laid constant stress on the importance both of worship and of social criticism.[109]

Historically the Anglican social tradition has been a mainly Anglo-Catholic phenomenon. Anglo-Catholicism, the strand within the Anglican church that lays particular emphasis on the catholicity of the church and its sacramental life, has its origins in the movement that began at Oxford in 1833. Some have spoken of "the social implications of the Oxford Movement,"[110] and it is certainly true that there was a radical dimension to that movement. The stress on the spiritual independence of the church and the rejection of "political religion" and the church's alliance with the Tory Party led some to a view of the church as a kind of counterculture. W. G. Ward, for instance, held that the church's "ordinary condition" was one of opposition to worldly power.[111] But to portray the early Anglo-Catholic movement as a radical, conflictual culture is not correct. From its beginnings there was much sickly piety within the movement, a kind of "bubble world . . . a state of abnormal, carefully cultivated religious excitement."[112] Henry Scott Holland was under no illusions about the false spirituality of much of the Anglo-Catholicism of his day. Lamenting the lack of involvement in social issues, Scott Holland told his readers, "And if you want to know why, you have only to look into the little books of holy devotion in their hands which were so wholly taken up with personal and individual details of self-examination, so preoccupied with self-direction, self-practices, self-oblation, self-correction that all memory of corporate and social responsibility had vanished away."[113] Of course, there were many exceptions. The saintly slum priest of Portsmouth Robert Dolling, writing in 1896, claimed that the purpose of the parish was to be "a common roof tree . . . the center of social righteousness in the whole district."[114] But for every Dolling, there were many priests of this tradition for whom spirituality was wholly inward, private, and unconnected with issues of justice.

The key figure in the emergence of a social theology within nineteenth-century Anglicanism was a theologian with little sympathy with the Oxford Movement: the Christian socialist F. D. Maurice. Maurice is important for a number of reasons: his rejection of a Fall-centered theology, his emphasis on the human craving for fellowship and rejection of individualism, his belief that the Kingdom of God was the fundamental reality underlying all human history.[115] The influence of Maurice, and of those who followed him and developed his thought in practical ways, was so significant that by the outbreak of the First World War a commitment to social reform, and a vague kind of socialism, was widely accepted in the Church of England. The Christian Social Union, dominated by such theologians as Scott Holland and B. F. Westcott, promoted this viewpoint. In a famous address Westcott contrasted individualism and socialism as representing opposite views of humanity.[116] The tradition of a moderate reformist socialism rooted in incarnational and sacramental theology was to dominate mainstream Anglicanism in England down to the death of William Temple in 1944. Temple, who was archbishop of Canterbury for the last few years of his life, was the last notable representative of the tradition before the impact of the war led the tradition into eclipse. It was he who, in 1929, coined the term "welfare state."[117] His 1942 book *Christianity and the Social Order* was an important critique of the view that Christianity was primarily concerned with the fate of the individual soul and with the next world, a view that was, Temple argued, "entirely modern and extremely questionable."[118] One of Temple's greatest contributions to Christian thought was his rejection of the false spirituality that divorced the gospel from material needs and demands. Christianity, he insisted, was "the most avowedly materialist of all the great religions."[119]

The tradition of "social concern" from Maurice and Gore to Temple was somewhat genteel and reflected a "trickle-down" theology in which all the thinking and action began with people in positions of power. But there also grew up within Anglicanism an alternative tradition, which offered a powerful integration of sacramental worship and social struggle, and which was rooted in the life and struggles of the poor. This tradition grew from a fusion of the theology of Maurice with the sacramentalism of the ritualists. Its public origin can be dated to 1877, when Stewart Headlam founded the Guild of Saint Matthew at Saint Matthew's Church, Bethnal Green, one of the poorest districts of London. The Guild was founded as a parish society with a commitment to eucharistic worship and a rule of life, but within a few years it had become the main socialist Christian movement in Britain.[120]

Headlam's stress on the unity of humanity, and on the conflict between the eucharistic community and the class structure of society, was in sharp contrast to the ritualists, with their obsessive concern for liturgical correctness. Headlam's impatience with ritualism is evident in all his work. "Let them postpone the question as to the exact spot by the Altar at which the Gospel should be said until each one of their dearly beloved brethren has a comfortable home, and their children a clean bed, and good fresh air to sleep in, and a moderate amount of healthy food. These are the real questions of church order and discipline."[121] Headlam's pioneering work inspired a number of other individuals and groups within this theological tradition. The most memorable of them was Conrad Noel (1869–1942).

Noel was parish priest in the Essex village of Thaxted from 1910 to 1942. His theology, expressed in a number of books but more in vast numbers of pamphlets and articles, stressed the "social God," a phrase that had been in use earlier.[122] The Catholic Crusade, a movement of Anglican priests that he founded, "looked forward to a new social order inspired by Catholicism of which the Holy Sacrament of the Altar was its symbol and life."[123] "We ... believe that our principal work is not 'social reform' nor pietistic exercises, but the stirring within the people of the hunger and thirst for that righteousness which shall fill them with the eternal things and a due measure of the things that are temporal."[124] Noel was fiercely opposed to "narrow sacerdotalism and next worldly pietism"[125] and to heretical religion that rejected political commitment. "Orthodox church folk recognize the statement that the church should have nothing to do with politics or with material life as a deadly and soul-destroying heresy, contradicting the Christian doctrines of creation, incarnation and of the resurrection of the body."[126] Pointing to the Hebrew Scriptures, which recognized "no divorce between things spiritual and material," Noel wrote, "Hebrew spirituality was concerned with the bodies, minds and spirits of men and translated itself immediately, as all healthy spirituality at all times must, into political action" (p. 41). At the root of Noel's spirituality was a profound sense of the world as sacrament, of the sacramental character of all reality. He spoke of the "sacraments of nature and of grace" (p. 143).

Reg Groves, Noel's friend and biographer, made a distinction between the "social democratic" type of Catholicism represented by Noel and the pietistic ritualism of other Anglo-Catholics.

> In believing the Church to be a fellowship pledged to strive for God's Commonwealth of social justice and righteousness, the social democrats were in open conflict with those Anglicans to whom the Church was an exclusive club concerned only with the spiritual exercises, necessary to secure for its members reserved places in a heaven above the clouds. In seeing ceremonial as the outward dramatic expression of the gospel and life of the divine commonwealth for which they were striving, the social democrats were in conflict with the Ritualists, to whom ceremony was a professional performance

of mysteries comprehensible only to the clerisy, mysteries of an unseen spiritual life which had to avoid contamination by remaining inside the church, having nothing to with life outside the holy temple.[127]

The Catholic Crusade stood for an alternative reality, and its churches were signs of contradiction to the established order. A visitor to Sneyd Church, Burslem, in the English Midlands in 1937 wrote, "Outside the smoke banners of the pot-banks: inside the whitewashed church, the gay flags and ensigns of a different world. Just to step into Sneyd Church therefore is to face a challenge, for the two pictures do not seem to belong to the same order."[128] Here then was a Catholicism of struggle, rooted in a commitment to the new world of God's Kingdom.

Anglican social theology has been firmly based on the central Christian themes of creation, incarnation, and redemption. The centrality of the Kingdom of God as a hope for the transformation of this world has been basic to Anglicanism from Maurice in the 1840s to Widdrington in 1922. Widdrington claimed that the rediscovery of the centrality of the Kingdom as the "regulative principle of theology" would bring about a Reformation compared with which the Reformation of the sixteenth century would appear a very small event.[129] Sacramental life was seen as ethical, worship as leading to politics. Writers within this Anglo-Catholic social tradition were inclined to be critical of liberal Protestantism, with its "lack of a sound dogmatic basis."[130] Evelyn Underhill, best known now for her works on mysticism, called for a "modified dualism" involving an "alternation of the transcendent and the homely."[131] But by the 1940s the tradition was in decay. In 1940 D. G. Peck was calling for "the recovery of a long lost tradition,"[132] while Temple lamented that few people had ever heard of the great figures of the Anglican social movement.

During the 1960s a major thinker within Anglicanism was John A. T. Robinson. Robinson was a New Testament scholar with scant acquaintance with the historical tradition, and, like most of his predecessors, he stood within an elitist academic context. However, during his period as a bishop in South London, he did attempt some engagement with urban issues, and, though his background was rarefied, he should be treated as one of the people who sought to develop a social spirituality for his day. Robinson was concerned with "worldly holiness" and saw prayer as engagement. He rejected the identification of church and Kingdom, seeing the church rather as the firstfruits (James 1:18). The major essay in Robinson's study *On Being the Church in the World* is entitled "Matter, Power and Liturgy," and it is a crucial document for contemporary spirituality. In this essay he stresses the unity of matter and spirit. "Christianity stands or falls by the sacramental principle that matter and spirit are not separate or antithetical."[133] Robinson saw the image of the church as the Body of Christ to be "the specifically Christian clue to the renewal of society" (p. 70).

This emphasis on the doctrine of the church is particularly important in Anglicanism, and it is evident in the context of Anglicans in situations of acute social and political conflict. John Davies writes of the church struggle in South Africa:

> The most powerful weapon in Catholicism's armory of imagery in the struggle against injustice is the doctrine of the Body of Christ. There has been nothing radical or intellectually daring about this: the South African situation has required Catholicism to be thoroughly conservative and oppose the novel nonsense of upstart racism with a traditional orthodoxy which insists that there must be a visible fellowship of believers and that Christian love must be acted out in visible terms.[134]

Yet it is important not to deceive ourselves. Though there are undoubtedly resources for resistance within the Anglican tradition, it is clear that many, maybe most, Anglicans have conformed to a vague liberal position. One sociologist, after surveying the perspective of Anglican clergy in East London, described it as "passionately idealistic liberalism" with a dose of "genteel socialism."[135] There are serious problems here. Yet we cannot deny that there are also important resources for a spirituality that has major social and political dimensions.

These are some among many elements within contemporary Christian movements that can be seen as resources for a new synthesis of spirituality and social commitment. In recent years a number of theologians have made significant contributions to the debates around this area: Harvey Cox, Dorothee Soelle, and Henri Nouwen in the

United States, Jurgen Moltmann and Wolfhart Pannenberg in Europe. There have been developments in social thinking within the Orthodox tradition with thinkers such as John Meyendorff, Stanley Harakas, and Archbishop Iakovos in the United States. Elsewhere we find John de Gruchy, writing out of the experience of South Africa, arguing that privatized piety becomes captive to the status quo and conformist.[136] We find people studying Bonhoeffer and Barth in the South African context.[137] And from Asia comes a sacramental thrust: "The central task for those who would discover a spirituality in the midst of Asia's struggles is therefore the linking of radical social involvement with a continuing exposure to biblical truth and sacramental action that may be signs of the Kingdom. In other words, an important aspect of Christian spirituality is the sacramental dimension of the struggle for social justice."[138] It is a call that is repeated all over the world where people are crying out for liberation, for the freedom of the children of God.

2

"LET THE OPPRESSED GO FREE"

Spirituality and Liberation

Living witnesses rather than theological speculation . . . are already pointing out the direction of a spirituality of liberation.

GUSTAVO GUTIERREZ

Furthermore Christians and their pastors should know how to recognize the hand of the Almighty in those events that from time to time put down the mighty from their thrones and raise up the humble, send away the rich empty handed and fill the hungry with good things.

LETTER OF SIXTEEN BISHOPS OF THE THIRD WORLD, 1968

He has sent me to proclaim release to the captives and recovering of sight to the blind, to set at liberty those who are oppressed, to proclaim the Acceptable Year of the Lord.

JESUS, LUKE 4:18–19

For freedom Christ has set us free; stand firm therefore and do not submit again to a yoke of slavery.

PAUL, GALATIANS 5:1

In one sense the theme of liberation dominates Jewish and Christian history. That history begins with the liberation of slaves from Egyptian oppression, and subsequent reflection and liturgical celebration are marked by the recurrence and centrality of the Exodus theme of deliverance from slavery. Though most English translations of both Hebrew and Christian Scriptures do not use the actual word *liberation,* preferring such words as *redemption, deliverance, freedom,* and so on, the recently published New Jerusalem Bible has opted for the word at various key points.

> You will declare this fiftieth year to be sacred and proclaim the liberation of all the country's inhabitants. (Lev. 25:10)

> When these things begin to take place, stand erect, hold your heads high, because your liberation is near at hand. (Luke 21:28)

Yet whether or not the word itself is used in English versions, the idea of liberation is at the very heart of the Christian gospel. Therefore Christian theology and spirituality are, by their very nature, liberation theology and liberation spirituality, for they are rooted in the saving events by which God has set people free.

In another sense, however, the theology of liberation does represent a minority and rebellious tradition within Christian experience, which has, throughout history, both taken the side of the oppressors and interpreted liberation narrowly in purely spiritual or individualistic terms. Thus an eighteenth-century Bishop of London assured his hearers that liberation was purely inward and did not affect external structures and conditions. "The freedom which Christianity gives is a freedom from the bondage of sin and Satan and from the dominion of men's lusts and passions and inordinate desires: but as to their *outward* condition, whatever that was before, whether bond or free, their being baptized and becoming Christian makes no matter of change in it."[1] As we shall see in this chapter, the recent history of Christian reflection on oppression and liberation has led to the insistence that what is often termed "integral liberation" must include liberation from social, economic, and political oppression as well as personal and "spiritual" liberation. Indeed, it calls into question a narrow definition of *spiritual* that restricts it to the inward sphere. A spirituality of liberation then must involve taking seriously, and with contemplative concern, the experience of human oppression and the cry for human liberation in all its forms.

Liberation means nothing by itself, apart from the experience of oppression. Only in the context of oppression, of bondage, of slavery, can liberation have meaning. In the Hebrew Scriptures bondage is seen as economic and political captivity, linked in the history of Israel with the constant temptation to idolatry. The cry "Let my people go" has as its purpose "that they may serve me." The deliverance is therefore both from slavery to the economic and political bondage of Egypt and from captivity to idols and false gods. The liberating God of the Exodus calls this oppressed and fragile people to serve that ultimate Freedom that is Godself. In the early Christian church, Paul sees the human liberation brought by Christ as part of a greater process, the liberation of creation itself. "For the whole creation is waiting with eagerness for the children of God to be revealed. It was not for its own purposes that creation had frustration imposed on it, but for the purposes of him who imposed it—with the intention that the whole creation itself might be freed from its slavery to corruption and brought into the same glorious freedom as the children of God" (Rom. 8:19–21, NJB). A spirituality of liberation will therefore need to take account of the creation, the environment, earth and seas, as well as of humankind.

The place of liberation as a key biblical metaphor for the activity of God is brought out well by one who speaks from the heart of the liberation struggle in South Africa, Archbishop Desmond Tutu:

> The liberation which God offers is a total and comprehensive liberation. He sets us free from sin (the negative aspect) and sets us free to be his children who will appropriate the glorious liberty that is theirs. He sets us free for service (the positive aspect). This follows the biblical paradigm for all liberation—that of the Exodus. There God set Israel free from bondage in Egypt and set them free so that they could serve him, to be his missionary agent, a light to the nations, not for their own aggrandizement. Consequently liberation theology

is profoundly biblical and must be tested and judged according to the extent to which it is consistent with what God shows himself to be in the Word of scripture and the Word made flesh.[2]

Liberation is thus at the heart of Christian spirituality, not a particular form of it. To be a Christian at all is to be part of this liberating movement of history and creation. Apart from such a movement the Christian mysteries cease to have meaning and cannot be understood. The theme of liberation within history is central to its Jewish and Christian usage, in sharp contrast, for example, to the theme of liberation as *moksa* that we find in Hinduism, an idea of release from the cycle of transmigration.[3] In Christian understanding, history is the context of liberating grace and liberating struggle.

The Rhetoric of Liberation

The word *liberation*, from the Latin *liberare*, "to liberate," was used in French by the fourteenth century. Though there are examples of its use in a personal sense, its regular meanings, from the fifteenth century down to the 1950s, were more likely to be military, economic, and scientific. Thus Bishop Clark in 1532 wrote of the liberation of Italy, Adam Smith in 1776 of "the future liberation of the public revenue," and Henry in 1800 of the need for gases to have red heat for their liberation. In 1875 Lightfoot, in his commentary on Colossians 2:15, wrote of "liberation from the dominion of the flesh."[4] But the main sense of the word remained a military one, and it was used a great deal in the post–1945 period both about the former Nazi-occupied territories in Europe and, in the 1950s, about Formosa, Korea, and other centers of conflict. It was during the 1950s also that the word came to be used in relation to struggles against colonialism in Africa.

In the late 1960s hints of a changed use began to appear. The term *liberation theology* seems to have been used first by Gustavo Gutierrez in a talk in Peru in 1968.[5] The American black activist George Jackson, in a letter of 23 February 1966, spoke of "the liberation that is planned for tomorrow." In 1967 The Dialectics of Liberation Congress was held in London, and within a few years *women's liberation* and *gay liberation* were to enter the popular vocabulary. Yet as late as 1989 the *New Encyclopaedia Britannica* had no article on liberation.[6]

The concept of liberation in its political sense as involving the struggle of a people is used in relation to such diverse situations as those in South Africa, Latin America, and, increasingly, Eastern Europe. Common to such struggles are themes of exploitation, repression, domination, subjugation, and oppression. These terms are often used loosely and interchangeably, but they have different emphases. *Exploitation* tends to be linked with economic power, specifically with the power of international capital. *Repression* is associated with political and military pressure from a state machine—the repressive power of the state—though it may also be used in a more psychological sense, particularly in relation to sexuality. *Domination* may, and increasingly is, used in connection with bureaucracies. *Subjugation* and *oppression* are likely to be associated with race and gender, oppression being used particularly within the women's movement and in debates on sexual politics. A term that came into popular use in the 1960s was *alienation*. Looser and weaker terms are *dissatisfaction, disenchantment, discontent, disaffiliation,* but there is no certainty that a liberation movement will arise from such experiences, though they may create communities of discontent on the fringes of nations and societies. Such communities may become communities of resistance within a particular context, particularly if mobilized by a charismatic leader.

Within Third World usage, *liberation* tends also to involve freedom from the dehumanizing effects of colonization, a theme central to the works of Frantz Fanon, and the creation of a "new humanity." If the term *spirituality* is used, it is in this sense of the new humanity that is being forged out of the experience of struggle. The spirit is perceived as dynamic, the driving force and visionary power of the movement. Only by involvement in struggle, only from within the movement itself, can a spirituality emerge. Christians in the "developed" world will learn what this means only by sitting at the feet of their brothers and sisters from the Third World, reading their writings, listening to their prayers and poems and songs, and trying, as best they can, to enter into the heart of their struggle for liberation and justice. Yet such struggles have been taking place within "advanced" Western societies for some time, the most notable being the movement of black liberation and the spiritual theology that has both motivated it and grown up around it.

Spirituality and the Black Liberation Struggle: A White Perspective

In 1700 Kimpa Vita, a Congolese girl, appeared as a prophetess and said that Christ was a black man with black apostles.[7] This event marked a significant moment of awakening for the black spiritual tradition, though it was much later that the movement for black liberation assumed concrete political form. The movement grew from a sense of solidarity in oppression rooted in skin color and aligned with slavery, poverty, and inequality. Black people were the first community to create a vocabulary to counter the oppression of those not defined by class. It was much later that concepts such as "sisterhood" and "gay power" helped to define the movements of other groups whose experience of oppression was rooted in gender and sexual orientation. But it was the black struggle that provided the impetus for the later movements. Perhaps the environmental movement alone was not dependent on black struggles.

In the archaeology of black radicalism, the slave revolts are crucial. There were slave revolts as early as the sixteenth century—in Colombia in 1530, 1548, and the 1550s, and in Venezuela in 1552. But the major risings were in the eighteenth and nineteenth centuries. In North America there were revolts in New York City in 1712 and in Stono, South Carolina, in 1739. During the eighteenth and nineteenth centuries there were over four hundred slave revolts in Jamaica, the main ones taking place in 1729, 1760, and 1831–32. The leaders of these revolts were almost all religious figures. And in 1791 there was the great rising in Haiti. In these risings, and the thinking aroused by them, we can see the origins of a black consciousness. The theme of "negritude," an early term for black consciousness, appeared in Caribbean literature in the nineteenth century. In these early protests of the slaves lie the beginnings of a black theology of liberation.

In 1829 David Walker issued his "Appeal to the Coloured Citizens of the World." This is a remarkable document and holds a central and abiding place in a black spirituality of liberation. Gayraud Wilmore has said of it, "Walker's Appeal is steeped in Biblical language and prophecy. It is certainly one of the most remarkable religious documents of the Protestant era, rivaling in its righteous indignation and Christian radicalism Luther's 'Open Letter to the Christian Nobility of the German Nation,' published in Wittenberg in 1520."[8] The Appeal was one among a growing number of assertions that the liberty by which Christ had set his people free was a liberty that was applicable to liberation from racial oppression. God was seen as taking sides in the struggle, as being on the side of the oppressed. In the same year Robert Alexander Young issued the Ethiopian Manifesto, an early Pan-Africanist document, with its message of a black Messiah. "God is a Negro," proclaimed Bishop Henry Turner of the African Methodist Episcopal Church in 1898. Turner (1834–1915) was a major figure in the emergence of a black liberation theology. Yet it was not simply a question of leading figures: there was a whole movement of black spirituality that was perceived as a motive force for liberation. As a result "black Christians who were ardent in their devotions had to be watched carefully."[9]

Over many years the black church, the only institution in the United States that was owned and controlled by black people, became both the main sphere for survival strategies and the context within which visions of liberation were nourished and expressed. In 1890 Levi Coppin of the African Methodist Episcopal Church claimed that if the world were to be converted to Christianity it would be through the blacks who were currently held in wretchedness and degradation.[10] For many, the church became an institutional bulwark against the meaninglessness and desolation of the ghetto, and black Christian discourse became the principal language of subversive dissent and visionary energy. The black church was, and in many places remains, a source of corporate and personal identity, a source for the definition of humanity, while to this day, all over the United States, the prophetic black church is a major source of political leadership.

Here too there grew up a culture in which music and rhythm was of central importance. In this community, where family bonds, language, culture, and freedom had been destroyed, there developed a musical tradition and an apocalyptic style that the white masters could not understand. Black worship became a subversive activity: the dance of liberation and the rhythm of surrender. The "sublimated outrage"[11] of the spirituals, the brutal pathos of the blues, and the joy and triumph of gospel music manifested a spirituality in which the journey from Calvary to the Resurrection was expressed in the songs of a pilgrim people.

The spirituals, often misunderstood by white people as individualistic and inward, are an assertion of personhood, of identity. They are sorrow songs, expressing a profound dialectic of lamentation and hope, frustration and longing, moaning, dread, and despair. Yet these songs, so intensely personal, within the context of black worship became revolutionary and formed the central element in a kind of grapevine of solidarity within an inhuman system. From the spirituals there was a movement to gospel music, the black Christian music of the urban settlements. Gospel music arose out of the Pentecostal Assemblies of the World, a church based in Indianapolis and with a massive presence on the South Side of Chicago. Here music that had its origins in West Africa became the foundation of a radical Christian presence in the inner cities. It was a music of hope and triumph. Typical of the sense of triumphal expectation was the song "I'll Overcome Someday." Composed by the black pastor Charles Tindley (1856–1933), it became the basis for "We Shall Overcome," one of the most inspirational songs of the civil rights movement in the 1960s. Tindley's hymn "We'll Understand It Better By and By" also conveys the sense of hope in spite of adversity that runs through the black spiritual tradition:

> Trials dark on every hand, and we cannot understand
> All the ways that God would lead us to that Blessed Promised
>   Land;
> But he guides us with his eye and we'll follow till we die,
> For we'll understand it better by and by.
>
> By and by, when the morning comes,
> All the saints of God are gathered home.
> We'll tell the story how we've overcome.
> For we'll understand it better by and by.[12]

It was during the depression that gospel music began to supersede the spirituals. The key figure, Thomas Dorsey, had been converted by Tindley, and he became the father of gospel music. Dorsey's song "Precious Lord" was translated into thirty-two languages.[13] What is often not recognized is that gospel music and social action often went together. One of the main centers of the gospel music tradition in Chicago is the huge Apostolic Church of God in the Woodlawn area, which has been led for many years by Bishop Arthur Brazier. Brazier, who stands firmly within the Pentecostal tradition of worship, was a close colleague of Saul Alinsky and wrote the history of the Woodlawn Organization, the most famous black community organization on the South Side. It is said that the powers that be in Chicago at the time were much more afraid of Brazier than of Malcolm X.[14]

From the Caribbean too comes music of the oppressed, music of rebellion. Out of Jamaican blues (blue beat) came reggae, and it was through reggae that Bob Marley gave a public and popular voice to the spiritual movement of Ras Tafari, the culture of the black redeemer. Jamaican rebel music unites the despair of the poor with defiance and hope. In the words of Linton Kwesi Johnson, "It is a music that beats heavily against the walls of Babylon that the walls may come a tumbling down; a music that chucks a heavy historical load that is pain, that is hunger, that is bitter, that is blood, that is dread. Yes, the popular music of Jamaica is full of dread for it is dread down Jamaica way this day: it is red down there I say."[15] In reggae, the experience of the Jamaican unemployed is expressed in biblical language, with imagery of blood, fire, brimstone, Sodom and Gomorrah, and Babylon. Ras Tafari is a movement that has drawn considerable support from the black youth of British cities.

In recent years the experience of black people, particularly in the United States, has found expression within the black theology of writers such as James Cone, Gayraud Wilmore, and Cornel West. Black, says Cone, is the color of oppression. God has made an unqualified identification with black people. If a theology is indifferent to liberation, it is not Christian theology. Black theology, then, is "a self-conscious effort to relate the experience of American blackness to the corpus of Christian theology."[16] From its beginnings it has been seen as a kind of liberation theology, as the title of one of Cone's early books, *A Black Theology of Liberation*, makes clear. Cone describes the contrast between black and white understandings of theology and, in so doing, makes clear the contribution of black Christianity to the Christian movement as a whole.

> White theologians built logical systems; black folks told tales. Whites debated the validity of infant baptism or the issue of predestination and free will; blacks recited biblical stories about God leading the Israelites from Egyptian bondage and Joshua and the battle of Jericho and the Hebrew children in the fiery furnace. While theologians argued about the general status of religious assertions in view of the development of science generally and Darwin's *Origin of Species* in particular, blacks were more concerned about their status in American society and its relation to the biblical claim that Jesus came to set the captives free. White thought on the Christian view of salvation was largely "spiritual" and sometimes "rational" but usually separated from the concrete struggle of freedom in this world. Black thought was largely eschatological and never abstract but usually related to their struggle against earthly oppression.[17]

For Cone, the blackness of Jesus Christ is a religious symbol both of oppression and of deliverance. In Christ there is a new humanity: we are "new creatures born in the divine blackness, and redeemed through the blood of the black Christ."[18] The experience of oppression is the ultimate authority for any Christian theological tradition. There can be no theology without this experience of an oppressed community. Cone is highly critical of those black churches that have moved toward conformity and away from a critical prophetic stance.

In Britain the largest and fastest growing black-led church is the New Testament Church of God. With headquarters in Cleveland, Tennessee, this church grew out of revivalist meetings in North Carolina and Tennessee in the nineteenth century. In the United States it is mainly white and conservative and only claims a mass black membership in Jamaica and England. Its growth in English cities is a post-immigration phenomenon. At the time immigration from the Caribbean began, the bulk of Christians in the islands belonged to the "mainstream" churches—Roman Catholic, Anglican, Baptist, Methodist, and Moravian—and less than 10 percent, mainly in Jamaica, to the "sideways" churches, principally of Pentecostal origin. Today in England almost the reverse is the case. Yet the white revivalist tradition fits uneasily with the bulk of the black membership, which is of urban working-class origin. Many of the younger members have become politically active and have begun to face issues that lie beyond the conceptual framework of the church hierarchy. One of its more radical members, Elaine Foster from Birmingham, England, writes, "The black religious experience in Britain today continues to be shackled by a theology essentially alien to the African experience, divorced from the pragmatics of life, bearing the values of the plantocracy and other white racist institutions."[19] It is by no means clear what the future holds for this and other black-led churches of Pentecostal origin. There could be a major split between the otherworldly, pietist elements and the more radical sections of the membership. Certainly the fusion of Pentecostal spirituality and radical politics carries a potentially explosive power, but the more militant among black youth on the streets of British cities are more likely to be attracted elsewhere.

For many black youth in British cities, as in Jamaica, it is the Ras Tafari movement that has created a kind of street liberation theology. Ras Tafari, or "Rasta," owes its origins to a fusion of the African vision of Marcus Garvey, the tradition of black folk religion, and political radicalism. It began as a millenarian movement among the very poor sections of Jamaican society in the 1930s, having been inspired by the coronation of the Ethiopian emperor Haile Selassie in 1930. The uprisings in Jamaica between 1935 and 1938 led to the emergence of Rasta as a political force. But Rasta is also a deeply spiritual movement. "The historical experience of the Afro-Jamaican is a deeply spiritual experience, a religious experience in the wildest sense of the word. . . . The historical phenomenon called Rastafarianism which is saturating the consciousness of the oppressed Jamaican . . . is in fact laying the spiritual and the cultural foundations from which to launch the struggle for liberation."[20] It was in the 1960s and 1970s, however, that Rasta became a mass cultural force, with Bob Marley and the Wailers providing the single most important impetus in the process.

White sociologists have portrayed Rasta as a culture of withdrawal, escape, and alienation and individual Rastas as people with "identity problems";[21] criminologists have interpreted the movement in terms of pathology and deviance, and doctors have spoken of personality disorders.[22] Such reductionist "explanations" fail to recognize the role of Rasta as a movement of spirituality and resistance. The red, black, and green flag symbolizes resistance and struggle.

> Red for the color of the blood which must be shed for their redemption and liberty;
> Black for the color of the noble and distinguished race to which we belong; and
> Green for the luxuriant vegetation of the Motherland.[23]

Linked with the flag are the symbol of the Lion and the chalice, the cultural and subversive force of the drum, the dreadlocks, and the language of the Rasta culture. Dreadlocks, the distinctive hairstyle of the Rastafarian, have their roots in dread, the central concept of the movement, with its suggestion of consciousness of power rooted in a dreadful confrontation with the denial of racial selfhood. But the historic roots of the movement lie in desperate poverty. The sociologist Ruth Glass portrayed the context of Rasta with great power in 1962 after a visit to the slum camps of Jamaica.

> Here there are flimsy miserable huts, thrown together; made of refuse—paper, cardboard, packing cases, bits of sticks and parts of discarded motor car bodies. Here there are open drains; no latrines; no sewage disposal. There is constant water famine; barely one standpipe for hundreds of people; it is a maze of sodden dirt tracks through a jungle of habitations, unfit for living creatures of any kind.

> There are similar shanty towns, squatters' colonies, ramshackle camps of urban hangers-on in other Caribbean territories, in other under-developed areas of the world, and in some regions of advanced countries too. But the Kingston jungles are exceptional both in extent and in the degree of abandonment they expose. There is nothing like them anywhere else in the West Indies nor in countries whose average income per head is lower than that of Jamaica. The Kingston slums are in a category apart not only because they exist in

juxtaposition to affluence but—more important—because they represent, unmistakably, the miserable chaos resulting from a system designed to produce human disintegration and still capable of producing it.

It is when you go into the slum camps of Kingston (and few outsiders from the comfortable areas of Jamaica ever do)—it is then that you are directly confronted by colonial history; you are in the presence of the aftermath of slavery. . . . People stop short in anger, seeing a white face: the symbol of privilege, the mark of Cain.[24]

What we are witnessing today is the reproduction of this culture of oppression and resistance within the deprived areas of Western cities.

What insights can white Christians gain from the black religious experience? What is the relevance of this experience for the struggle to find a spirituality for social and political commitment?

The first lesson to be learned is the need to unite hope and protest. It is this unity that is so clearly present in black Pentecostal worship, with its sense of joy in the midst of anguish and pain. Cornel West has spoken of "subversive joy and revolutionary patience" as characteristics of black spirituality.[25] The act of worship is of its very nature a protest, the assertion of the lordship of Christ over all claims of earthly lords and masters.

A second area is that of the expression of pain. In the spirituals and the blues, the depths of pain are plumbed, and black spirituality has a special place for the funeral. The anguish of suffering and death are not banished to the private realm but are expressed powerfully in the words and music of the worship service.

Third, there is the stress on the power of the Word. Preaching plays a central part in black worship and black struggle. It is an activity that involves a communion of the preacher with the Word of God and that demands a response from the hearers. In contrast to the perfunctory, emotionless ten-minute homily of many mainstream white churches, the black sermon is a lengthy, sustained, and powerful liturgical action.

A fourth area concerns the use of the body. The worship of the black church involves the whole body—the emotions and feelings, the voice, arms and legs, the entire personality. The centrality of the feet washing in many black churches expresses both the importance of the physical and the dimension of lowly service to the community. Linked with this is the sense of dance and rhythm, the "soul power" and dynamic energy of hymns and songs.

Finally, it is important to see that the theology that is held within the black liberation tradition is a theology of the liberation of the poor. "In all roles the theologian is committed to that form of existence arising from Jesus' life, death and resurrection. He knows that the death of the man on the tree has radical implications for those who are enslaved, lynched and ghettoized in the name of God and country. In order to do theology from that standpoint, he must ask the right questions. . . . The right questions are always related to the basic question: What has the gospel to do with the oppressed of the land and their struggle for liberation?"[26] If white Christians are to learn from the black experience, they will need to see that their historic relationship to their black brothers and sisters has been one of oppressor to victim. Spiritual renewal can come only by ending this relationship, and this involves turning to the victim and seeing in that victim our only hope.[27]

"Another Country": The Spiritual Significance of Lesbian and Gay Struggles

The word *homosexual* owes its origin to the Hungarian physician Karoly Benkert in 1869.[28] From its first use in the nineteenth century it was not a neutral or value-free term but reflected the current ideology within biology and psychology as well as the social need to classify a new type of deviant. On the other hand, *sodomite* and *bugger* had been in use from medieval times. An act of 1290 decreed that convicted sodomites were to be burned alive, and, although Henry VIII in 1533 changed the mode of execution, death remained the penalty in Britain until 1861 and life imprisonment until 1967. To this day the death penalty for homosexual activity is still demanded by some American Christians. Homosexuals have been among the most persecuted and brutalized groups within "Christian" societies, not least as victims of the Nazi holocaust. From the perspective of a theology of liberation, therefore, the central issue is very simple. Whatever the moral status of "homosexual genital acts," the evidence shows that this community has been among the most oppressed, persecuted, and victimized groups in human history. Any theology of liberation must be tested against the response to this community and its struggle against such oppression.

The modern gay liberation movement is usually dated to the police raid on the Stonewall Cafe in New York in 1969, which led to an annual celebration of "gay pride." However, there had been activity within the Christian church prior to this, including the founding of Dignity, the gay supportive and pressure group within the Roman Catholic church in the United States, and the Metropolitan Community Church, a gay Christian communion, in 1968. Later came Integrity, the American Episcopal group, and the Gay Christian Movement (now the Lesbian and Gay Christian Movement) in Britain.

The gay liberation movement arose as a resistance movement against the persecution, stereotyping, and prejudice directed against gay people. Since those days the arrival of the AIDS epidemic, wrongly associated by many people exclusively with gay men, has further stigmatized this community. Gays are increasingly portrayed by sections of the media, and viewed by many people, as a contaminating influence within society. They have joined the ranks of the scapegoats. For many centuries people have sought scapegoats, particularly when confronted with disease or disaster. The Jews were blamed for the Black Death and later (by Hitler) for syphilis. In England the Tudor and Stuart plagues were blamed on "blasphemers," and the nineteenth-century cholera on "the great unwashed." The attack on gay people today could be extended to other vulnerable groups. Such stigmatizing and victimizing presents a major challenge to Christians as disciples of Christ the victim, who, like the scapegoat of Leviticus, bore our sins in his own body to the tree (1 Pet. 2:24; cf. Lev. 16:8–10).

At the present time people with AIDS suffer a multiple stigma. They suffer as gay people or as drug addicts (another group among whom the virus has spread). They suffer as a result of physical marks—the blotches of Kaposi's sarcoma and other skin lesions, as well as the loss of weight, the general physical deterioration, and the enforced isolation from "respectable" circles. In a real sense they have become the equivalent of the ancient lepers, the unclean and despised, the outcasts of society.

However, it is not simply people with AIDS but people in the lesbian and gay community in general who have suffered in the recent upsurge of what is, somewhat misleadingly, termed "homophobia."[29] In particular, they have suffered the effects of a frightening increase in violence and harassment within the "Christian" nations of the United States and Britain. The documentation of such attacks in recent years is considerable and terrifying: an attack on two gay men with garbage cans in Greenwich Village on a crowded Friday night in 1986; two gay men decapitated in Queens in 1986; two men cut up and set on fire in a garbage can in New York City in February 1986; six to ten reports of violence each day in New York City in 1987; swastikas with antigay slogans on the Episcopal chaplaincy at the University of Chicago, with signs saying "Fight AIDS, Castrate All Gays," and so on.[30] In the United States, recorded attacks grew from 2,042 in 1985 to 4,946 in 1986 and have continued to rise.[31] At Yale, nearly half the lesbian and gay students in one survey said that they had experienced harassment, and other surveys have shown similar results. In Britain there were seventeen murders of gay men, or men believed to be gay, in two years; three gay men were murdered in west London in 1990.[32] The increasingly hostile attitudes of the media and sections of the government have helped to create a climate in which violence can flourish. In Britain the notorious Clause 28 of the Local Government Act of 1988 attacked those who were "intentionally promoting homosexuality" and what was termed the "pretended family relationship" of lesbian and gay couples. There is no doubt that the atmosphere has become increasingly oppressive.

This growing climate of intolerance and hatred has not left the Christian community unaffected. Indeed, in some respects the attitude to gay and lesbian people within some sections of the churches is more hostile and more rooted in fear and loathing than it is in the wider community. The call by the Moral Majority for a "war against homosexuality," with its injunction to "stop homosexuals dead in their tracks,"[33] has been followed only too literally by some people. The ferocious hatred that one finds in some types of fundamentalism is one facet of our religious problem, and it is clear that lesbian and gay people have most to fear from the recent upsurge of the Christian Right.[34] In Britain one observer has spoken of the resurgence of homophobia as "the most sordid and squalid campaign of bigotry and scapegoating which this country has seen since the heyday of Mosleyite enthusiasm."[35] (Sir Oswald Mosley was the leader of the fascist movement in Britain in the 1930s.)

In the Church of England, the response to homosexuality has been more genteel and hypocritical, lacking in both pastoral sensitivity and theological seriousness. In 1988 the legal officers of the Diocese of London, a diocese with very large numbers of homosexual clergy, including many in very senior and influential positions, initiated proceedings to evict the Lesbian and Gay Christian Movement from its premises in Saint Botolph's Church, Aldgate, a church with a long record of compassionate and caring ministry. The saga of the proceedings, and the behavior of the officials, makes very sad reading.[36] At one point seventy clergy wrote a letter pointing out that "members of the LGCM are our brothers and sisters in Christ, and the rest of the church should listen to them with respect and love, especially at this time of increasing hostility to gay people. But again the church has been seen as intolerant and rejecting, driving gay people out both physically and symbolically."[37] But the letter made no impression, and the church bureaucracy and hierarchy colluded with the secular mood to reinforce the growing bigotry.

I want therefore to argue that the movement for the dignity of lesbian and gay people, and the history of their treatment at the hands of violent and oppressive forces—both inside and outside the church—is a critical test case for Christian spirituality and Christian concern for justice. It raises many issues that go far beyond the confines of the homosexual community.

It raises, first, the binding obligation upon Christ's disciples to stand by the stigmatized and the afflicted, following Christ's own example of solidarity with outcasts. Wherever men and women are despised, rejected, and abused, there is Christ. Such solidarity with the victims of injustice and oppression must always override any temptations to judge or condemn. It is a critical test of fidelity to the way of Christ.

Second, the struggles of lesbian and gay people pose in a fundamental and painful way the whole issue of honesty within the church. It is well known that churches have contained "practicing" homosexuals for centuries and that many of these members have been ordained to the ministry. Yet bishops and senior church officials continue to speak as if this were not the case. As a result, lesbian and gay people within the churches are often forced into a position of silence and secrecy and may feel obliged, under pressure, to vote against their own identities as a way of protecting themselves. Indeed, many parts of the church seem to encourage concealment and dishonesty and to reward effective concealment with promotion, while handing over to the bigotry and cruelty of the secular press those who do not succeed in this charade. This climate of doublethink undermines the church's claim to be a zone of truth; honesty becomes impossible within the church community, with tragic consequences not only for lesbian and gay people but for the integrity of the entire community. A spirituality of liberation cannot be built on dishonesty and the refusal to confront the realities of human life.

These struggles, and the responses to them, reveal a third issue of enormous concern for the future of spirituality: the resurgence of right-wing fundamentalism in a specifically antihomosexual form. At the heart of the fundamentalist tradition is a posture of utter certainty and an exclusion of doubt and darkness, and it is not surprising that intolerance of dissent and deviance should form a central part of the movement, particularly when it is allied to a conservative political crusade. Sara Diamond is correct to see lesbian and gay people as "the most vulnerable targets of Christian Right venom."[38] Biblical fundamentalism has normally been accompanied by manifestations of bigotry, intolerance, and often violence, and there is little doubt that in the present climate fundamentalism and antigay politics go hand in hand. Fundamentalism of this kind is a serious danger to Christian spirituality as well as to the health of any community in which it is present. It is a pathological growth upon the Christian movement, and it calls for very serious and thoughtful responses. The worst kind of response would be a reverse intolerance by which fundamentalists became the new outcasts and a demonology was created around them. Indeed, there is considerable evidence that many of those attracted by fundamentalist claims are people who feel left out, undervalued, insecure, people whose voices have not been heard. The resurgence of fundamentalism is a challenge to all Christians to reexamine the roots of their faith and discipleship.

Fourth, the struggles of lesbian and gay Christians raise a central issue for spirituality: the relation between orientation and practice. It is curious that in most areas of the Christian life—social justice, political action, the life of prayer, for instance—the unity of being and doing, inner disposition and outward practice, are stressed. The test of our devotion is practical action, faith is manifested in works, and so on. Only, it seems, on the matter of homosexuality is a sharp moral division made between being and doing. What we seem to be saying is that God has created a community of people whose psychosexual identities are such that they can have no physical outward manifestation, a community for whom orientation and practice must forever remain divided.[39] The tragic feature of this approach is that, though promiscuous and irresponsible relationships can always be forgiven, and so "pastoral care of the homosexual" can be sustained as a Christian norm, the real victims are those people in stable, loving, and responsible lesbian and gay relationships, people who feel no need of repentance. These are the people for whom the church has nothing of positive value to say: they remain "intrinsically disordered," their condition one of "symbolic confusion."[40] Surely Christian spirituality can offer a more hopeful path to perfection.

There is a fifth issue that is raised specifically by the spread of AIDS. In bringing AIDS into the discussion at this point I do not wish to reinforce the view that it is a "gay plague" or that only gay men are affected by it. Indeed, the point of raising the question is to emphasize the creative and positive response of the gay community to the disease and the transforming effects within those sections of the Christian church that have responded, not with panic, fear, and loathing, but with compassion, love, and gentleness. It has been said that the Roman Catholic Holy Redeemer parish in San Francisco came to life through its experience of AIDS,[41] and the responses of love, compassion, and understanding that resulted. There are many other examples. Two members of another San Francisco parish have written of their experience of having come alive through AIDS. "We have come to understand ourselves as a church with AIDS. This doesn't mean that our church will soon be dead and gone. No, in fact it means that we live more deeply. The whole gay male community is undergoing a parallel transformation. A lifestyle characterized by carefree promiscuity has given way to dating and friendship. Many people are seeking intimacy and spirituality, which has had the effect of a revival."[42] At a more personal level, a London pastor writes of his experience of working on the AIDS ward at San Francisco General Hospital and the impact of this on his spirituality.

> After seventeen years as a London parish priest, where my ministry has been built upon the ongoing building up of relationships and community development centered on the eucharistic community, I have found it especially hard adjusting to the ministry on the AIDS unit . . . where each encounter must stand on its own; where each opportunity is special; and where time is not on our side. Learning just "to be" exposes me to my own frailty, loneliness and nakedness, especially perhaps as a stranger in a far country. I have always been a great fixer, both as social activist seeking to change the world and as the priest-actor-manager, offering a sacramental merry-go-round of exciting worship and meaningful spiritual comfort. Only now am I slowly, falteringly and fearfully facing the challenge of staying where the suffering really is; of not knowing the answers, and being honest about this; of allowing others to set the agenda for ministry; and even admitting that I receive from them as much as I can ever give.

This priest continues:

> The impact on me is not the numbers of people dying of AIDS but the stunning example of so many learning to live with AIDS, learning to live well, maybe not for long, but with a quality, a richness, a depth of loving not often experienced in young or comparatively young people, so many of whose lives have often, by nature of homosexuality, been clouded by prejudice, fear and oppression.

> Pastoral involvement means learning what it is to share the powerlessness, the fear and the degeneration which HIV brings to innocent sons and daughters made in the image of

God. It is a road to Calvary, not knowing answers; moving slowly, falteringly, and fearfully, staying with pain as it really is; with the rotting bodies, the decaying brains, the disabled forms; the prematurely aging human frames, the broken hearts of the medics and nurses as well as the dying and their loved ones; the terrified youth realizing he's almost dead before beginning to live. There can be no neat answers, no religious platitudes. Yet in some mysterious way we are used as icons, sacraments, models of the God who hung on the cross.[43]

These are not untypical testimonies from those who, through the experience of HIV and AIDS, and through ministering to those affected, have been drawn into a more profound spirituality, an encounter with the mystery of dying and rising, with the very heart of our faith. They have come to experience what Christian preachers have always said, that there can be no way to resurrection except through the encounter with death. To speak of such mysteries and to experience their reality are quite different, and it is of the nature of *krisis* and *kairos*, as the Scriptures see them, to make these truths real in all their disturbing nature.

Finally, the struggles of lesbian and gay people point us to the problem of difference and to the need to see the response to difference as central to our politics and our spirituality. The issues that arise around difference and diversity have been a major concern of the black American thinker Audre Lorde. In her book *Sister Outsider*, Lorde writes of the inability of our society to relate to difference in a way that is based on equality and respect.

Institutionalized rejection of difference is an absolute necessity in a profit economy which needs outsiders as surplus people. As members of such an economy, we have all been programmed to respond to the human differences between us with fear and loathing, and to handle that difference in one of three ways: ignore it, and if that is not possible, copy it if we think it is dominant, or destroy it if we think it is subordinate. But we have no patterns for relating across our human differences as equals. As a result, these differences have been misnamed and misused in the service of separation and confusion.[44]

The project of "relating across our human differences" is really basic to Christian life. Nothing was more striking about the ministry and teaching of Jesus than his insistence on the need to move from differences and strangeness to solidarity and communion. Instead of seeing one another as threats or as sources of contamination, we need to learn to recognize, value, and support one another as sharers in a common life and partners in a common struggle.

For these and for other reasons, I believe that the recent history of the movement for lesbian and gay rights carries important lessons for the practice of Christian spirituality and for the Christian commitment to social justice. Here particularly we see the coming together of the quest for personal identity and the need for political struggle. Yet here too we see how so much of the confusion about sexuality in the Western world has been projected upon the gay community, so this history also brings to the surface with a renewed significance and urgency the very old issue of the relationship between sexuality and the life of the spirit.

"The Carnality of Grace": Liberation and Sexuality

There is, to put it mildly, something rather odd about the claim in a recent American church report that "it is somewhat difficult in today's world to relate one's Christian spirituality to decisions involved in living as a sexual being."[45] Christian spirituality, indeed the Christian faith as a whole, is based upon the belief that the Word became flesh (John 1:14). Yet this religion of the incarnation, with its high valuation of matter, the flesh, the physical, does seem to have real problems in dealing with the issues of human sexuality. The persistence of the Gnostic and Manichaean heresies, with their view that the flesh is inherently sinful, has had devastating effects on Christian attitudes to sexuality, even though the "mainstream" Christian tradition has officially repudiated them. There is no doubt that Augustine's association of original sin specifically with sexual intercourse has seriously damaged the Christian approach to this area. A dualism dividing flesh from spirit, and interpreting sexuality in terms of the "lower nature," has made deep inroads into Christian spirituality and pastoral practice.

The erotic and the emotional life have come to be suspect. Sensuality, passion, and wildness are seen as threats both to the purity of the faith and to the decent order of moral life. So in the late nineteenth century an Anglican parish priest in Cornwall blamed the increase in "illegitimate" births on the influence of Methodism, which, he claimed, encouraged young peasant girls to give way to their emotions![46] Sex and the spirit are simply not seen to belong together.

The disgust at sexuality—or at least the uncertainty about whether Christianity really approves of it—is linked with the retreat from political involvement. Robert Lambourne, a priest and physician, used to speak of "the fear of flesh and politics"[47] as a distinguishing feature of conventional Christianity. Both the flesh and the polis are seen as equally threatening, equally contaminating, to the purity of the soul. So it is not surprising that many Christians have found their tradition deeply deficient in its ability to view sexuality other than as problematic. Recently this deficiency has come to be recognized and articulated in the writing of some (though only a few) theologians. Margaret Miles speaks of the "threadbare inadequacy of Christian tradition on these issues";[48] Carter Heyward has written with even greater emphasis:

> Christians who are committed to constructing a sexual ethics of liberation and tenderness, of friendship and touching, need to be aware that our religious heritage will serve us primarily as a foil in this particular task. For some issues, such as war and peace, traditional Christian teachings can play a more ambivalent, even perhaps a creative role. The shaping of a humane, body-affirming, relational ethics of sexuality, however, is not an enterprise in which traditional Christianity has either experience or knowledge. Like all pioneers, we Christians who venture into this terrain will do well to stick together, or we most likely shall get lost.[49]

The Christian tradition, on this view, is more than unhelpful; it is positively damaging. A spirituality of liberation, therefore, must honestly recognize the oppressive elements within the tradition and make a commitment to move beyond these to a more hopeful and affirmative position.

Heyward is one of the few Christian theologians who has devoted attention to the links between sexuality and justice, seeing lovemaking as a form of justice making and as a source of energy for the work of justice in the world. She points to the fact that the quest for justice in sexual relations has been trivialized, feared, and postponed. Yet she believes that this area is of fundamental importance for the future of the Christian movement, and her work is addressed to those who are "committed to making connections between sexuality, spirituality, and the ongoing struggle for justice for all."[50] In her account of the damaging effects of much in Christian tradition, she fails to give adequate recognition to the positive resources in Christian theology that might be mobilized.

Any project to nourish a spirituality of liberation must take very seriously the fact that the soul does not float freely, that grace comes through the body. This truth lies at the heart of all incarnational and sacramental theology: the principle of spirit through matter, God in the flesh, God in the sacrament. And yet we have created a gulf between the event of God in Christ and the activity of the grace of God in our bodies, between "the Sacraments" and the sacramental character of all creation. As a result we have lost the link between grace and the body. Over twenty years ago Sam Keen, in his important study *To a Dancing God*, posed the central question that confronts us still.

> What has happened to me? How am I to understand this warmth and grace which pervades my body? As I begin to reflect, I realize that neither the Christian nor the secular culture, in which I have been jointly nurtured, have given me adequate categories to interpret such an experience. Neither has taught me to discern the sacred in the voice of the body and the language of the senses. In the same measure that Christian theology has failed to help me appreciate the *carnality of grace*, secular ideology has failed to provide me categories for understanding the *grace of carnality*. Before I can understand what I have experienced, I must see where Christian theology and secular ideology have failed me.[51]

Of course, the pursuit of this project does not imply an end to the serious problems that affect the sexual lives and relationships of Christian people. Yet we are more likely to be able to make sense of them if we have begun to value and reverence the body, the flesh, and to enter into "the body's grace."[52]

Christian spirituality at its best is materialistic, a spirituality of the whole person in communion. It is not a static essence, a purely inward encounter, a flight of the alone to the alone, but a movement of persons in solidarity. It can be a liberating movement only if it is formed and directed by a genuine materialism, rooted in the truths of incarnation, resurrection, and sacrament. It is materialistic, for it believes that, in the words of Irenaeus, if the flesh is not saved, then the Lord has not redeemed us.[53] It holds, with Gregory Nazianzen, that "what he [Christ] has not assumed, he has not healed"[54] and that this includes our sexual natures.

One major and continuing obstacle in the path of a healthy and affirming view of sexuality is the tendency to see both sex and the passions as belonging to a "lower nature" and to associate the image of God and "spirituality" with mind and reason, the "higher nature." In our day the New English Bible, by translating "flesh" as "lower nature" has perpetuated this long-entrenched misunderstanding. In New Testament thought, the "flesh," as used by Paul, means unredeemed human nature. There is nothing here of the dualism that was later to distort the understanding of the wholeness of human personality. Yet dualism and denial of the flesh were not totally victorious. Patristic writers such as John Chrysostom and John Climacus insist that physical human love, *eros*, is analogous to divine love. God, says Chrysostom, is "more erotic than bride and groom," and Climacus speaks of the love of God as being "an abundance of eros." Symeon the New Theologian calls the relationship with God "intercourse" and speaks of sleeping with Christ.[55] In the thirteenth century both Aquinas in the West and Gregory Palamas in the East stress the central place of the passions and insist that body and emotions share in the divine nature. As Palamas says, "The passionate forces of the soul are not put to death but transfigured and sanctified."[56]

Reverence for the body goes hand in hand with reverence for creation: the rejection of, and contempt for, the body is linked with the rejection of, and contempt for, the created world. A spirituality of liberation must therefore involve a renewal of the doctrine of creation as a living and dynamic component of Christian discipleship.

The Greening of the Spirit: Spirituality and Creation

The word *ecology* was coined over a century ago by the German scientist Ernst Haeckel (1834–1919), but it took a hundred years for it to enter the *Oxford English Dictionary* (though it did get into the 1933 *Supplement)*. Concern about the environment, and the possible threats to it, long antedates the counterculture of the 1960s, as it does the other liberation movements. Indeed, some would argue that the "green movement" should not be included among liberation struggles, because its origins, and much of its ethos, are so different. Certainly much of the concern about ecological doom and the pollution of the environment is rooted in a profoundly conservative view of the social and economic order. The very language used is that of preservation, conservation, and survival—hardly that of radical politics. Green concerns may very easily go hand in hand with a very conservative view of the world, and in practice much environmentalism is content to tinker with the structures and does not seek to challenge either the underlying ideology of industrialism or established hierarchies of domination. So, for example, the British Conservative Party uses an environmentalist rhetoric but fails to make connections with its strongly held commitment to nuclear weapons and nuclear power. Nevertheless it has become clear in recent years that another trend within the movement is far more radical, and that the green agenda points to a deep critique of the fundamental values of Western society. It is impossible to consider a Christian spirituality of liberation without taking into account, with the utmost seriousness, the question of the liberation of the creation from its oppressive and potentially fatal bondage.

In shaping current concerns certain books and reports are important landmarks. Rachel Carson's *The Silent Spring* (1962) pointed to the misuse of chemicals and the possible extinction of wildlife. But it was 1972 that was to be the crucial year. In this year *The Limits to Growth* was published by the Club of Rome, and *Blueprint for Survival* appeared in *The Ecologist*. These and other studies argued that industrial expansionism was not sustainable. The same year saw the publication of *Only One Earth* by Barbara Ward and Rene Dubos, and a conference of that name took place in Stockholm. The following year

E. F. Schumacher produced his book *Small Is Beautiful,* which was soon to become "the Bible of the green movement."[57] Within a short time it had been translated into thirty-four languages. Schumacher's book was not simply an argument for a reduction of scale: it was an attack on materialism and a call to a new spirituality, nourished by Buddhist ideas of reverence for life.

Since those early years, concern about the pollution of the rivers and seas, about the threat from toxic waste (the United States dumps billions of pounds of such waste into the waters every year), about the disappearance of forests and plant and animal species, about acid rain and global warming—such concern has accelerated, as have the number of groups committed to ensuring that it becomes a major part of the political agenda. Of course, political will has not kept pace with the seriousness of the issues or the strength of the feeling. Thus in the United Kingdom in 1988, although there were 23,253 recorded cases of water pollution, only one percent resulted in prosecutions. In Europe, there has been massive outrage about the pollution of the Rhine and Danube rivers, and it is from Europe that the most significant change in the political climate has come. In the European Parliament elections of 1989, green candidates won 15 percent of the votes.

However, alongside the development of green political structures has come the quest for a new spirituality. This quest was evident as early as Schumacher's book, and Schumacher was followed by Theodore Roszak with the claim that the needs of the person and the planet are one.[58] In the United States the scientist Paul Ehrlich has called for a "quasi-religious transformation of contemporary cultures,"[59] while Jonathon Porritt, the leader of the British group Friends of the Earth, has attacked contemporary capitalism as "a system without a soul" and stressed the need for "a new sort of politics that opens itself to the spiritual dimension."[60] Porritt relies on a number of other green thinkers, including Fritjof Capra, who emphasizes the unity of personal and political in a new holistic spirituality. "With the holistic sense of spirituality, one's personal life is truly political and one's political life is truly personal. Anyone who does not comprehend within him- or herself this essential unity cannot achieve political change on a deep level and cannot strive for the ideals of the greens."[61]

That the movement for ecological renewal has led to a renewed interest in spirituality is beyond doubt, but it is equally clear that most of that spirituality is not Christian in its origins. Indeed, many within the green movement see the Christian tradition as one of the major forces that has encouraged human domination of the natural world, encouraged those very forces of exploitation that lie at the heart of our current problems. This view was stated as long ago as 1967 by Lynn White in a famous article in *Science* that has been reprinted many times.[62] White argued that interpretation of the Old Testament, and specifically the language of Genesis 1:26–28, had led to a view of the relationship between humanity and the creation as one of domination. There is certainly a good deal of truth in White's view, and the record of the Christian church on environmental issues is highly ambiguous. However, it is important to recognize that there is not one approach to "nature" in the Bible but several, and the testimony is much more positive than is often claimed.

There is no Hebrew word for nature in our modern sense. There is, however, a profound recognition that the earth belongs to God (Exod. 19:5; Deut. 10:14) and is held in trust: it is not, as rival theories of the time held, a tradable commodity, but a gift and an inheritance.[63] Human beings, according to the Jewish Scriptures, are part of the solidarity of all life: with rocks, deserts, seas and floods, whales, and birds of the air, we praise the Lord. Psalm 104 and the Song of the Three Children (Benedicite) are among the many testimonies to this deeply sacramental view of the created world. Christians who have responded to White's thesis have pointed to that central theme in the Scriptures which stresses the covenant with the earth (Gen. 9:13). Relationship and companionship with nature lie at the heart of Jewish theology, as emphasized in Genesis 2, the older strand of the creation tradition. Nowhere is this sense of solidarity in covenant more powerfully expressed than in Hosea 2:18–19: "And I will make for you a covenant on that day with the beasts of the field, the birds of the air, and the creeping things of the ground; and I will abolish the bow, the sword, and war from the land; and I will make you lie down in safety." On the other hand, to break the covenant has its consequences in a broken earth; in Isaiah 24, Yahweh lays waste the earth and makes it desolate.

The earth lies polluted
under its inhabitants;
for they have transgressed the laws,
violated the statutes,
broken the everlasting covenant.
Therefore a curse devours the earth,
and its inhabitants suffer for their guilt;
therefore the inhabitants of the earth are scorched,
and few men are left. (Isa. 24:5–6)

In this passage a close link is made between the mourning of the wine and languishing of the vine, and the sighing of the merry and silencing of the mirth of timbrels and lyre (verses 7–8). The earth is described as "utterly broken . . . rent asunder . . . violently shaken" (verse 19). Ecological disaster is seen as the consequence of human infidelity to the covenant between God and the earth.

The positive and affirming attitudes toward creation in the biblical record are continued within later Christian history: in the tradition of the Benedictines, who worked with their hands, of the Cistercians, who cleared and cultivated the marshlands, of the Franciscans, with their joy and celebration of the natural world, and of the Diggers and Levellers, with their belief that salvation involved a restored and rejuvenated earth. "True religion and undefiled," said the Digger leader Gerrard Winstanley, "is to let everyone quietly have earth to manure."[64] Winstanley was a contemporary of the Anglican metaphysical poet Thomas Traherne, who saw identification with the natural order as the necessary foundation of a life of prayer and praise. Traherne wrote, "You never enjoy the world aright till the sea itself floweth in your veins, till you are clothed with the heavens and crowned with the stars; and perceive yourself to be the sole heir of the whole world: and more than so, because men are in it who are everyone sole heirs as well as you . . . till your spirit filleth the whole world, and the stars are your jewels, till you are familiar with the way of God in all ages as well as with your walk and table . . . till you delight in God for being good to all: you never enjoy the world."[65] Traherne stands within a long tradition of celebration of the creation with its roots in the Hebrew Scriptures and in the sacramental theology of the church. Modern Western attempts to restate a creation spirituality go back to the last century. Something of the necessary and powerful mingling of creation and redemption in Christian mystical theology is expressed in a beautiful poem by J. M. Plunket (1887–1916):

> I see his blood upon the rose
> And in the stars the glory of his eyes,
> His body gleams amid eternal snows,
> His tears fall from the skies.
>
> I see his face in every flower;
> The thunder and the singing of the birds
> Are but his voice—and carven by his power
> Rocks are his written words.
>
> All pathways by his feet are worn,
> His strong heart stirs the ever-beating sea,
> His crown of thorns is twined with every thorn,
> His cross in every tree.[66]

During the same period Conrad Noel, the parish priest of Thaxted in Essex, was emphasizing the importance of placing a radical understanding of the Eucharist and of the sacramental life within the framework of the sacramental nature of all created things:

> The poets speak of flowers as suggesting thoughts that lie too deep for tears, of the flower in the crannied wall as microcosm of God and man, of God's holy sacrament of spring, of the wayside sacrament of our hedgerows. Poets and mystics understand that God is really present to bless men under forms of bread, wine, oil, salt, flowers, water, fruit; that the color of the tulip, the scent of the rose, the sound of the sea, the grace and symmetry of the human body, are effectual signs of the presence of the God who prevents and follows us as the waters cover the sea.[67]

Later came Pierre Teilhard de Chardin, with his Hymn of the Universe, J. V. Taylor with his "theology of enough," Paulos Gregorios from the Syrian Orthodox tradition, and, most recently, the American Dominican Matthew Fox.

Fox's central point is that the Christian tradition has been dominated by the doctrines and ethos of Fall and atonement, and that only in the last decade has the doctrine of creation come into its own, principally through his own writing and promotional campaigning. Through his well-marketed "creation-centered spirituality," Fox has certainly helped to recover some neglected dimensions in Christian spirituality, though there are dangerous signs that his movement has become a cult, with all the problems of uncritical devotion to the leader, simplistic and idealized accounts of complex phenomena, and a green mysticism with only a minimal degree of political awareness. As with the earlier cult of Teilhard, adherence to latter-day gurus such as Fox and Thomas Berry can easily lead to neglect of the need to root ecological politics in scientific rigor. A rereading of the late Sir Peter Medawar's critique of Teilhard, in which he emphasizes these points, might be helpful in the current climate.[68] Yet the fact that creation-centered spirituality is clearly a marketable product within the flourishing eco-bourgeoisie must lead not only to a critical assessment of its claims but also to recognition that it is a response to a real hunger.

In fact the green movement as a whole raises a vast range of issues for Christians, but four stand out in relation to spirituality. The first is the importance of recovering the sense of the holiness of matter. Christians cannot despise matter, for, as Irenaeus put it, if the created world is no more than decay, ignorance, and passion, then it is a sin to offer its fruits to God; or, in the more affirmative maxim of Saint John of Damascus, Christians hold that it was through matter that our salvation came to pass. But Christian spirituality is not simply about celebration of the creation; it is about its liberation from slavery and oppression. And here some words of John Robinson are relevant. Writing of the stress in the eucharistic offertory on production and the role of the manufacturing process (bread and wine, not wheat and grapes), Robinson claimed that it was this stress that distinguished Christianity from "pagan religion and from much harvest festival religion."

> When men are not altogether averse to any connection between matter and religion, they lean to the idea that God can be encountered in "nature"—that is, in unspoiled nature. "God made the countryside, man made the town" is a theme that evokes a response in all of us. Bread and wine seem to take us further from God than earth and water, not nearer to

him: the element of production bars more than it mediates the divine encounter. At harvest festivals we fill our churches with vegetable marrows to the exclusion of the much more questionable manufactures which bear the smear of trade and industry. In this way we seek to find a way to God through matter that bypasses the need for redemption.[69]

A Christian spirituality of creation must take seriously the need for the redemption of the creation.

It is important, second, to stress the links between the oppression and exploitation of the earth and other forms of oppression. Rosemary Ruether is one of a small number of theologians who have pointed to the connections between the oppression of the earth and the oppression of women. Since Ruether's study *New Woman New Earth* in 1975, the term *ecofeminism* has entered the vocabulary as a way of expressing these connections.[70] But as in the work of Fox, it has not always been clear that those who claim to be ecofeminists have understood the economic and political issues.

And so, third, it is essential to place the concern about the environment within a wider political vision. New Age spirituality may have its attractions, but, at the end of the day, it is as dangerous and misleading a path as the earlier paths of esoteric mysticism and other-worldly pietism have been. "Deep ecology" and "earth wisdom" can easily degenerate into what Murray Bookchin terms "ecolala," the spirituality of the elitist dropout, which substitutes a romantic earth mysticism for any real engagement with the politics of hierarchy and domination.[71]

Finally, therefore, it is vital to connect the movement for ecological renewal with that of liberation from violence. An ecological spirituality must be a spirituality of resistance to violence and a spirituality of liberation from violence. It must recognize that "the 'principalities and powers' that oppress the poor also oppress the earth and other living beings. In light of this widespread abuse of life and environment, the theme of liberation must itself be extended to include the earth and other living creatures. As liberation theologies enter the twenty-first century such extension . . . is a next step in liberation thinking."[72] Today's environmental movements have arisen under the shadow of the nuclear threat, the symbol both of human violation of the creation and of the potential destruction of human life itself. "The bomb" continues to dominate all serious reflection on the future, whether of the earth or of humankind within it. It represents total violence, violence beyond bounds and constraints. But it represents an even more deadly reality for the Christian community: the violation of, and obliteration of, human and social values. No spirituality of liberation can survive that does not face this ultimate challenge to seek peace in the climate of nuclear terrorism.

Not Peace But a Sword: Spirituality, Violence, and Nonviolence

All thinking about human liberation today takes place within the context of violence: violence against the environment, violence against Third World peoples, violence against the poor, racial violence, violence against women, and so on. Violence is not an aberration within our society: it is endemic, it is normal. Yet we persistently ignore the systemic violence of the state, manifested in so many forms, while we deplore the violence of individuals against the state machine. Here the tradition of Catholic social thought is important in recalling us to foundational principles. The notion of systemic or structural violence is not new. Saint Thomas Aquinas taught that unjust laws were acts of violence; the French Catholic personalist thinker Emmanuel Mounier, writing in 1933, pointed out that attention to acts of violence tended to deflect attention from the more fundamental problem of states of violence—unemployment, dehumanization, even death.[73] The claim made by the bishops at Medellin in 1978 that Latin America was a "continent of violence" was well within this traditional way of thinking.[74]

Religion, and Christianity in particular, has been linked historically with violence. The church of the medieval West blessed the warrior class that emerged from the twelfth century. Indeed, the military orders, such as the Templars or the Knights of St. John, a fusion of the Germanic warrior and the Latin *sacerdos*, were central to medieval culture. They had been blessed by the church from the start and were a major factor in undermining the whole idea of the just war. The just war theory, concerned with means and limits, grew up *within* Christendom. But if one is fighting for absolutes, as in the "religious wars" of the sixteenth and seventeenth centuries or the ideological wars of the nineteenth and twentieth centuries, all means become legitimate.[75] Churches often claimed that wars cleansed and created a new and more religious society. In fact, the opposite was the case.[76] The contribution of war to the erosion of spiritual and moral values is very great.

Our history since 1945 has been dominated by the memory of violence on a more massive scale. Beginning with Auschwitz and Hiroshima, it has been within the political and spiritual climate created by the violence of the death camps and the bomb that we have had to struggle to live out our Christian discipleship. There are many who have questioned whether Christian faith can be maintained with integrity after the holocaust, just as there are many who have found that the "way of life" structured around the philosophy of nuclear deterrence has made any life of faith impossible.

Auschwitz took place in total silence, away from the sight of humanity. Only a few cried out, and their voices were not heard. Hiroshima took place with great clamor for all the world to hear, yet the scars and deep wounds of the Nazi holocaust are in some ways more abiding than even the effects of the bomb. We still live under the shadow of the total violence and destructive power of these two evils. At the basic physical level, ours is an age in which great damage has been done, and continues to be done, to the planet, damage greater than at any time in the previous sixty-five million years.[77] There have been scientific blunders, industrial crimes, numerous errors of judgment. The creation itself suffers violence, and is in travail, awaiting its deliverance from this slavery and oppression. We now have the materials to wipe out the world one hundred fifty times over.

But alongside the physical contamination and other damage there is the growing insecurity that the nuclear arms race and its spin-offs have created. From the Mershon Report of 1960 to the study by Professor Norman Rasmussen in 1974, the danger of nuclear accident has been well documented. The dishonest and increasingly incredible claims for the adequacy of "civil defense" made by successive governments in Britain and the United States no longer convince people. Britain, which has one of the highest concentrations of nuclear bases, would fare very badly in a nuclear attack. Even a one-megaton bomb on one city would kill one-third of the population of Great Britain immediately; it has been estimated that a 167-megaton attack would lead to 6.8 million deaths in the first month and 38 to 40 million in the first year.[78] The seriousness of nuclear damage is recognized by virtually all scientists as well as by leading military historians and experts on war. Thus Sir Michael Howard has written, "Few of us believe that there would be much left of our highly urbanized, economically tightly integrated and desperately vulnerable societies after even the most controlled and limited strategic nuclear exchange."[79] So we live in a climate marked by both accelerating expenditure and accelerating insecurity. Not only has insecurity increased as a reality, but the consciousness of insecurity has also increased, and as a consequence intensified despair and hopelessness.

In moral and spiritual terms, what is most alarming about the nuclear state and the culture of deterrence is the combination of secrecy, lying, and linguistic corruption. The nuclear industry was raised in secrecy, though it is only recently that the degree of this structural secrecy has been appreciated. In Britain, from the Atomic Energy Act of 1946 right through the 1950s, the growth of the industry took place beyond the sphere of democratic control and accountability. Even today the British government denies the existence of some U.S. military facilities (though they are listed in British Telecom directories!). The climate of secrecy and deception is not an accidental accompaniment of the nuclear weapons industry but is fundamental to its nature. Robert Jungk, in *The Nuclear State*, claimed that an industry based on plutonium was incompatible with democracy, and his claim was reinforced by warnings of dangers to civil liberties contained in reports from the U.S. Nuclear Regulatory Commission and the (British) Royal Commission on Environmental Pollution. The Royal Commission's study *Nuclear Power and the Environment* (1976) warned of increasing restrictions on rights of movement, the suspension of habeas corpus, and so on.[80]

The nuclear state is a repressive and authoritarian state by its nature. But it has increasingly become a state in which lying and the corruption of language have been institutionalized. A climate of illusion has been created in which our leaders are no longer believable. The importance of this for spirituality is clear, for a central task of spiritual tradition in the past has been to uphold the integrity and moral credibility of language. In the climate created by "nukespeak," a climate alien to all spiritual values, this task can only be pursued as a subversive one, for nukespeak has made ordinary straightforward and honest talk a virtual impossibility. "In *nukespeak* atrocities are rendered invisible by sterile words like *megadeaths;* nuclear war is called a *nuclear exchange.* Nuclear weapons accidents are called *broken arrows* and *bent spears.* Plutonium is called a *potential nuclear explosive.* The accident at Three Mile Island was called an *event,* an *incident, abnormal evolution* and a *plant transient.* India called its nuclear bomb a *peaceful nuclear device.*"[81] In this climate of *nukespeak* the question raised by Dietrich Bonhoeffer in the Nazi period becomes a cosmic question: nourished and distorted by the culture of duplicity and dishonesty, are we still able to be of service to the God of peace? Bonhoeffer wrote,

> We have been the silent witnesses of evil deeds. Many storms have gone over our heads. We have learnt the art of deception and of equivocal speech. Experience has made us suspicious of others and prevented us from being open and frank. Bitter conflicts have made us weary and even cynical. Are we still serviceable? It is not the genius that we shall need, not the cynic, not the misanthropist, not the adroit tactician, but honest straightforward men. Will our spiritual resources prove adequate and our candor with ourselves remorseless enough to enable us to find our way back again to simplicity and straightforwardness?[82]

Today Bonhoeffer's question must be asked again and again by Christians in the corrupting climate of the nuclear age.

So oppressive and degrading is this climate that increasingly those who seek to follow and serve truth, as well as justice and peace, find themselves turning to, or being led to, "holy disobedience." Through their obedience to Christ they become part of that network of "dissident groups" about which the Home Office *Training Manual for Scientific Advisers* warns its readers. The nuclear issue has presented Christians with a real diagnostic test of spiritual fidelity. "Blessed are the peacemakers" has today to be worked out in the framework of a spiritual formation that seeks to disaffiliate from the dominant culture of violence and destruction. Within this culture of total violence, with its threats to the planet itself as well as to human life and human values, the many signs and symbols of localized violence, whether in terrorism, vandalism, or urban uprisings, are not surprising. It is not odd that some young people should wish to smash up decaying and dehumanizing buildings when they have been brought up to accept the threat to smash up the world as a matter of course. Violence is indivisible: it cannot be condoned at one level and attacked at another. Planetary violence has its localized spin-offs because patterns of destruction have an increasingly global character. Yet much spirituality and church life lacks this global perspective and seeks to resist cosmic forces of destruction with weapons derived from an earlier, preglobal perspective.

I believe, therefore, that one of the contributions of the nuclear climate to Christian consciousness lies in the recovery of the meaning of nonviolence, not simply as a tactic but as an expression of what it is to follow Christ today. It is interesting to recall that the ancient writer Celsus's main complaint against the Christians was that they refused to fight in the army, and he saw this as being related to their claim to possess some special revealed truth.[83] Certainly Celsus was correct to see that the refusal to fight was more than a rejection of the Roman imperial claims to obedience. Nonviolence was a manifestation of obedience to the teaching and example of Christ. In a similar way today the Christian community is called to practice and manifest nonviolence at the heart of its spirituality.

What does this involve? Those who seek to practice the nonviolent life must have faced the reality of violence, both within themselves and within the society of which they are part. Nonviolent spirituality cannot be built on innocence or on a failure to deal with the roots of violence; it can only be built on the foundations of a recognition of, and transcendence of, both the power and the limitations of violence. Only those who have faced, recognized, and rejected the violence in themselves can be truly nonviolent. Only those who have understood the pressures that lead to violence can credibly struggle to be nonviolent. For it is struggle, liberating struggle, with which we are dealing, struggle that calls for a greater degree of love than does the commitment to violence. As Simone Weil observed, if we are merely incapable of the same degree of brutality as our enemies, there is no guarantee we will prevail.[84] A greater intensity and power of countervailing love is called for. Nonviolence is rooted in such intense love, in purity of heart and interior struggle. It is a whole way of life, the only way of life that is compatible with Christian discipleship.

A life of nonviolence cannot then be a passive life. In his "Letter from Birmingham Jail," Martin Luther King described nonviolent action as a crisis force whose aim was to bring a community to confront issues that it would rather avoid.[85] Earlier Gandhi had written of it in terms of liberating force, that force of truth which is the original meaning of *satyagraha*. For truth and peace are integrally connected. Peace can only be achieved through the transforming power of truth. Stanley Hauerwas is therefore right to say that nonviolence is integral to the shape of Christian conviction and stands at the heart of the Christian understanding of God.[86] Christian theology is the theology of the Prince of Peace; Christian spirituality is a spirituality of peacemaking, of nonviolent struggle to bring about God's will on earth as in heaven. That struggle cannot be pursued by violent and destructive methods that, though they may rearrange the structures of power, do not effectively change the nature of power. The Second World War did not bring an end to fascism. That struggle is still with us, as is the struggle for peace and justice. It is a struggle that goes to the very heart of Christian faith, a warfare of the spirit, the conflict with principalities and powers, calling for the most heroic discipleship.

At the heart of the nonviolent tradition is the conviction that politics is not simply about method and organizing, but also about lifestyle, identity, and supportive solidarity. To practice nonviolence is to be a particular kind of person, to be part of a nonviolent community, a community of peace. In recent years the connections between politics and lifestyle, between personal and political, have been made most powerfully and consistently by feminists, both inside and outside the religious traditions, and it is important to examine the contribution of feminist experience and reflection to a spirituality of liberation.

"Only Justice Can Stop a Curse": The Challenge of Feminism

Contemporary feminism did not arise from nowhere. It has roots both in the earlier movements for women's emancipation and in the counterculture consciousness of the 1960s, with its rejection of conventional middle-class lifestyles, its focus on the personal aspects of liberation, and its concern for justice.[87] The theme of the personal as political, though it is rightly associated with the women's movement, in fact antedated it and was an integral part of the thought of Jean-Paul Sartre, R. D. Laing, and Herbert Marcuse as well as other writers of the late 1960s. But the specific origins of modern feminism in Britain are usually located in the four demands of the Women's Liberation Movement, a feminist network that began in 1970: equal pay, education, and job opportunities; free contraception; abortion on demand; and free twenty-four-hour nurseries. Later a number of other demands were added: legal and financial independence; an end to discrimination against lesbians and the right to define one's sexuality; and, in 1978, freedom from intimidation, violence, and sexual coercion. Behind these demands lay a deeper concern for an end to the oppression of women within Western social, political, and economic structures.

The women's movement arose out of such concrete and practical struggles. The year 1971, which saw the effective origins of the movement in Britain, was also the year in which Chiswick Women's Centre was formed, the first of a number of refuges throughout the country. By 1975 the National Women's Aid Federation had been formed, a federation of thirty-five such centers. In the same year the first Rape Crisis Centre also appeared. Modern feminism had its origins in such responses to specific examples of sexual and domestic violence and economic exploitation. To say that it was a practical movement before it became a literary and reflective one would be to oversimplify the position. It would be more correct to say that it was a movement rooted in a unity of practice and theory. From its early years there were organs of feminist opinion and debate. In 1972 the best-known British feminist magazine *Spare Rib* began. Since then there have been many debates about white domination of the movement. In 1982 Outwrite, a multiracial collective, was formed, and black feminist groups have grown significantly during the 1980s. In addition to the changing racial character of feminism, four other developments within the recent movement are important: the growth of political lesbianism after 1978; the rise of eco-feminism; the rise and decline of socialist feminism; and the growth of the women's peace witness, particularly since the creation of the peace camp at Greenham Common in Britain in 1981 and the numerous movements of women against nuclear violence in the United States.

If I, as a male writer, am to reflect on, and respond to, the challenge of feminism, I need—as do my readers—to be clear about what I am doing and to be aware of some dangers. Most male writing on this and other issues is based on the very notion of neutral objectivity that feminists reject. Thus male writers will discuss "feminism" in a lofty, complacent, and detached, though "concerned," way as if it were simply another subject on the academic (male) agenda. To contribute to this process would no doubt earn me a reputation for scholarly objectivity—and it would be to misunderstand totally what the feminist challenge is about. However, most male writers, and especially those within the churches, seek to respond to feminist issues in this classical liberal way: by seeking to identify specific demands and then campaigning to have them placed upon the existing agenda. In this way feminism can, it is assumed, be absorbed into the already fixed framework of the (male) establishment. I have placed "male" in brackets because it is a feature that is normally hidden. The fact that an agenda, or an establishment, is male-dominated is not normally seen as more than an incidental feature of its status. It is simply part of the way things are: it is not questioned, and a whole range of issues (including feminism) are discussed and debated within its accepted framework. In this way an illusory objectivity is created, the male viewpoint being seen as the norm. This phenomenon has its liberal form: today it is not at all uncommon to find writings by men that purport to summarize, evaluate, and contain movements of thought (such as feminism) within their already formulated agendas. It is not unknown for male writers to extol the virtues of feminist thought with virtually no reference to any feminist thinker.[88]

I believe that one of the most important contributions of feminist thinking is its recovery of the concrete origins and character of knowledge and its rejection of the abstract self of the Enlightenment. Notions of a "received correctness"[89] are rejected, along with those familiar ideas of complete objectivity that merely lead to isolation and estrangement from lived consciousness. I believe that feminism has contributed greatly to any understanding of liberation in the current climate, and so, encouraged by Beverly Harrison, who urges men to do feminist theology,[90] and by other feminist thinkers, I offer the following reflections.

Feminism offers an alternative vision of the self to that of liberal individualism: a view of the self as foundationally social. As women and men, we are historical beings and can only be understood in terms of that history and of the relationships that have developed within it. In the early years of the women's movement, this social consciousness was communicated in the concept of sisterhood. Since those years there has been much criticism of this notion, with many pointing out that, though it has been a valuable rallying cry, it has obscured important differences between women through an overemphasis on Western middle-class white lifestyles. In spite of this, the themes of solidarity and friendship as basic to politics and spirituality are among the major contributions of the women's movement to contemporary understandings.[91]

The slogan "The personal is political" (which antedates feminism) has been a crucial element in challenging a politics that treats people as agents rather than subjects. In emphasizing the central place of the personal in politics, feminists have demanded more of themselves and have called for more exacting inner standards of political commitment. In a feminist perspective, politics absorbs more of one's being than has been the case in political life since the early days of the labor movement.

Of course, there are real dangers in so strong an emphasis on personal awareness and identity. As Bonnie Zimmerman has written, "There is a price to pay for a politics rooted so strongly in consciousness and identity. The point of diversity has as its mirror image and companion the powerlessness of fragmentation. Small autonomous groups can also be ineffectual groups."[92] Though fragmentation need not follow, the power structures are always ready to absorb and marginalize such groups, so concern for liberated lifestyle can replace the struggle for liberation as such. Yet in the recovery of the personal dimension in politics, there has come to the surface a feature of liberation struggle that is vital and yet is all too easily forgotten in much fashionable militancy: the value and dignity of every human being, however degraded and broken. Feminist politics arises from very basic and painful experiences of oppression, and it is this rootedness, this solidarity in pain, and the organized response to it, that makes the commitment to the least powerful so passionate and so persistent. Consider these words from an account by women who were former inmates of a psychiatric hospital:

> We know that it is important to recognize the value of the least powerful among us not only because we care about our sisters, but because it is in our own self-interest to stay together. If lesbians are unsafe and unvalued, every one of us is in trouble. If the rape of women of color is condoned, then all women are potential victims. If we fail to recognize that a husband forcing sex on a woman is rape, then we are saying that the men we choose always have access to our bodies. If it is acceptable to rape or beat up prostitutes, then not a single one of us is safe. If madwomen, "retarded" women, or women prisoners are acceptable targets for violence, we can all be subject to assault. We speak here because silence is complicity, and we will not consent to assault on any women. Each of us is precious, unique and valuable.[93]

In these words a vital dimension is restored to the politics of liberation.

For liberation does not occur at the level of ideas and feelings but at the level of actual people and of concrete institutions and structures. At the core of contemporary feminism is a profound commitment to people combined with a critique of existing institutions that oppress and damage people. Its analysis of the family is of critical importance and is basic to all feminist analysis. Feminists rightly see the family as a central site of oppression and reject the dishonesty and hypocrisy that surrounds much idealizing and ideologizing of the family within Western societies. A critical approach to the family is particularly necessary for Christians, who have often naively accepted the modern nuclear family as if it had appeared fully grown from the Garden of Eden, though it is in fact extremely modern and Western. No one can take feminism seriously without understanding how central is its critique of the family as the basic material structure that embodies female dependence on the male and of the dominant ideology of motherhood and domesticity. It is, in short, the embodiment of domination, and any critique of domination has to begin there.

But feminist social and historical criticism goes beyond the nuclear family to include "an enormous interrogation of the past."[94] There is a concern to recover the lost voices of women, to reclaim lost history, to let suppressed voices from past and present be heard. There is a concern to unmask the history that has been written from the perspective of its male participants. Here the resistance to violence, whether at Greenham Common or in the large number of refuges for victims of rape, incest, and domestic violence, plays a crucial part in the shaping of the contemporary women's movement for liberation. A feminist spirituality of liberation involves the healing of lives that have been disfigured and crushed by the cycle of male violence and cruelty.

In recent years I have played a small part in bringing to public attention two studies, one of rape and one of violence against black women.[95] I believe that it is essential for men to hear these voices and take account of these struggles and not to seek either to contain them within an acceptable, male-absorbed form or to listen only to the gentler, sanitized voices of the reformist liberal feminists who are often encountered in churches. By failing to let the movement speak for itself, we miss the pain and anger of the feminist liberation struggle. Some of the most powerful influences on my thinking have come from socialist feminists, those women who seek to pursue the struggle for women's equality within the framework of the socialist tradition. The socialist feminist voice is currently muted, as feminists share in the general confusion and perplexity of the left in the 1990s. Yet there is much that feminists have to contribute to current discussions about the future of socialism, about the state and society, about the inadequacies of the Leninist tradition, about the need for vision and for the utopian dimension in radical thought, about unexplored dimensions of Marxism, and so on. It could be argued that the future of the left in Europe and North America may depend on its ability to hear the feminist analysis and critique.

Feminists within the church too stand in a critical relationship to the tradition. Beverly Harrison has made the point that in the church women have heard "a story of liberation that we were not intended to hear."[96] Christian feminists represent a neglected, suppressed, marginal tradition of Christianity and are under no illusions about the degree of hostility toward their testimony and about the weight of the historic tradition that is held against them. The language that sees women as "the devil's gateway," as the "advance post of hell," as misbegotten males, the tradition of Tertullian, Jerome, and John Chrysostom, of Augustine and Aquinas, is not easily overcome. Even much so-called progressive or radical theology ignores both the position of women and its own gender base. At the Second Vatican Council no women were allowed to give papers, and there were strong attempts to ban women journalists from attending the Council Masses and from receiving communion.[97]

It is not surprising that many women, and probably most feminists, have abandoned the Christian tradition as irredeemably patriarchal.[98] Those who have not, and have chosen to remain, have set about interpreting the Bible as a liberating source and researching Christian origins to identify the egalitarian roots of the movement. Following Valerie Saiving's famous article of 1960, often seen as the beginning of the discipline of feminist theology,[99] they have devoted attention to a reinterpretation of the understanding of sin and ethics in the light of women's experience. Some, like Sharon Welch, have written of "joy in the wonder of life" as the heart of feminist spirituality and ethics.[100] Others, like Beverly Harrison, have written of the creative power of anger as part of the work of love and as a source of great strength in struggle.[101] Rejecting the anti-body dualism in which lie the roots of both misogyny and homophobia, writers such as Carter Heyward argue that the association of sin with sex has led to a repressive, guilt-inducing ethic that in its turn has produced a pornographic culture of sexual violence.[102] And there has been a tremendous concern with development of liturgical forms, models of spiritual direction, and ways of prayer that reflect women's experience.[103]

I doubt if most men realize the courage and persistence, not to mention the capacity for coping with weariness, that is required for such women to remain faithful to a church in which they constantly find themselves "overwhelmed by a linguistic form that excludes them from visible existence."[104] For such women the Eucharist, which is meant to be a focus of unity and solidarity, becomes a point of paradox and contradiction. It is desperately important that men try to understand the intensity of the darkness into which many women are plunged in their encounter with the Christian tradition. In Carolyn Osiek's words, "It is a death experience, a dark night, to which all the descriptions of such abandonment and desolation in the spiritual classics are applicable. . . . It is a spiritual crisis of enormous proportions and must be understood and treated as such."[105] One of the characteristic features of the dark night of the classical tradition is that all concepts and assumptions go into solution, all existing securities and certainties are purged and reevaluated. There is a thorough ascesis of soul and society in which everything has to be looked at afresh. Reality is never the same again. I believe that the feminist revolution is of such a character, and it is necessary for men to learn to listen, to hear, and to reflect on the significance of this revolution. It has to be part of our liberation too.

Feminist theology then stands within the movement of liberation theology. It is a theology rooted in the commitment to justice for all, for, as Alice Walker has written, "Only justice can stop a curse."[106] And, like all genuine liberation theology, it starts from the bottom, starts where the pain is. Carter Heyward has put it in this way:

> I see more vividly than before that our redemption requires that this power come to us, and through us, in healing and liberation, advocacy and friendship, love and sisterliness, in the most badly broken and frightening places of our life together and as individuals. In a racist, heterosexist, class-injured world, God is likely to meet us often in images associated with children, poor women, black, brown, yellow and red women, lesbian women, battered women, bleeding women and women learning to fight back. Dark images. Like Mary's poor little boy, God is seldom welcome in reputable places. The story is not a nice one. Good theology is not respectable.[107]

A Spirituality of Liberation

"The Christian faith has always understood itself as a means to human liberation," writes the English theologian Colin Gunton,[108] and, of course, he is correct at the level of rhetoric. At the same time it would be incorrect and dishonest not to admit that for much of its history the church has interpreted liberation in entirely inward and personal or futuristic terms and has denied, or devoted little attention to, the relevance of liberation to the social, economic, and political structures of this world, to the freedom of oppressed minorities, to the attack on racial oppression, or to the physical future of the planet itself. There has been a particular resistance to the notion that liberation involves dealing with the specific and concrete demands of specific groups of oppressed people. Many of those who speak airily of "human liberation" show little practical concern for the liberation of anyone in particular. Thus, however much lip service has been, and is, paid to the language and idea of liberation, Christians who pursue a theology of liberation in the ways that I have discussed in this chapter, and in the way in which the tradition has been developed in Latin America and elsewhere, represent a minority tradition within Christianity. They reflect "one stratum within the Christian tradition,"[109] one that preserves dangerous memories and that keeps alive the hope that sustains resistance and struggle.

In spite of the massive and growing industry of books about liberation theology, there remains a large area of ignorance, confusion, and misrepresentation of this movement. Some writers see it as a movement that replaces spirituality with political action, in spite of the overwhelming evidence to the contrary—for rarely can there have been a theological movement that is so clearly and so deeply rooted in spiritual experience. Many continue to see it as nothing more than Marxism in theological dress, although it has been shown that the contribution of Marxist theory to most work within the liberation theology tradition is very slight.[110] We are in fact dealing with a theological tradition that takes as its starting point the experience of oppression, that is rooted in the sharing of the life of very poor people, and that exists in an atmosphere of great physical danger; a tradition that seeks to break with the narrow academic captivity of theological work, that is partisan in its understanding of solidarity, and that seeks to unite contemplation and political struggle; a tradition that has been most marked since its early years by its concern for the deepening of spiritual life.

In his first book in 1973, Gustavo Gutierrez referred to a "serious crisis" relating to prayer. He went on to suggest that this crisis could lead to a purification of the life of the spirit, but that there was a need to break new paths and to live new spiritual experiences. The recovery of the contemplative life was central. He then claimed that there was a "great need for a spirituality of liberation," for a new tradition within which conversion to the people would be fundamental.[111] Gutierrez has been one of the most prolific and most consistent writers within the liberation theology movement. He has always insisted that any authentic theology must be a spiritual theology, and his writings are steeped in a mystical theology that unites prayer and action in a way that few contemporary Christian writers can match. In a study in 1984 he pointed out that there had been a marked growth in spirituality over the years among Christians within the liberation tradition: "a growing maturity in their solidarity with the commitment to liberation has . . . brought with it a new emphasis on prayer as a fundamental dimension of Christian life."[112] To the oft-repeated maxim that theology is the "second act," Gutierrez, writing in 1988, added the vital truth that contemplation and practice together constitute the first act.[113]

Since Gutierrez's early call for a spirituality of liberation, many writers have devoted attention to this theme. The Chilean pastor Segundo Galilea is one who has constantly focused on the need for a rich devotional life. Galilea is steeped in the Spanish mystics, and his work, in contrast to the large (and sometimes turgid) prose of other theologians, consists of small but profound devotional studies on the nature of contemporary discipleship and prayerfulness. Galilea in 1975 wrote of a "crisis of spirituality" associated with the split between contemplation and politics. He believed that liberation was fundamentally a problem of spirituality, and that there was a need for a meeting of mystics and militants.[114] Christian mysticism is a mysticism of commitment, and it is in commitment that contemplation and action come together. Throughout his work Galilea's central concern has been "how to bring a strong spirituality into the liberation theology thinking and its ensuing commitments."[115]

Both Gutierrez and Galilea see liberation and the spirituality of liberation as corporate activities, involving commitment, mutual support, and networks of solidarity. And here they connect with one of the key problems in Western political activity, the problem of the lonely militant about which Sheila Rowbotham has written.

This individual militant appears as a lonely character without ties, bereft of domestic emotions, who is hard, erect, self-contained, controlled, without the time or ability to express loving passion, who cannot pause to nurture, and for whom friendship is a diversion. . . . Left to carry the burden of a higher consciousness, members of this elect will tend to see the people around them as, at worst, bad, lazy, consumed with the desire for material accumulation and sundry diversionary passions; at best, ignorant, needing to be hauled to a higher level. In the hauling, the faint-hearted fall by the wayside, the cuddly retire into cosiness, and all the suspicions of the elect are confirmed. Being an elect they can rely on no one, and being an elect means they have to do everything.[116]

Rowbotham here identifies a serious problem that affects both political movements and the religious community. The movement for human liberation cannot be built by lonely militants in isolation from the common people. It is a movement that can be built only on solidarity and comradeship among people. It calls for the creation of what the philosopher Alasdair MacIntyre has called networks of small groups of friends, local forms of community within which the virtues and the vision of a human future can be sustained.[117] Nicholas Lash, reflecting on MacIntyre's proposal, calls for a "transcultural global 'network' of local communities" that can sustain hope and stimulate resistance, communities of disciples on a journey, nourished by the eucharistic food.[118]

A spirituality of liberation must be characterized by solidarity, for the work of liberation is corporate work, not private enterprise. Those involved in this work are called into comradeship, into communion. They will need a common spirituality that nurtures and strengthens a community of disciplined commitment. A central feature of such a spirituality will be the creation and strengthening of these networks of friends and pilgrims in truth and love, networks of people who guide and help one another. Spiritual direction will assume new and more mutually nurturing forms within the liberation tradition.

A spirituality of liberation will be marked by discontent and dissatisfaction combined with joyful longing. It is not a spirituality for those who would be at ease in Zion. It is rooted rather in that seed of restless questioning, sanctified unease. It is this seed that contains the hope of the future, the hope of that liberated zone which inspired Bernard of Cluny when he sang of

> the home of fadeless splendour,
> of flowers that fear no thorn,
> where they shall dwell as children
> that here in exile mourn.[119]

3

STEPPING OUT OF BABYLON
Politics and Christian Vision

Those who can live in it may be purified; those who look on are usually defiled.

C. E. RAVEN, ON THE EXPERIENCE OF WAR

Don't talk to me about politics: I'm only interested in style.

JAMES JOYCE

Realism is dependent on the possibility of access to the forces of change in a given moment of history.

FREDRIC JAMESON

In this chapter I do not aim to diagnose the contemporary political scene as a whole, or to offer a detailed agenda for the churches in confronting principalities and powers. My purpose is rather to examine the theological and spiritual roots of political commitment and political action, the spiritual challenges that are presented by political systems, and the spiritual resources necessary for an understanding of Christian discipleship that takes political vision and political struggle seriously.

Calls that the church should "keep out of politics" or cease to "meddle" in the political arena change little over generations or even centuries. There is an assumption that the church's proper realm is moral and spiritual, and that this realm can be clearly separated from the realm of the political. There is an assumption that to "keep out of politics" is actually possible, and that those churches (and Christian individuals) that avoid any public attack upon, or criticism of, existing political institutions have somehow managed to achieve this feat. There is an assumption that to enter into politics is to "meddle," or "dabble," with all the connotations of amateurism and illegitimate interference that go with those loaded words. And there is an assumption that the lines of demarcation between that which is moral and spiritual and that which is political are fairly clear. In fact, each of these assumptions is highly questionable, and I believe that each of them can be shown to be fallacious. In fact the ways in which churches have related to political issues and political institutions have varied enormously over the centuries.

Strangers and Sojourners: The Christian Community and "the Powers That Be"

From the point when a form of Christianity became the official religion of the Roman Empire in the fourth century, the church's political action has most commonly conformed to, and acquiesced in, the dominant structures and ideology of the day. The church has been the defender, the spiritual cement, of the established order. That is, after all, the easiest response, and the one that calls for the least intellectual or moral energy. To accept the status quo is often assumed not to be a form of action, but to do nothing is an extremely effective way of maintaining things as they are. It is not surprising, therefore, that "nonpolitical" Christians have a remarkably consistent record of turning out to be conservatives.

Often the practice of conformity is defended by a theology of otherworldliness, a theology that makes a sharp division between the demands of the Kingdom of God and the dilemmas of this world. We find such a theology in the writings of the English right-wing conservative politician Enoch Powell. On Powell's view, there is a radical discontinuity between the two kingdoms. Jesus' mission was not in any way relevant to politics or economics.[1] From a similar theology marked by sharp contrast, the Anabaptists were led to a view of the gospel that called for a radical conflict between the two realms; but for Powell, and for most of the proponents of "two kingdoms" theology, the direction taken is one of disconnectedness. Not surprisingly, the theology of the "two kingdoms" has a troubled and tragic history. Its popularity among the Lutherans of Nazi Germany was one of the factors that made it so easy for Hitler to displace the church. Richard Neuhaus has written of "the doleful history that has, in many minds, entirely discredited the notion of two kingdoms."[2] But in most cases, Christians who support the established political order within which they find themselves do not do so on the basis of any clearly thought out theological rationale; they simply take the easy route, that of inactivity.

A different kind of theology is that which sees the role of the church as one of baptizing and sanctifying the social order. The practical consequences of this approach will differ from a "two kingdoms" theology insofar as there is a clear social and political mandate for the church within the social order. Though the basic framework of the social order is accepted, the role of the church in maintaining that framework is more than incidental. This kind of establishment political theology has a long history, not least within English Anglicanism from the sixteenth century to the nineteenth. To Richard Hooker (1554–1600), church and commonwealth were a unity; in the twentieth century T. S. Eliot argued for a Christian organization for society.[3] The theme that the church should be a civilizing influence and thus a means to the preservation of social order is one with deep roots in English social history. The Sunday schools of nineteenth-century

Manchester were defended as "the cheapest way to civilize the poor, to make them less dangerous to society, to render them more useful workers, and incidentally to save their souls."[4] The church was valued then, as it is today by most political regimes, for its ability to suppress trouble spots, contain and control agitators, sedate the masses, and reinforce national and global defenses. Its essential role was preservative.

These two views of the church may have the same results in practice—support of the prevailing political order—though those who take the latter view will see a greater role for churches in shaping that order. Neither view is likely to see much scope for a prophetic or conflictual role for the church; indeed, such a role is systematically excluded, not least by those who would see their general outlook to be "progressive." Thus Robin Gill, a pastor and sociologist of liberal position: "Churches, as churches, can be prophetic in society only in the most unusual circumstances. Usually their relationships to particular societies is too close to allow them to be independently prophetic."[5] However, a general consensus within the "mainstream" churches in recent years has agreed with Karl Rahner that "the critical function of the church in society cannot have as its true and own responsibility the defense of a socio-political status quo."[6]

Within a broad framework of conformity, many Christians have operated ameliorative services, various kinds of "ambulance ministry," aimed at rescue of individuals. Large numbers of those who have become involved in rescue ministry find it has been a key stage in the deepening of their political consciousness. Dick York, pastor of the Free Church of Berkeley, California, who was involved in 1968 in such ministry on Telegraph Avenue, realized that "you cannot minister to alienated runaways, drug users, and street people without addressing yourself to the causes of that alienation."[7] Yet there are hundreds of thousands in whom that consciousness is never awakened, and for whom there is no progress beyond rescue of individuals.

It is within the area of rescue and ambulance ministry that politicians tend to see the church's contribution. However, they would also offer a second sphere: that of moral judgment. Douglas Hurd, the British Home Secretary at the time, addressed the General Synod of the Church of England on 10 February 1988, putting this viewpoint.

The church, he argued, was often concerned with "lesser matters"—after all, it had spent much of the previous day attacking the government's poll tax. Its true role, Hurd claimed, was to "rebuild moral standards and values which should form the sure foundation of a cohesive and united nation." In the *Church Times* of 9 September 1988 Hurd developed his ideas on church and state. "Each sphere shares areas of interest and responsibility," he claimed. "Clergy were entitled to express their views on political and social issues. But it follows that any cleric, be he primate or parson, who ventures down from the pulpit into the scar pit of political controversies needs to be aware of what he is doing. His surplice will offer him no protection." A clergyman "who intervenes" in political debates, according to Hurd, must expect "treatment and public criticism of a sort which his sermons will probably rarely engender." Politicians in their turn may "trespass on the church's home pitch of moral guidance," but they have "no special authority" to do so, for "that authority rests firmly with the church."[8] Allowing for the somewhat archaic and patronizing style, this presentation of the role of the church is probably not untypical of that held by many public officials in many countries.

Once politicians have reached the point of accepting that church leaders—the ordinary member of the Body of Christ hardly ever figures in these debates—have some kind of right to comment on political issues, they tend to assume that the contribution the church can make consists of recommendations for improvement of the existing system. One long-time exponent of this reformist view of Christian social ethics is Sir Fred Catherwood, a British industrialist who is now a leading figure in the European Community. For Catherwood, the present system contains much Christian idealism, and Christian action should be action aimed at modifications and improvements within this system.[9] Professor Brian Griffiths, a leading evangelical economist who until 1990 directed Margaret Thatcher's Policy Unit, has often expressed the view that Christianity and capitalism are not incompatible and can work together for the good of humanity.[10] This tradition of "baptizing" the current secular ideology is not new. In an earlier era, Anglican social theorists expressed a high view of the role of the state as, for example, in the volume *Lux Mundi* of 1889. According to these thinkers the role of the church is to sanctify the social order. From

William Temple, archbishop of Canterbury in the 1940s, to the *Faith in the City* report of 1985, the idea that the church's central political task is to inculcate Christian principles has dominated the conventional Christian agenda. Temple believed strongly in "Christian principles" and in "the task of reshaping the existing order in closer conformity to those principles." According to this view, theology is about ends, politics about means. So the church should aim "to influence all citizens and permeate all parties."[11] This is the tradition within which Robert Runcie, the recently retired archbishop of Canterbury, stood. Runcie, like Temple, held that "archbishops should stick to principles," and he was strongly committed to what he saw as the "middle ground."[12] We find this reformist approach in the work of many mainstream Christian social thinkers, like the English theologian John Atherton, with his vague theology of the common good.[13] Such exponents, though they recognize that there are times when the church needs to take up a critical position in relation to government, tend to regard these as exceptional occasions and to yearn for better times. Thus the bishop of Saint Albans predicted in 1989 that "after Thatcher the Conservative Party may find its natural center again, and then the church will not need to be in opposition and can do its own job."[14] Thus speaks the voice of the church pragmatic here on earth.

There are, of course, situations in which the church sees its role as one of commitment to revolutionary change. In South America and the Caribbean, there has been a long history of churches playing a dynamic role in popular revolts,[15] and the place of the church in the liberation struggles in Southern Africa is well known and continues to this day. The Christian commitment to revolution is a political expression of commitment to a new world, rejecting ideas of modification or improvement. Such a commitment to revolution requires faith, for the new order is not conceivable, not available in blueprints, and can only be spoken of in parables and hints. A corporate Christian commitment to revolutionary change is in practice a minority position, for institutional churches tend to side with the existing power structure. Some groups, however, may choose to fight for the restoration of a "Christian order" of the past. In the United States today many Christians see moral and spiritual decline as a result of the influence of liberalism, the teaching of the theory of evolution, and the spread of various schools of psychology. It was in fact out of the concern about liberalism and evolution that what we now term fundamentalism grew up in the early years of the twentieth century. Recent Christian "Reconstructionists" seek to restore lost positions and rebuild a society according to these positions. Such groups and individuals would see themselves as "radical" in their desire for a break with the liberal and secular values of the present, though in their identification of Christian principles with earlier cultural styles, they may be as guilty of assimilating the gospel to the spirit of the age (in this case an earlier age) as those whom they criticize.

There are Christians for whom the alliances with secular political ideologies, whether of "left," "right," or "center," represent a betrayal of the nature of the church as an alternative form of politics. These Christians see the church as a counterculture, a community that stands, by its very nature, in conflict with the established political and cultural order of its day. There have been many examples of this conflictual view of the church's political witness, from early monasticism through a range of medieval movements to the Anabaptists, the Diggers, Levellers, and Fifth Monarchy Men of seventeenth-century England, down to contemporary groups such as the Amish and Mennonites, the Catholic Worker communities, and numerous individuals inside and on the edge of all the churches.

The Methodist theologian Stanley Hauerwas is currently a popular exponent of this position. Consistently critical of most forms of the church's expressions of "social concern," Hauerwas argues for a radical discontinuity between Christians and any given culture. The church, on his view, should offer a "contrast model," "a political alternative to every nation."[16] He believes that the nature and form of the church is the central issue in social ethics. Christians, he argues, "must be uninvolved in the politics of our society and involved in the polity that is the church."[17] According to Hauerwas, Christian social ethics can only be done by those who are not in control of world history. The church's role in politics is dependent on its servant and minority status. Hauerwas is a strong opponent of the Constantinian approach to Christian social and political witness. In his view the church's main failure has been its inability to offer a radical alternative view of the nature of the political. Hauerwas is critical of the mainstream Christian approach to the political world, as expressed, for example, in the "lifeless abstractions" of the papal social encyclicals.[18] Instead of issuing such vague pronouncements, the church should be urging a defiance of economic injustices created by class and nation, a defiance rooted in the sense of being a community of contradiction.

Hauerwas has been accused of offering a theology of withdrawal, a sectarian position. He has strongly denied the first charge, but his theology certainly favors the view of the Christian community as a minority dissenting group within society. He is deeply influenced by the Mennonites and by theologians like John Howard Yoder, who sees the church as the primary social structure and agent of change.[19] In a book published in 1989, Hauerwas claims that Christianity is "mostly a matter of politics." However, he stresses that the church is "a countercultural phenomenon, a new *polis.*" Rejecting the approach of Jerry Falwell, whom he sees as a modern equivalent of Reinhold Niebuhr, and of other exponents of "public religion," he argues that "the political task of Christians is to be the church rather than to transform the world."[20]

In practice, Christians tend to move between these varied positions. To sustain the role of a counterculture is not easy, and most Christians accept the values and practices of the dominant social order, at least to some extent. It is not uncommon to find Christian groups who combine short-term rescue work with an overall commitment to political change. It is often said that "it is all a matter of emphasis." But emphasis can make a tremendous amount of difference. A great deal depends on where the emphasis lies.

Babylon in Confusion: The Strange Shape of Modern Politics

Martin Buber, drawing on the work of the American sociologist Robert MacIver, claimed that the grossest of all confusions was that between the social and the political. Whereas the political principle was based on power, authority, and domination, Buber claimed, the social principle was based on mutuality and the common interest.[21] His distinction would have puzzled Aristotle, for whom the concept of the political was much wider. The word *social* is in fact of Latin origin and has no Greek equivalent, though the Latin *societas* has a more political meaning than our word *society*. For Aristotle, to be political, to live within a *polis*, meant that issues were decided not by violence but by argument and persuasion. In sharp contrast to modern polarized notions, contemplation *(theoria)* was an essential part of political vision, indeed, was the highest human activity. Politics was concerned with the attainment of the highest good of individuals within the *polis*. It was concerned with excellence as a corporate value. To say that human beings were political animals was therefore to say something about their commitment to conversation and dialogue, and about their capacity for excellence and for vision of the good life. It is from this conception of politics that we derive the idea of civility as a discipline of conversation and an alternative to warfare and conflict.[22]

To turn from this ancient understanding of the political realm as a realm of dialogue to the strange and tormented face of modern politics is to enter a wholly different world, in which the whole notion of politics has been distorted and diminished. The increased globalization of politics has led not to an enriched and expanded vision but rather to an increased sense of disconnectedness. Politics ceases to be about the concerns, hopes, and aspirations of ordinary people, bound together within a *polis*, and becomes something done by professional elites for the people. Politics is something done by experts, supported by a massive army of civil servants who, it is believed, combine value neutrality and manipulative power. Whatever dialogue takes place is a dialogue among government, business, and various elites and takes place over the heads of the people. Only these elites, it is claimed, have sufficient grasp of the complexities of the political world, sufficient knowledge of the data, to make any significant decisions. They must be trusted to act on our behalf: as the Douglas Jay, a British Labour politician, once said, "The man from Whitehall does know best."[23] Yet it is clear that, in today's world, the claim of the experts to understand has come to be more and more incredible.

Part of the explanation lies not in the personal incompetence of public figures but in the fact that debates about political systems are marked by a persistent sense of insecurity and uncertainty—about the fate of liberalism, socialism, Marxism, capitalism. Things that were considered solid are now eroding away, while within the ruins and the chaos of their disintegration we see the resurgence of racism and racist forms of nationalism, not least in states that were until recently considered Marxist. There are constant reports of the reappearance of Nazi-type movements in various countries of Europe, while old and new forms of fundamentalism, religious and political, are emerging as individuals and communities search desperately for new certainties and securities to replace those that are gone.

Yet it is only some thirty years since we were told that we had entered the age of the "end of ideology," and that consensus had been achieved on most major issues. The debates about political issues in the future, it was claimed, would be debates about pragmatic questions, about technical matters, not about fundamental matters of principle. Today we seem to be faced with new and fiercer ideologies existing alongside a general and more pervasive sense of bafflement, a sense of being in a political and moral wilderness. In the West there is a frequently expressed unease with the ideology of liberalism, the philosophy that grew from seventeenth-century Puritanism and from the Whig tradition that dominated English politics from 1688 to 1832. No one doubts that the contribution of the liberal tradition to Western societies has been considerable. But today there is clearly much dissatisfaction with the individualism that characterizes most forms of liberalism. Classical liberalism was based on the belief in individual rights, including the right to unlimited amounts of property. Yet voting rights for the poor were seen to threaten this belief, and John Stuart Mill opposed extending the right to vote to the illiterate on the grounds that this would likely lead in the direction of equality. The holding together of freedom and equality within a comprehensive social vision has been beyond the conceptual framework of the liberal mind. Modern liberalism has become divorced from structures that might realize some of its ideals. It has, in the words of C. Wright Mills, "no theory of society adequate to its moral aims."[24] It asserts rights but ignores resources. It maintains devotion to ideals but is so committed to change without conflict that it always tends to side with the existing structures of power. But the fundamental problem is that liberalism seems to have no core political vision, no idea of the kind of community within which its individuals might flourish. Even Francis

Fukuyama, who came to brief fame in 1989 for his claim that Western liberalism had triumphed among world ideologies and had thus brought about "the end of history," recognized that there was an "emptiness at the core of liberalism."[25]

We should not be too swift to proclaim the death of liberalism. Earlier predictions have proved to be premature: Horkheimer began an essay of 1941 with the words, "At the close of the liberal era . . ."[26] Human beings can live with a certain degree of muddle and emptiness for quite a long time. Yet it does seem that the recognition of the inadequacy of liberalism's political vision has led many, on both the left and the right of politics, to begin to look afresh at the meaning of citizenship and community. In Britain there has been rhetoric in the last few years about the "active citizen," but it has tended to be reduced to the idea that those who have the money and the leisure to do so should do volunteer work. It has in fact been privatized. Even so, market research in the *London Times* in 1988 showed that "there is a shift away from [an] individualistic and narcissistic ethos toward a much more collective attitude . . . from the current every man for himself survivalism to a new community awareness."[27] It is not, however, clear how this concern for a new sense of community can be translated into effective political action.

In the meantime we have been disturbed to see that, in both Britain and the United States, there seem to be a growing number of people who believe that the choice between political parties makes little difference. In 1951 in Britain, 20 percent of the population thought that it mattered little which party was in power. By 1959 this had grown to 38 percent, and by 1964 to 49 percent.[28] The percentage appears to have continued to grow. Of course this is not new. James Thorold Rogers said in 1884 that most English people saw politics as a game and held that "it signifies little which gets a temporary ascendancy."[29] In the United States, evidence suggests that voting is related to security of income. Of those earning over $50,000 per year, 76 percent tend to vote, compared with 38 percent of those earning under $5,000.[30]

It would seem reasonable to conclude that political activity has come to be seen by many people as irrelevant. And so it is not surprising that there is considerable ignorance about the political world.

The ignorance of young people is very apparent. In one British survey, 50 percent of young people leaving school, age sixteen to eighteen, did not know the name of their member of Parliament; 44 percent thought that the IRA was a Protestant group; 20 percent thought that nationalization was Conservative policy; and 6 percent did not know the name of the prime minister. Later studies showed that 77 percent did not know what NATO was (1979) and 10 percent did not know the name of the president of the United States (1983).[31]

The ignorance and disillusionment is more than a loss of trust in the parties and the personalities: it is connected with the nature of politics itself. Alasdair MacIntyre has said that "modern politics is civil war carried on by other means." But he goes on to recognize that there is "no tolerable alternative set of political and economic structures which could be brought into place to replace the structures of advanced capitalism."[32] Capitalism itself is in flux, and there are debates about "new times," "post-Fordism" (the end of the mass assembly line age in industry), "postmodernism," and so on. These debates bring together economic ideas (the shift away from vertical power and the mass-scale standard product, an economy modeled on the army, to the decentralized, cellular structures of new technology) as well as political, cultural, and philosophical ideas about the nature of "modernity."[33]

The entire political scene has been dramatically affected by the collapse of communism in Eastern Europe. Does it mean the end of Marxism as a system of thought and analysis, or simply the end of a particular type of political structure? Many argue that much of Marxist theory must now be abandoned, such as the Leninist approach to revolution based on the assumption of the decomposition and collapse of the capitalist world system. Some would see Stalinism merely as a "dark interval" within socialist history.[34] However, there is a growing consensus among many British Marxists (and some who continue to call themselves Marxists with no clear reason for doing so!) that sees 1989 as "the end of the whole 1917 tradition."[35] The historian Eric Hobsbawm has described the period from 1917 to 1989 as a "long detour."[36] Hobsbawm makes his point very strongly: "We are seeing not the crisis of a type of movement, regime and economy, but its end. Those of us who held that the October Revolution was the gate to the future of world history have been shown to be wrong." Hobsbawm is clear that 1989 marked the end of "really existing socialism." "The socialism born of the October revolution is dead," and there now remains no alternative system to that of capitalism.[37] The recognition of this fact must have major implications for communist parties that have been built on the basis of 1917, like the Communist Party of Great Britain, with a membership now down to six thousand and a most uncertain future. It is significant that the only communist parties anywhere in the world with any mass support are in Italy, South Africa, and India.

In fact the abandonment of Marxism by European socialists antedated the events of 1989. There was never much Marxist influence on British socialism. Marxist theory was abandoned by the German SPD at Bad Godesberg in 1956. In 1970 the Italian Communist Party declared Marxism-Leninism to be an optional creed. And it is certainly difficult to find much Marxist thought in the *Manifesto for a New European Left* of 1986.[38] As the historian Sir Michael Howard has observed, "Where Marxism survived, it was as a wholly admirable passion for social justice and a valuable tool for social analysis rather than as a creed with predictive powers based on a unique insight into the historical process."[39] Certainly the belief in Marxism as a total worldview has disappeared in most places. Yet, with the collapse of the Marxist worldview, there has also been a collapse of vision, and a lack of coherence; Marx was, after all, the first major critic of European cultural disintegration,[40] and the ending of an era of Marxist thought has coincided with a new and uncertain era for Europe. Part of this uncertainty is about the future of socialism as a project. Many writers now see socialism as a "visionless movement."[41] But this is hardly peculiar to socialism; the sense of loss of vision is perhaps the most striking feature of the contemporary Western political scene. Older positions have been overtaken and made obsolete by historical events. Previously held certainties have been eroded. And this sense of bafflement and perplexity reveals itself as a spiritual vacuum. For what has been lost is more than an intellectual grasp of appropriate strategies and tactics; the loss is far deeper: it is a loss of any sense of meaning, any vision of a more human, more wholesome, future. There is a terrible vacuum, and it opens up an ominous and potentially lethal prospect.

Seeds of Disintegration: Europe and the Spiritual Roots of Fascism

It is in such times as these, times of alienation and disenchantment, of insecurity and anxiety, that populism may combine with militarism, nationalism, and overwhelming fear of some kind of apocalypse to produce a kind of political movement that relies more on heroes and adventurers than it does on clear ideology or great organization. Helped by theories of corruption and conspiracies, of degeneracy and decay, what we now know as fascism may establish deep roots within a population. Historically fascist movements have found their home in the heart of Christian culture, Catholic and Protestant; hence it is vital that Christians reflect on the spiritual roots of the fascism of the 1920s and 1930s if we are to understand the dangers in our own age.

It was of Europe in 1940 that Bishop Bell of Chichester wrote, "The masses are in despair. The old assurances are undermined. The old loyalties have lost their former authority. There are no common standards—no mutual trust—but everywhere a going to pieces."[42] Bell believed that if the Nazi regime were followed by no more than a spiritual and cultural vacuum, a nostalgia for lost identity, then the last state of Germany might be worse than the first.[43] Today some right-wing German writers are expressing similar anxieties. Thus Hans-Jurgen Syberberg sees the postwar German condition as one of sickness and degeneracy. It is, he claims, "the Jewish epoch of European cultural history," an age without spirit or meaning. In similar vein, Gerd Borgfleth attacks the "cynical Enlightenment" and its progeny of "returned Jewish left-wing intelligentsia" who have sought to remake Germany according to their own cosmopolitan standards. As a result there is "no independent German spirit at all."[44] To read these and similar writings is to enter a worrying world, not dissimilar to that of the 1930s.

The rise of fascism in Italy and of Nazism in Germany were, of course, related to massive economic and political upheavals within European society. Yet it is clear that there were also profound spiritual, intellectual, and cultural factors that helped to provide the climate within which these movements grew and flourished. The beginnings of that climate can be seen in the nineteenth century. The German

Romantics of that period were outsiders, aliens within an emerging industrial society that had no need for their imaginative and creative work. Writers of differing outlooks saw the dangerous effects of this new mass society on the human spirit and on future political developments. Jacob Burkhardt warned of the likely growth of political extremism in Europe, with highly militarized states and a tendency for "saviors" to replace political principles.[45] The Norwegian novelist Knut Hamsun—described by Isaac Bashevis Singer as the "father of the modern school of literature"—anticipated the era of the natural despot and the return of "Caesar" figures. Hamsun was one of the few public figures who remained loyal to Hitler to the end.[46] Certainly the *volkisch* youth movements of the 1890s can be seen as antecedents of the later fascist groups. Prophecies of apocalyptic doom were not uncommon, as adventist and millenarian movements flourished, while in Vienna the satirist Karl Kraus wrote of "the last days of mankind."[47]

In particular, the failure of the risings of 1848, and of the movements inspired by the revolutionary ideals of those years, had led to a whole series of speculations about the "decline of the West." Oswald Spengler, whose book of that name was published toward the end of the First World War, was deeply pessimistic about the future of European civilization. Spengler, who was influenced by the writings of Nietzsche and George Bernard Shaw and who in turn was a major influence on the thinking of Oswald Mosley, believed that truth and justice were illusory and that only reality lay in force. The times demanded hero figures. But such figures would not be social transformers or world improvers; instead, they would be tough, brutal, Caesar figures who ruled by sheer power and mystical violence. It was the age of the "man of destiny"; indeed, Spengler predicted, "If you listen closely you can already hear the tramp of the Caesars who are coming to take over the world."[48] Fascism was a remaking of politics according to Spengler's vision.

The atmosphere of cultural despair that paved the way for fascism was linked with fears of national and cultural degeneracy that went back to Darwin and his heirs, the founders of the science of eugenics. One strain of this thinking resulted in the racial hygiene movement of the Nazi period, though the Nazi phase represented the culmination of ideas and approaches that had been around for some time.[49]

The positive dimension of evolutionary vitalism was expressed musically in Wagner's operas and in the prose of Bernard Shaw's *The Perfect Wagnerite,* another major influence on Mosley.[50] However, around these scientific and pseudoscientific developments, forces of irrationality flourished. Both Wilhelm Reich and Carl Jung wrote of the upsurge of the dark forces of the unconscious in the preparation of the symbolic world of Nazism. There was an unpredictable dimension about the European revolt against rationalism, liberalism, and positivism, the revulsion against the machine age and mass society that characterized the culture of the Weimar Republic. For this was an age of restlessness, of striving, and of a dream of spiritual rebirth. But that dream which haunted Weimar culture could not be earthed in any concrete movement. By 1932 an exhaustion of spirit had taken over. It was into this vacuum created by exhaustion and irrationalism that fascism entered, with its politically organized contempt for the mind.

Italian fascism and German Nazism were similar movements, but there were crucially important differences, not least in their philosophical foundations. Mussolini was an idealist, striving always for higher spiritual forms, nourished by a heroic vitalism and by notions of self-sacrifice. There was an organic spiritual character about the fascist vision that bore witness to its Catholic origins. By contrast, Hitler was a crude materialist, influenced by Darwin and the Aryan myths. Biological determinism, rather than spiritual idealism, was his driving force; he saw struggle as the basis of politics. Yet in both its Italian and German forms, fascism was a response to chaos and functioned in many ways as a religious movement. It sought to bring an end to history, for the messianic ruler was the primary source of significance and inspiration. Both the hierarchical authoritarianism of Catholic Europe and the irrationalism and individualism of Luther and of later Enlightenment thinkers were part of the prehistory of fascism.

The religious character and appeal of the movement is seen clearly in Hitler, with his sense of being the child of providence, the savior of his people. The whole movement was steeped in religious ecstasy and mystical symbolism of great power. Hitler saw entry into the Nazi movement as "a form of conversion, a new faith."[51] The British member of Parliament Sir Arnold Wilson wrote of the solemnity and emotional impact of the Nuremberg Rally of September

1936.[52] The fusion of the mystical and the messianic was central. Holding a Manichaean view of reality, in which the Jews appeared as devils, Hitler had no need of the moral restraint or the sense of hope that Christian tradition had offered. Hope was fulfilled in him, and morality had no meaning apart from his decrees. There was a complex dialectic of tradition and newness in the Nazi system. On the one hand, there was a strong sense of the need to maintain and strengthen those parts of the tradition that were seen as basic to the stable order. The role of women, for example, as "breeders for race and nation," was clearly delineated. Hitler believed that the masses had a "feminine" character: women, he claimed, were always the first to follow the strong leader.[53] On the other hand, there was a commitment to the future, the new order that had been achieved. The future was known and thus closed, for the new age, the millennial kingdom, the *reich*, had come.

It is often said that Nazism was a pagan movement, deeply anti-Christian in its foundations and its practice. Certainly there were pagan dimensions. Many of the leaders of the Nazi movement had been members of the Thule Society of Munich, with its occult symbolism and fascination with the ancient German alphabet. In this philosophy the struggle between Aryan and Jew was seen as a struggle between gods and beasts.[54] In Nazism there was a crude mingling of racism, social Darwinism, and the occult and theosophical. The notion of a "secret doctrine," a body of truths known only to the initiated elect, was a contributing factor to the mythology of racial purity.

However, the contribution of Christianity to fascism in all its forms was considerable, and must never be ignored. Mosley in 1933 claimed that fascism was a synthesis of Christian and Nietzschean values, self-sacrifice and virility, though after the war he was more likely to stress the influence of Goethe's Faust as a symbol of heroic achievement.[55] The authoritarian structure of the Roman church was part of the tradition out of which Mussolini's movement grew. Christopher Dawson pointed out that the social teachings of Popes Leo XIII and Pius XI were much closer to fascism than to socialism.[56] On 20 December 1926 Pius XI called Mussolini "the man sent by providence," and many Italian bishops were profascist down to the 1950s.[57] The majority of Roman Catholics in Europe supported

Franco in Spain. Cardinal Hinsley, the leader of Britain's Catholic community, had a photograph of Franco on his desk; *The Tablet*, a leading British Catholic journal, in 1939 urged Roman Catholics "not to join or encourage this anti-fascist crusade."[58]

In Germany itself the church support for Hitler was almost unanimous. The German Evangelical Church sent a telegram to Hitler in 1934 assuring him of their loyalty and hailing him as the defender of European Christian civilization.[59] Theologians supported the idea of the *volk*, the community of blood and race, as the basis of all human community. Friedrich Gogarten believed that the Nazi state preserved the Christian order against the destructive powers, Paul Althaus spoke of the "German hour of the church," and Gerhard Kittel saw Nazism as a *volkisch* renewal movement based on Christian foundations and the Jews as an alien force.[60] The "German Christians" held that the church had taken concrete form in the Nazi movement and its "positive Christianity." This was the official line, though in truth the Nazis despised Christianity, seeing it as a threat to the German way of life, a belief clearly evident in the textbooks of the period.[61]

Nor were the fascist movements lacking in Christian sympathizers in other countries. Among English Anglicans, Bishop Headlam of Gloucester was an enthusiastic supporter of Hitler in the early years, while Bishop Garbett of Winchester, later to be archbishop of York, saw Hitler as a bulwark against communism.[62] *The Cicestrian*, the journal of Chichester Theological College, commended fascism in 1936.[63]

Purely economic explanations of the rise of fascism are simply not adequate. Fascism appealed to a wide section of the community, and its success was on moral, cultural, and spiritual fronts. It was aided by academics who refused to accept their political responsibility, who helped, by active support or by silence, the promotion and glorification of "German virtues," and who maintained a remote and politically irrelevant curriculum.[64] It was aided by disillusionment with the alternative political parties and by loss of faith in the possibilities of reform. Not surprisingly, it grew among the dispossessed and the despairing. It grew up from below, attracting shopkeepers, professionals, artisans, small landowners, pensioners, and the "lumpen." Social discontent, confusion, apathy and anxiety; the rootlessness of suburbia; the hopelessness of the socially "nondescript," people with no status and no future: all these were important factors.

Fascism appealed to, and was supported by, ordinary, decent, good people. Hitler may well have been driven by pathological forces, but to identify fascism with psychological derangement and delusion, as if emotionally stable, sane, balanced, and "reasonable" people would never be drawn in by its claims, is extremely dangerous and misleading. There was a high degree of respectability and propriety about the appeal of the fascist parties. The Nazi Physicians' League, while it was playing its role in preparing for the Final Solution, was also promoting the use of whole grain bread and mineral water.[65] Most of all, fascism appealed to youth, not least because, as George Orwell pointed out in 1940, whereas socialism and capitalism offered no more than alternative ways of getting "a good time," fascism offered struggle, danger, and death.[66]

Is any of this history still relevant? Is fascism still a real threat? Observers of trends in Europe since the 1970s see growing evidence of anti-immigrant feelings and behavior, racially motivated violence, support for racist and fascist movements, and signs of the resurgence of neo-Nazism. Concern at increased hostility toward immigrants goes back at least to the early 1970s, when there were racial disturbances in Rotterdam and Marseilles. At that time the Runnymede Trust, a British information unit, warned of the growing threat to migrant workers and of the ominous rise of a (then) little-known racist politician called Le Pen in France.[67] Since then the numbers of immigrants, migrants, and refugees in Europe has grown to over sixteen million. They constitute a kind of "thirteenth state" within the European Community, and many of them have no citizenship rights. Le Pen's movement, the National Front, has grown and is represented in the European Parliament. Attention to the removal of trade barriers and harmonization of tariffs has led to concern about the creation of a "Fortress Europe" with an increased racial thrust. Immigrants are seen, along with drug traffickers and terrorists, as threats to the stable order, as in Margaret Thatcher's speech at Bruges in September 1988, when she spoke of the need to "stop the movement of drugs, terrorists and illegal immigrants."[68] In the same speech she stressed the "common experience" of Europe and linked this with Christianity, ignoring the enormous Jewish, Muslim, and other populations.

None of this spells fascism, but there is what Ralf Dahrendorf terms an "uncanny resemblance to the 1920s."[69] Today, however, it is not simply Jews who are under attack but minorities from many countries, like the poor Turkish workers described as the "lowest of the low."[70] The growth of the neo-Nazi skinhead culture has been marked both in France, where hundreds of attacks on North Africans, blacks, Jews, drug addicts, tramps, homosexuals, and punks have occurred, and in Germany. Anti-Semitism itself has grown, with an increase in attacks on synagogues, cemeteries, and Jewish individuals, while the "holocaust denial" movement promotes its revisionist history. There are ominously close parallels in the United States.[71]

It has been said that the holocaust "sought to expunge from the life of Europe any witness to a religious component by which its behavior might be judged."[72] Today Europe is an increasingly secular culture. The spread of "Western values" to the east may go deeper than porno cassettes, fast food, cosmetics, McDonald's, and Kentucky Fried Chicken, but there is no certainty that it will. Once again there is a spiritual emptiness at the heart of Europe that is crying out to be filled.

In 1931 the German philosopher Karl Jaspers wrote *The Spiritual Situation of the Age.* In 1978 Jurgen Habermas invited fifty German thinkers to write an essay on the same subject.[73] In light of the increase of poverty and deprivation, of intolerance and racism, and of insecurity and anxiety, a more sustained reflection is an urgent task that confronts us all.

Portrait of a Decade: The Thatcher Phenomenon in Christian Perspective

The years from 1979 to 1990 in Britain were the years in which the government was led, and mainstream politics dominated, by the figure of Margaret Thatcher. They coincided with the rebirth and strengthening of right-wing forces in many countries, including the Reagan administration in the United States. They are years that offer a major challenge to, and important lessons for, the Christian community in its struggle for political fidelity.

My purpose here is not to analyze the economic and political ideology of Thatcherism but to focus on its claim to be a Christian ideology and to examine this claim in light of the Christian tradition. I want to attempt to assess the nature of the current and continuing conflict between the churches and the Conservative government; to describe briefly what I take Thatcherite ideology and practice to be; to identify those elements in Thatcherism that derive from, or are alleged to derive from, Christianity; and to suggest that what we saw in those years, and are still seeing with some modifications, is something very far removed from Christian orthodoxy. I shall argue that, in this and similar political formations elsewhere, we are seeing an ideology that pays lip service to a Christian and moral vocabulary while denying its substance at every important point. But I shall also suggest that these distortions do have their roots in a specific type of Christianity, and that the church has only itself to blame for this particular mutation of its faith. In discussing "Thatcherism," therefore, I am indirectly discussing a range of manifestations of right-wing Christianity throughout the world, though the details vary from place to place.

It is often assumed that there was a deep conflict between the churches and the Thatcher regime. For most members of the churches, in fact, there was no conflict at all. Most ordinary members of the Church of England, for example, are still attached to the Conservative Party.[74] Churches tend to reflect the dominant values of their society, and I see no evidence of any widespread revolt against Thatcherite values in the churches as a whole or in the Church of England in particular. There "the Tory Party at prayer" is still a valid description of the laity, if slightly less so of the clergy.

Nevertheless conflict there is, in the sense, first, that most mainstream Christian churches, through their leaders, synods, and boards, have found themselves in opposition to government policy on issues involving nuclear weapons, South Africa, child benefits, the community charge or poll tax, the National Health Service, the British Nationality Act, and urban policies; and, second, that there is undoubtedly a process of "radicalization" going on among Christians of all traditions (as there is in the United States), and this process has been aided, and in some cases initiated, by the experience of the Thatcher (and the Reagan) years. This is particularly interesting because the Thatcher government, more than any other British government since the war—and possibly this century—claimed to be a government rooted in Christian principles. One religious journalist said in 1978 that Thatcherism was "consciously and explicitly theological in its foundations"; a sociology weekly called the Thatcher regime "the most determinedly Christian government since the war."[75] The Christian links, and especially the links with the Church of England, of course, go back to the party's origins. It was originally a church party. It is fascinating today to read the official Conservative Party policy document for 1949, *The Right Road for Britain:* "Conservatism proclaims the inability of purely materialist philosophies to read the riddle of life, and achieve the necessary subordination of scientific invention and economic progress to the needs of the human spirit. Man is a spiritual creature adventuring on an immortal destiny, and science, politics and economics are good or bad so far as they help or hinder the individual soul on its eternal destiny."[76]

In her insistence on maintaining a link with Christianity, Mrs. Thatcher was well within the Tory traditions. This was not the case with her economic policies and her political philosophy (which, ironically, owed something to the eighteenth-century Anglican clergymen Malthus and Paley!). It was in fact in her break with traditional Tory paternalism, which had dominated the party from Disraeli to Macmillan, with the High Church party of hierarchy and old wealth, that some of the roots of the present conflicts with the Church of England are to be found.

For the hierarchy of the church has not suddenly shifted to the left, still less adopted a Marxist perspective. There are many discernible influences on recent church social utterances, but Marx is certainly not one of them. Rather has the church remained faithful to the paternalistic social liberalism of an earlier conservative age. One newspaper described the Church of England as "a citadel of exiled liberalism,"[77] one of the few large British institutions that did not succumb to Thatcherism. However, one by-product of Margaret Thatcher's revolution was to force Christians in all the churches to rethink the theological roots of their social concern, and this led to, among other things, a revival of the socialist Christian tradition. Now, in the aftermath of the Thatcher era, we have the paradox of a government that continues to emphasize religion and morality confronted by churches that, at all significant points, reject its perspective and its practice. We see, in short, two conflicting understandings of what Christianity is.

Mrs. Thatcher and some of her cabinet were probably taken aback by the strength and persistence of the opposition from the Church of England (even though its bishops were still willing to run to Downing Street when summoned at short notice!). For the opposition was certainly strong and persistent: the attack on the Nationality Act and on the abolition of the Greater London Council, led by the bishop of London; the report *The Church and the Bomb;* report after report on issues of poverty, unemployment, and social welfare; opposition to the war in the Falkland Islands; the report *Faith in the City* on the urban crisis; the churches' criticisms of the government in the miners' strike; Archbishop Runcie's claim that Britain had become a "Pharisee society"; and so on. It was for this reason that by 1989 we saw attempts by both Margaret Thatcher and Douglas Hurd, then her Home Secretary, in addresses to the Church of Scotland and the Church of England, to regain lost ground. But the attempts were not successful. On the contrary, they only served to emphasize how wide was the gulf between Thatcherism and the churches, at least at the official level.

I am assuming that Thatcherism did exist, which would be denied by many Conservatives, as well as by the socialist Tony Benn (for whom capitalism is capitalism is capitalism) and by David Selbourne (who speaks rather of working-class Toryism). But the fact that Margaret Thatcher, alone of all twentieth-century prime ministers, gave her name to an "ism" does suggest that there is some basis for it. I use Thatcherism to mean a body of thought and practice that combines economic liberalism and authoritarian conservatism in a somewhat unstable fusion. The two tendencies were in conflict from the early days of Thatcher's rise to power. It was the neoliberals, the economic disciples of Friedrich von Hayek, Milton Friedman, and the London-based Institute of Economic Affairs, who promoted her to power, but in 1978 the social authoritarians produced a symposium called *Conservative Essays*, which shifted the focus from economic liberty to political authority. The history of Thatcherite ideology and practice was in large part a history of tension and struggle between these two tendencies.

The Thatcherite commitment to the dominance of the market derived from the thinking of the Institute of Economic Affairs and its journal. As the lady said, "All policies are based on ideas. Our policies are firmly founded on those ideas which have been developed with such imagination in the *Journal.*"[78] The social authoritarian wing of the movement, however, was nurtured by the gurus of Peterhouse, Cambridge—Maurice Cowling, Peregrine Worsthorne, George Gale, and Roger Scruton and the *Salisbury Review* group, with their stress on social discipline rather than individual freedom. "The most important need today," wrote Worsthorne, "is for the state to regain control over the people";[79] Scruton has argued that most sections of local government should be eliminated.[80] The years since the 1981 uprisings, the miners' strike, and the abolition of the Greater London Council and the metropolitan councils saw the strengthening of this aspect of Thatcherism. "Never let anyone say I am laissez-faire. We are a strong government."[81] From a minimalist doctrine of state intervention in public welfare there was a rapid move to a centralized and authoritarian state in its exercise of political and social control, and it was this move, with its accompanying intransigence and its intensified brutality against the poor, that was a major factor in her downfall.

What connection had Thatcherism with Christian ideas and values? Some argue that Thatcherism (and indeed capitalism as a whole) is fundamentally anti-Christian, an utterly ungodly system of mammon worship. At one level I would agree. Yet it is foolish for Christians to deny that, both in ideology and in practice, the Thatcher regime drew on strands within Western, and particularly post-Reformation, Christianity. Ironically, it was precisely at those points where it was most faithful to the theology of the Reformation that it came into conflict with a Christian community that had moved beyond that framework. The crucial period for the re-forming or renewing of Christian social consciousness, among both Roman Catholics and evangelicals (the Church of England catching up later), was the 1960s, the era of Martin Luther King, of the peace movement, of the Second Vatican

Council, of John Robinson and the rediscovery of Bonhoeffer, and so much else. But this creative period, the most creative spiritual and social decade of postwar Christianity, is for Margaret Thatcher, Norman Tebbit, and their heirs a period of "fashionable theories and permissive claptrap. . . . We are reaping what was sown in the sixties."[82] The rejection of the values and insights of the 1960s is crucial to Thatcherite and post-Thatcherite conservatism, as it is to the New Right in the United States.

However, there is a sense—though perhaps not the sense that Margaret Thatcher intended—in which she was right. For Thatcherism, with all its harshness and materialism, was a predictable reaction to the often naive optimism, utopian socialism, and apolitical spirituality of the 1960s. But that is another and longer story. The historical point about the church-Tory conflict is that its seeds were sown in the radicalizing trends of that decade. Although the Thatcherites found themselves in conflict with mainstream Christianity, they certainly drew on elements within Christian theology and Christian tradition, specifically on that of the sixteenth-century Reformation, with its stress on the individual, on original sin, and so on.

They are, in the first place, individualists. As Margaret Thatcher said in a famous interview: "Really, you know, there is no such thing as society. . . . If the families and the church and the great voluntary organizations were really doing their job, there would be no need for governments to intervene."[83] Mrs. Thatcher had said earlier that she regarded individualism as a Christian mission and claimed that the New Testament was "preoccupied with the individual" and that all biblical principles referred back to the individual.[84]

The contrast between this and traditional Catholic Christianity could not be more dramatic. As a former archbishop of Canterbury, Michael Ramsey, pointed out in 1936, there is no place for individualism in Christianity: the one is implacably hostile to the other. The New Testament says virtually nothing about personal spirituality or personal salvation; all its emphasis is on the Body of Christ, the Kingdom of God, the New Humanity in Christ. One of the key biblical studies of the 1960s was John Robinson's *The Body,* which stressed how central is the theme of solidarity (a word unknown in Thatcherite vocabulary) to the New Testament. The postwar period has seen a major critique of and rejection of individualism by thousands of Christians, especially by evangelicals, who have seen it to be unchristian, unbiblical, and untrue.

So Thatcherism and its heirs have come preaching an individualist gospel at a time when Christians, evangelical and Catholic, have rediscovered the importance of society, social justice, and human interdependence.

Second, Thatcherites have a low and pessimistic view of human nature, especially of human beings in groups. The view of human society as nonperfectible is shared by critics of Thatcherism, more traditional conservatives like Sir Ian Gilmour. "Human nature is not perfectible," he says, "and . . . government has no business to seek to alter it."[85] Mrs. Thatcher and her disciples often link original sin and imperfection with the impossibility of utopias and of any significant social transformation: people are basically sinful and must be firmly disciplined, taught to obey and kept under control. This view is stated most clearly in Nigel Lawson's tract *The New Conservatism* (1980). Human imperfection, he claims, is the basis of conservatism.

The Christian church, however, though it accepts the doctrine of original sin, does not offer this as the basis of policy, and it rejects a politics rooted in a belief in irredeemable human degeneracy. It rejects a static view of "human nature" as unchangeable. Both human beings and human society are constantly open to the possibility of transformation and fulfillment, and this calls for both spiritual and political struggle. To say that they are not easily perfectible is not to say that they are not perfectible at all. And again it is precisely in the period that Margaret Thatcher was calling for obedience, treating the people of the nation as immature, rebellious children, that churches were coming to stress the importance of questioning, of criticism, of doubt, and of other adult virtues.

Third, in spite of their belief in human depravity, these conservatives also have a central belief in freedom, but it is freedom of choice for individuals. And this is linked with the rejection of the notion of equality in Margaret Thatcher's thought. "Free choice is ultimately what life is about. . . . From saying we are all equal it is only a small step to saying that we cannot make any choice for ourselves." She has even claimed that "the right to choose is the essence of Christianity."[86] However, freedom is the freedom to maintain existing privileges or to restore lost ones.

Now, of course, the Christian church also believes in freedom. The biblical word is *redemption*, best translated "liberation," and it is essentially about the setting free of a people from oppressive forces. In the New Testament it is used both of the human community and of the creation itself. It is a theology very far removed from the Conservative privatized view of enterprise by which the upwardly mobile leave the rest behind. And here again lay a major source of political conflict, for the churches at the grass roots have had a better and clearer view of what free choice means in terms of human bondage than Mrs. Thatcher ever did. They saw that freedom for some could mean misery for others, and they therefore went back to the biblical teaching that what happens to the poor is the criterion of how authentic our freedom is.

Fourth, they hold an Erastian view of the church as an agent of social control and as moral cement for the established order. It was the former MP and political journalist Brian Walden who said in 1985, "If the working classes in our cities . . . are not restrained by Christian morality then they are not restrained at all."[87] There is no reason to doubt that this reflects mainstream Tory thinking about religion. The church is primarily a force for stability and for social control. It should provide the moral and spiritual resources for national unity. That it failed to do so was at the heart of the row over the Falkland Islands service. Here church leaders insisted on stressing penitence rather than triumphalism. Denis Thatcher was quoted as saying, "I've just been with the Boss [he did not mean God] and she's hopping mad." It came out very clearly also in Douglas Hurd's address to the General Synod of the Church of England in February 1988 that was quoted earlier. Here Hurd advised the body of clergy to stick to morality and not to be so concerned with "lesser matters." Church and state should work together to rebuild moral standards and values.

The refusal of the church to be nothing more than the religious arm of the civil power periodically sends sensationalist tabloid newspapers like the *Daily Express* and the *Daily Mail* into apoplexy. These papers are not afraid to face the issue of what happens when morality and politics conflict. Tony Dawe wrote in the *Express* after the Falklands service that "instead of a triumphal service thanking God for our victory the congregation was treated to a sermon on the morals of war."[88] Morals! What a thing for a church leader to talk about on such an occasion!

There is a second, and secondary, role for the church in current conservative philosophy: caring for the casualties of our society, even the casualties of government policy. Caring for the poor is conceded to be part of the church's job. (The government's job, it may be suggested, is to ensure that there is a constant supply of them to care for!) But it is emphatically not the church's job to ask questions about the causes of poverty. There is no notion of the church as a critical community with values that are different from those of the state and that perhaps conflict with them.

Finally, Thatcherites hold a "two kingdoms" theology of the type that was held by the German churches at the time of the rise of Nazism and that made the Nazi conquest of the church so easy. In this theology, church and state, God and Caesar, have clearly defined and differentiated roles: moral and political. God must not trespass on the territory of Caesar, and vice versa. "Render to Caesar" (the first part of the sentence at any rate) was one of Mrs. Thatcher's favorite texts. As she said over ten years ago in an address in the church of Saint Lawrence Jewry in London, "For the truth of the matter is this: the Bible as well as the tradition of the church tell us very little directly about political systems or social programs. The nearest we get is Christ telling his disciples to render unto Caesar that which is Caesar's and unto God that which is God's."[89] Even clearer was the very right-wing Norman Tebbit in his reply to some London church leaders who had expressed their views on the future of the Greater London Council: "I am sure you will continue to follow the injunction to render unto Caesar what is Caesar's but resist the temptation to initiate a comparative search of the testaments to justify our positions. Whilst this government, concerned as ever to operate within the widest consensus, asked for comments on its white paper, I see no reason why the churches should enter a specifically political arena."[90] Jesus "got it about right," Mrs. Thatcher told us in 1984, when he said, "Render unto Caesar."[91]

Mrs. Thatcher repeated her sentiments when she addressed the Church of Scotland on 21 May 1988.[92] Her address ended with the recital of words from the hymn "I Vow to Thee, My Country."

> I vow to thee, my country, all earthly things above,
> Entire and whole and perfect, the service of my love.

It was a revealing choice of hymn. For not only is the hymn deeply heretical in its otherworldliness and its sharp distinction between this world and "another country," but it is also uncritical in its devotion to the fatherland. Indeed the fatherland is all but deified.

> The love that asks no question, the love that stands the test,
> That lays upon the altar the dearest and the best.

In Thatcherite theology Caesar clearly wins the victory.

I have so far looked at conservative thinking as it relates to Christian theology. In identifying the principal features of the Thatcherite theology, I am writing not of an era that is past but of present-day British conservatives in the post-Thatcher period. For though there have been changes in style and emphasis, the substance remains the same. However, it should be stressed that Christians do not judge governments by what they say alone but by what they do: by their fruits we shall know them. And in fact the principal reason for the conflict between the church and the present government in Britain does not lie at the theoretical level; it lies in the fact that churches on the ground, especially in the inner cities and in the run-down economies of the north, have seen the devastation and the cruelty as well as the demoralizing effects of Thatcherism in practice. They have seen that the government's assurances that all is well do not correspond to their own experience, and they therefore raise the issues of truth and illusion. When church leaders from Liverpool, Manchester, and the East End of London have talked to the government, it has been as if they were talking to people on Mars, so great is the comprehension gap. For many of these Christians, the government has become, in the literal sense, incredible: members of the government do not speak the truth that these Christians perceive. Instead they bear false witness. But more than that: for in biblical terms, the truth is not spoken, it is done. It is those who do justice who know the Lord. And so these Christians have gone back to the Scriptures and found such words as "Woe to those who decree iniquitous decrees . . . those who grind the faces of the poor." They have read again about the fate of the alien, the orphan, and the widow; the condemnations of riches and of the service of mammon. And they have realized that Caesar, far from sharing a divided realm with God, is often an enemy at whose over-throw the saints rejoice. They have read Revelation 19, the lament over Babylon, the prosperous city that trafficked in human souls, and seen renewed relevance.

At this point it is important to remember that in the inner urban ar-eas of many British cities, the majority of practicing Christians are black. And they too have seen the effects of Thatcherism in practice: not only in unemployment and despair, but in the operation of the im-migration rules by which the "party of the family" persistently keeps Asian families divided, in the insecurity and inferior status created by the Nationality Act, and in the explicit and crude racist nationalism of some Tory politicians, many councillors, and most of the right-wing press. Here a crucial reference point is Mrs. Thatcher's "swamping" in-terview on Granada TV on 30 January 1978. What is remembered is the reference to the British (that is, the white British) fear of being "swamped" by an alien influx that tipped the polls within days in fa-vor of the Conservatives. But in that interview Mrs. Thatcher was also asked whether she wanted to bring the support that had gone to the fas-cist party, the National Front, back to the Conservative Party. She replied, "Oh, very much back, certainly." And that is what happened. In 1979 the National Front vote collapsed due to public identification of the Conservative Party with a "tough" line on immigration. There were massive swings to the Conservatives in all the areas of NF sup-port, from Islington Central through the East End of London to Dagen-ham. The National Front was marginalized and fragmented because the Conservative Party had made them obsolete.[93]

And here we need surely to recall that devout British Christian who can claim to be the father of Thatcherism, for the Gospel according to

Saint Margaret was originally written in the Book of Enoch. As the journalist Peregrine Worsthorne wrote,

> It was Enoch Powell who first sowed the seeds whose harvest Margaret Thatcher reaped last Thursday. What is now called Thatcherism was originally known as Powellism: bitter tasting market economics sweetened and rendered palatable to the popular taste by great creamy dollops of nationalistic custard. In his case immigration control was the custard and it was a bit too rich for any but the strongest digestions. She was lucky to have the Falklands campaign handed to her on a plate which did the same job more effectively, turning fewer stomachs. . . . But the original formula was Enoch's.[94]

I believe it is a very serious mistake to treat Powell as a rejected and tragic wilderness figure of no further political significance. The Conservative Party had officially rejected him in the late 1960s—though whether it would have done so had Thatcher been the leader at the time instead of Heath is open to question—but it has taken many of his key ideas on board, not least on matters of race and nation. It has done so at a time when Christians are more and more conscious of both their international solidarity with their black brothers and sisters and the destructive power of institutional racism.

The churches then have witnessed the effects of the Thatcher regime and its successor on the most vulnerable sections of the community. They have remembered Tawney's words that the test of any philosophy or system of government is how it responds to those who fall by the wayside. They have seen the devastation of the inner cities and the incomprehension and perplexity of those politicians who have descended, heavily guarded, usually after some disturbance. They have watched the decline in health care, documented in report after report, and the refusal of the government to accept the evidence. They have watched the marked shift from struggle to complacency and the institutionalization of selfishness. (On the same day as Thatcher's address to the Church of Scotland, a Harris Poll showed that 61 percent of people believed that Britain was a more selfish society.) They have seen the growing materialism. They have seen the young housewives from the north forced into prostitution in London ("Thatcher's girls" they were called in the King's Cross district of London), the bitter flip side of the consumer culture. But, in a sense, in the crude materialism of Thatcherite values, we have all become prostitutes. Even the Good Samaritan is only remembered for his money. "In the Thatcherist view there *is* nothing else beyond the satisfaction of desires. . . . In the Thatcherist society we each become a Faust whose endless and innumerable desires can all be satisfied provided only that he gives up his identity, his soul."[95] At heart the Christian critique of the Thatcher years has been a spiritual critique: it represented a specific form of mammon worship, rooted in the mortal sin of avarice, an assault on human dignity that erodes the human spirit.

The revival of conservative politics in Britain, North America, and elsewhere has been a complex phenomenon. Undoubtedly there has been a resurgence of right-wing fundamentalism and of conservative and reactionary trends within the "mainstream" churches, leading many Christians to a strong support of the conservative regimes. The theological defense of Thatcherism was somewhat different from that of its Reaganite equivalent in the United States. Because there is a lower level of religious allegiance and a greater degree of secularization in Britain, and no mass fundamentalist movement on the scale of the United States, Thatcher's religious appeal was much vaguer. In addition, the tradition of social criticism in the Church of England has been strengthened in response to the experience of the Thatcher years in a way that has no exact American parallel. In both countries the social conscience of evangelicals has been raised. Many Christians, however, have become disillusioned and despondent about any hope of large-scale change and have retreated into forms of pietism, small and local projects, and internal concerns. The "alternative" approach, as represented by Hauerwas, has become more popular, and for some it has provided a way of adopting a radical and even revolutionary style of rhetoric without any serious commitment to political change at any recognizable point.

Most of all, the traditional "Christian left" has found itself bewildered and stranded, as the upheavals in Eastern Europe and the well-funded machines of the New Right in the West have helped to undermine the credibility of the socialist project. Yet there has been in the past a theologically deeply rooted tradition of socialist Christian thought and action, and it is important to examine the present state of that tradition as we face the twenty-first century.

Christians and the Left: The Dissident Anglo-Catholic Experience

"The political forces of the Left in the Western world are fragmented and have quantitatively minor influence. And they are so far failing to throw up commanding leaders who can rally them to future constructive forward movement." This remarkably contemporary comment might have come from any number of writers on the current state of the Left during the last few years. In fact, they come from the Anglo-Catholic Marxist priest Frederick Hastings Smyth, writing in August 1950.[96] Smyth faithfully reflected one strand within the Anglo-Catholic movement that had begun at Oxford in 1833. But the Oxford fathers would have been confused and baffled by him, and, had they understood his thinking, horrified. Smyth's *Manhood into God*[97] was the first major attempt to integrate Thomist theology and dialectical materialism. He was one among many Anglo-Catholics who combined a revolutionary political position with a Catholic theology. The Second Vatican Council was to make it possible for that strand to become a world tradition.

It has also been the tradition that has nourished and inspired my own life and ministry. My aim as a Christian writer is to articulate a vision of human society arising from and nourished by a Catholic socialist perspective. Yet in doing so I am presented with a twofold problem. First, I am not sure that Anglo-Catholicism as a discrete phenomenon still exists, but, second, if it does, I am quite sure it offers no radical social vision. So I speak of resources that need to be recovered rather than of a movement with a confessing agenda.

When we speak of the Anglo-Catholic tradition within the Anglican churches we may mean one of at least three movements. There is, first, the Tractarian movement, which began at Oxford in July 1833, focusing on the spiritual autonomy of the church and looking back to the early fathers, emphasizing catholicity and the revival of the sacramental life. Second, there is ritualism, which began with the spread of sacramental religion to the new towns and to city slums such as London Docks in 1856. Ritualism became a political issue, and priests were imprisoned for ritual and ceremonial offenses under the Public Worship Regulation Act of 1874. We may think, third, of the Catholic socialist tradition, which began with Stewart Headlam and the Guild of Saint Matthew in the 1870s and continued with Conrad Noel, John Groser, Stanley Evans, and many others in the twentieth century.

What became known as Anglo-Catholicism was a fusion of the first and second movements. It was a form of Christianity that emphasized the centrality of the sacraments, especially of eucharistic worship and sacramental confession, and the need for intense personal devotion. Many of the positive aspects of that tradition have now been absorbed into post–Vatican II Roman Catholicism and into many Protestant traditions. Anglo-Catholicism as a separate phenomenon continues to exist as a kind of marginal movement that is increasingly cut off from all the creative currents in the Christian world. It represents, in my view, an exhausted religious culture, and yet out of it may emerge some fruits. Samson's experience when investigating the carcass of the dead lion is not without its relevance.

It was in the third phase of the movement, from the late 1870s onward, that a new theological synthesis was created through a fusion of the theology of F. D. Maurice with the sacramentalism of the Oxford Movement. It was this fusion that created the phenomenon of Anglo-Catholic socialism, most clearly manifested in the establishment of the Guild of Saint Matthew (GSM) at Bethnal Green in 1877, the first explicitly socialist group in Britain, and that led to the volume *Lux Mundi* and the establishment of the Christian Social Union (CSU) in 1889. From Headlam and the GSM there grew up a rebel tradition associated with such figures as Thomas Hancock (who spoke of "the banner of Christ in the hands of the socialists" and called the Magnificat "the hymn of the universal social revolution"), Charles Marson, author of *God's Cooperative Society,* and Conrad Noel, parish priest of Thaxted and one of the founders of the British Socialist Party. From the CSU developed a more genteel and liberal tradition of social critique, pragmatic and reformist in its approach and very Anglican in its style. Its key figures were B. F. Westcott, Charles Gore, and Henry Scott

Holland. This tradition of social incarnational sacramental religion dominated mainstream Anglican thought from the 1880s to the death of William Temple in 1944. The publication of *Lux Mundi* in 1889 and of Gore's Bampton Lectures in 1891 were of crucial importance. As Michael Ramsey wrote, "It was an outcome of the *Lux Mundi* appeal to the Logos doctrine that both democracy and socialism were held to be expressions of the working of the divine spirit."[98]

The socialism of which these thinkers wrote was of an evolutionary and reformist kind. Westcott defined it as the principle of cooperation as against that of individualism, and said that socialism and individualism corresponded to two conflicting views of humanity. It is true that Westcott gave Christian socialism respectability and legitimacy, and in the process he diluted it. That tradition, articulated most memorably in the thought of William Temple, provided the specifically Christian basis for the welfare state.

But the Catholic tradition also nourished on its periphery a more revolutionary movement. Conrad Noel ridiculed the CSU as a mere talk shop. "Here's a pressing social problem: let's read a paper about it." These people, Noel complained, believed that the mighty would be put down from their thrones so gently that they would not feel the bump when they hit the ground. Noel's Catholic Crusade, formed in 1918 after the Russian Revolution, was committed to involvement in revolutionary struggle. Though on many issues it was naive and uncritical (though no more than many others), it represents the libertarian and prophetic tradition of Anglo-Catholic socialism at its best. Rowan Williams has claimed that of all the early leftist movements it comes closest to today's liberation theology.[99] The Crusade finally collapsed in the aftermath of the Stalin-Trotsky dispute. When George Orwell wrote that Anglo-Catholicism was the ecclesiastical equivalent of Trotskyism, he was correct in ways that he did not intend: one reason given by the Communist Party for the expulsion of the early Trotskyists was their association with Noel and the Crusade.[100]

There were then two traditions of Anglo-Catholic socialism: a middle-class, reformist, liberal tradition of social reform and a more grass roots tradition, rooted in concrete struggles, a tradition of "socialism from below." And, as in all movements, there were significant weaknesses. As a movement and a tradition, Anglo-Catholicism had some serious weaknesses, and at times one must speak of pathological growths. It was a very English movement, at times arrogantly nationalist in its perception of Catholic identity. It promoted clericalism, that distortion of priesthood that has so defaced and damaged the Christian church. In its English and its exported forms, it was not untainted by racism, even though the majority of Anglo-Catholics are black and its traditional strongholds are in Central and South Africa and the Caribbean. Yet in its public face it has manifested the perspectives and the interests of white men of English and North American backgrounds (though it should be noted that the first female bishop in any church within the Catholic tradition is a black woman of Anglo-Catholic background, Barbara Harris of Massachusetts). Specifically, Anglo-Catholicism has been associated with three features that have, at certain times and places, assumed the dimensions of a serious illness.

The first is a profound inability to cope with issues of human sexuality, leading to a dread of women that often reaches the point of real gynophobia. The central problem here lies in the historic and ambivalent relationship between Anglo-Catholicism and homosexuality, a relationship that goes back to the early years of the movement, and that calls for further discussion.[101] The second is an organic and rigidly hierarchical view of both church and society that veers toward a kind of fascism. As I showed above, the European roots of fascism lie in part in a Catholic social vision, articulated most memorably in the encyclical *Quadragesimo Anno* of 1931. Many Anglo-Catholics, particularly those of a papalist outlook, have shared in this view of the social order of which the fascist state was the culmination.

There is a third serious problem within the Anglo-Catholic culture, however: its creation of a world within a world. Valerie Pitt has described the growth of Anglo-Catholicism as a type of cultural distortion that deviated more and more from the world of reality. By creating a world within a world, she claims, they "unconsciously made religion a life substitute rather than a life revealer, not a way into the splendors of the visible world but a way out. That habit of mind is fixed in us still, and ultimately it is destructive of religion itself."[102] I believe that a critical encounter with the distortions of this and other historical formations is an important way of understanding our own dilemmas and challenges. In the history and dilemmas of Anglo-Catholicism we see features that have characterized and disfigured religion as a whole in the modern world.

For, in spite of all this, we are speaking of a tradition of great richness, theological depth, and vision. It offers a way of being a Christian that takes account both of the need to have doctrinal and spiritual roots in a historic tradition and of the need to develop a dialectical encounter with the agenda of contemporary society. In the light of this tradition I offer three suggestions.

First, I suggest that socialism, a form of society in which wealth is owned by the community and the productive process is controlled by the workers, is compatible with a Catholic view of humanity and the social order in a way that capitalism is not. Even the strongly anti-socialist encyclicals of the popes from Leo XIII to Pius XII are much more anticapitalist (even though it is a precapitalist critique of capitalism). Since Vatican II and the currents of thought that have come from Latin America, the possibilities for a creative movement of Catholic vision in shaping a socialist society are much greater, and I believe that there is much within the Anglo-Catholic tradition that could support this movement theologically. The failure of the socialist experiments in Eastern Europe and the Soviet Union lend no support to a movement backward but only to a more committed and self-critical quest for a democratic and human socialist society.

Second, I suggest that the only way out of the present crisis of the church in the West is through transcendence of the conceptual limitations of Reformation theology, especially its individualism. But this cannot be accomplished by a return to medievalism or to the Catholicism of the European Counter-Reformation. The only hope for a Christian response to the contradictions and dilemmas of contemporary capitalism lies in a renewed Catholicism that is able to engage with the structures of advanced technological society. I believe that the tradition that combines a Catholic theology with an openness to modern critical thought and experience is the most hopeful way ahead.

Third, I suggest, with the American black theologian Cornel West, that, though Christianity and Marxism are the most distorted traditions in the modern world, an alliance between prophetic Christianity and progressive Marxism offers the last humane hope for humankind.[103]

For many years the only serious attempt to relate Christianity to Marxism in practical terms was among Anglo-Catholics. In spite of its manifest failures, limitations, and weaknesses, the theological framework of Anglo-Catholicism offers the best hope in this area. Therefore we need to ask, What kind of social vision emerges from the Anglo-Catholic tradition?

First, it is a corporate vision. It is a social vision, a vision of a co-operative society, a community bonded together by a fundamental and unbreakable solidarity, a community of equals. Central to Anglo-Catholic theology is its emphasis on the church as the Body of Christ and as an integral element in the proclamation of the gospel. Michael Ramsey's book *The Gospel and the Catholic Church* (1936) was of fundamental importance in shaping a theological tradition that took seriously both the New Testament and the liturgical renewal and did so in an ecumenical way. It undermined the liberal tradition, with its impatience with doctrine and its division between gospel and church, and it prepared the theological ground for what became known as "Christian sociology." Many years after Ramsey's book, John Robinson was to claim that the doctrine of the Body of Christ was "the specifically Christian clue to the renewal of society."[104] It is worth remembering that the best-known Anglo-Catholic bishop in the world today is Desmond Tutu. Apartheid involved the belief that Christian love did not have to be expressed in visible material structures. Against this twentieth-century version of the Eutychian heresy, the very traditional Anglo-Catholics of the Reeves-Huddleston generation insisted that Christianity demanded a material and social embodiment. A high doctrine of the church became a key element in the resistance to what John Davies has termed "the novel nonsense of upstart racism."[105]

It was in its stress on the body, on communion and sharing, and in its rejection of individualism in religion that the link between Anglo-Catholicism and socialism was forged. "Those who assist at Holy Communion," insisted Stewart Headlam, "are bound to be Holy Communists."[106] It was not possible to maintain the eucharistic principles of common life and equality without those principles being extended to the social order outside the sanctuary—unless, of course, one maintained a kind of dualism that preserved church and society in separate compartments.

Second, it is a materialistic vision. It is a vision that is deeply and unashamedly materialistic, that values the creation, that rejoices in the physical, in the flesh, in human sexuality, and that is rooted in the principle that matter is the vehicle of spirit, not its enemy. When Temple said that Christianity was the most materialistic of all religions, he stood within a long tradition of incarnational and sacramental materialism. This tradition not only saw bread and wine as symbols of the transformation of all human resources; it saw the material world as the primal sacrament from which all others derived. Anglo-Catholic theology refuses to tolerate a division between matter and spirit, or any disparaging of matter or the physical. To despise and undervalue the creation is to despise its Creator. Catholic Christianity stands or falls on this sacramental principle, and this must involve a break with those movements of Christian thought that see the spiritual as the antithesis of the material and that see concern for social and economic justice as a hindrance to true spirituality. Such dualism is deeply alien to a sacramental materialism. Anglo-Catholic social theology is basically at odds with philosophical idealism and is rooted instead in a realist and materialist approach to the world.

At the very core of Anglo-Catholic spirituality and of the Anglo-Catholic social tradition is the doctrine of incarnation. But the tradition has not simply emphasized the Word made flesh as the basis of a movement of compassion, care, and service; it has emphasized equally the "taking of manhood into God," the theme of the incarnation as a continuing process of transformation. It therefore offers a type of Christian theology and Christian practice that does not lay so much stress on human fallenness and original sin that it undermines the basis for Christian social action. Rather, it lays stress on grace operating in and through the material and historical processes, and on the image of God in all people. It works with a high and optimistic view of human potential and of the power of grace to transcend the limitations of nature. All this has important political implications.

Third, it is a vision of transformation, of a transformed society, not simply an improved one. At the heart of Anglo-Catholic spirituality is the eucharistic offering, with its twofold emphasis on offering and consecration. Bread and wine, fruits of the earth *and* work of human hands, products not only of nature but of the industrial process, are, at the eucharistic offertory, brought within the redemptive process. In Smyth's words, "The bread and wine at the offertory set forth structures in history which have been brought out of the fallen world into the first stage of its redemption."[107] In contrast to Andrew Carnegie in 1889 and to Margaret Thatcher in 1989, both of whom insist that Christian ethics are only concerned with the second stage of wealth, its use, the liturgical offertory sees the movements of creation and of production as equally important. For it is impossible to offer to God the fruits of injustice and oppression, as Irenaeus saw in the second century. Eucharistic worship implies, and indeed depends upon, the process of production as an element in the divine encounter. It involves a rejection of pagan harvest festival religion, which avoids the hard questions of manufacturing industry and seeks a way to God through matter that bypasses the need for redemption.[108]

The Eucharist, however, is not only about offering to God the fruits of labor: it is about the transformation, in Thomist language the transubstantiation, of matter to become the material of the resurrection. At the very heart of worship is the reality of change, of the sanctifying power of the Spirit to transform both the material things and the community. A theology that places the transformation of material structures and of human relations at the heart of its liturgy and life should be a theology that is open to the need for such transformation in the economic and political life of society.

Fourth, this tradition is a rebel tradition. The Tractarian movement began as a critique of the church-Tory alliance and as a protest against state control of the church. In no other sense can it be said that the Tractarians were social radicals. But in their rejection of the politics of the ecclesiastical establishment, they sowed the seeds of a tradition of nonconformity and dissent in other areas. And this culture of dissent was intensified when ritualism became a criminal offense in the second phase of the movement. Thus Anglo-Catholicism and a rebellious spirit became allies. The fact that the rebellion was about the details of church furniture and fashions is not the point; once a movement of nonconformity has been inspired in one area, it can spread to others. It is clear that in a number of slum neighborhoods—in Hoxton and Haggerston in East London, in Portsmouth, in Moss Side and Ardwick in Manchester, in Sunderland, and elsewhere—Anglo-Catholicism became the religion of the poor and despised, a poor people's church, a church of the back streets. Ritualism was, as the churchwardens of Saint Alban's, Holborn, told the bewildered Archbishop Tait, "a working men's question."[109] And this history points to a crucial element in Anglo-Catholic history: the Anglo-Catholic movement in many places broke the identification of the Church of England with the establishment and with bourgeois conformity. Back-street Anglo-Catholicism in some places had a closer affinity with the very poor and dispossessed, with the lumpen, than conventional Anglicanism, the political parties, or the trade unions.

But the Catholic socialists of the tradition of Conrad Noel, John Groser, and Stanley Evans saw pastoral ministry to the poor as only one aspect of the church's social task; there was the equally important task of nourishing a culture of resistance, a culture that would challenge and confront the false values of mammon. So Father Adderley spoke of the Eucharist as "the weekly meeting of rebels against a mammon-worshiping world order."[110] At churches like Thaxted in Essex and Burslem in the Potteries, the liturgy was seen as a foretaste of the coming age of justice. These Christian communities recognized that vision, and struggle to realize that vision, must be nourished at the local, concrete level. Without that contextual base among the people, no social program could succeed.

One aspect of this rebel tradition has been its ability to establish links of solidarity with marginalized groups without losing its own identity. Recent examples include the support for Viraj Mendis, the Sri Lankan immigrant who was eventually deported, at the Church of the Ascension in Hulme, Manchester; the solidarity of the church at Goldthorpe, Yorkshire, with the miners' strike; the identification of Saint Botolph's Church, Aldgate, with the gay community; and the close involvement of Anglo-Catholic parishes in Liverpool, Brixton, and Bristol in the urban uprisings of 1981 and their aftermath. This solidarity can, of course, be exaggerated. But it is interesting to see the way in which Catholic sacramentalists have been involved at key points in the struggles of oppressed and marginalized groups and communities in our society, especially in the inner urban areas.

Finally, the Anglo-Catholic social vision is one that moves beyond the Christian community and is concerned with the working out of God's purposes in the upheavals and crises of world history. It is a Kingdom theology rather than a church theology. The centrality of the Kingdom of God as the regulative principle of theology was a consistent theme of Anglo-Catholic social thought from the time that Percy Widdrington first used that expression in 1922. "For generations past the church has preached what is called 'the Gospel.' The call today is to return to what the New Testament calls 'the Gospel of the Kingdom'—the Kingdom of God, the cardinal doctrine of our preaching, regulative of our theology, and the touchstone by which all the activities of the church are tested. This will involve a Reformation in comparison with which the Reformation of the sixteenth century will seem a small thing."[111] In the 1950s Stanley Evans, an East London parish priest, picked up the theme: the real division in the Christian world, he claimed, was about the Kingdom of God.[112] To read Widdrington and Evans today is to see how extraordinarily prophetic and visionary they were, for this is precisely our situation as we confront the new forces and new alignments within the Christian world.

In a sense the relationship of church and Kingdom and the issues around Kingdom theology—whether the Kingdom of God is this-worldly or otherworldly, social or personal, present or future, and so on—are the key issues in determining whether Christians have *any* vision for society and, if they do, how vision and reality connect. Much depends on how we envisage that relationship. The dismissal of utopia and the pejorative usage of the term—both by Marx and by his critic Karl Popper—has its parallels in Christian irritation and embarrassment with eschatology. The view that eschatological ideas, millenarianism, adventism, any focusing on the future, is irredeemably escapist, unreal, and destructive of concrete political struggle needs to be questioned. No doubt much visionary thinking is of this kind, but the Anglo-Catholic socialist tradition, with its deep sense of the life of the age to come and its conviction that the Kingdom of God is not a purely otherworldly hope, stands as a challenge to contemporary socialism, with its conspicuous lack of vision.

One of the key insights of the Anglo-Catholic socialist tradition is the recognition that visions and dreams, though a necessary part of a politics of struggle, must be constantly tested against experiences of real people and their struggles—against the realities of homelessness, racial oppression, the collapse of communities. Anglo-Catholic social vision has always been worked out in the back streets, in specific neighborhoods, in and through involvement with very concrete struggles. It has begun with the specific and the concrete. The two most crucial challenges to the thinking of both Anglo-Catholicism and the socialist movement today come from the black community and from feminism. There is no way that either Catholic Christianity or the Left, Christian or secular, can survive those challenges without either significant transformation or significant wounding. And this rootedness in concrete struggles is of crucial importance, for in every generation movements, religious and political, face challenges to their thought, their identity, and their inner strength—challenges that, if not faced or not absorbed, will lead to serious damage and possibly decay. The future of Anglo-Catholicism is still uncertain.

Political Holiness: Resources for Struggle

The uncertainty and insecurity that surrounds the Anglo-Catholic left is a microcosm of the uncertainty surrounding the political world as a whole. This uncertainty is not simply an intellectual problem. There is a widespread failure of the imagination to conceive of transformation on any significant scale. The sense that "there is no alternative" to the present system has become a form of slavery, a captivity to the status quo, an inability to envision anything beyond the present reality. Politics for most people has been reduced to impotent observation. Most people have abandoned altogether any belief that they can play a part in effective political action. Those who continue to pursue the political path either enter the world of the professional reformist or of the party machines, or move toward moralistic types of nationalism, often supported and reinforced by religion. Others may retreat into sectarian fundamentalisms that enable doctrinal purity to be maintained at the cost of relevance, or into nihilistic terrorism that may seem to offer some hope of success.

There is a climate of autism, a paralysis of the spirit, a deep sense that work for fundamental change is a futile activity. In part this sense is a result of realistic assessment of the problems confronting us. The sheer size and complexity of the issues of global politics leads us to the view that individuals are helpless and individual action ineffective. And this view is partly correct. There are many issues in both global and national politics on which action by individuals will not be effective and will serve only to waste or divert energy. But this does not mean that action of any kind is doomed.

The present state of Christian political response is to a large extent the result of various responses to the complexity and size of world problems. Many people have given up altogether, having convinced themselves that nothing can be done. Others throw themselves into single-issue campaigns, in the belief that effective action can be taken in relation to specific issues, if not about the state of society as a whole. Because of this shift, much political activity has moved from the political parties into pressure groups and movements such as Oxfam, Friends of the Earth, Greenpeace, antinuclear campaigns, and so on. Others, particularly churches, have begun, or intensified, "soup kitchen" and ambulance styles of action and have often earned government praise for doing so. Indeed, one serious danger on the present political scene in both Britain and the United States is that, because the problems of homelessness, hunger, and sickness have grown so much worse, churches may resign themselves to such ministry as their major contribution to the political realm. There is simply too much to do, so care for casualties takes precedence over any sustained critique of the system that produces them and replaces any sustained commitment to political change. The words of Percy Widdrington, addressing the Church Socialist League in 1913, have added impact in the present climate.

> The church has been too long the Church Quiescent here on earth, content to serve as the scavenger of the capitalist system. If it refuses the challenge it may survive as a pietistic sect providing devotional opportunities for a small and dwindling section of the community, a residuary solace for the world's defeated, administering religion as an anesthetic to help men to endure the hateful operation of life, an ambulance picking up the wounded, entered on the Charities Register—an institution

among institutions. But it will cease to be the organ of the
Kingdom, building up the world out of itself: it will have abandoned its mission and become apostate.[113]

Today Widdrington's prediction has become a reality in many towns
and cities where this ameliorative work has become the sole manifestation of the church's "social action." Indeed, it has been extended
from churches and voluntary groups to the political world itself as
more and more energy is taken up in defending inadequate health care
and welfare systems against threats to reduce them even further. In
this context holding on to what is left can become a full-time activity,
a constant case of defending the bad against the worse. Confronted
by powerful conservative regimes, "progressive" political groups are
often forced into being little more than what the British socialist politician Tony Benn has called "intensive care units for capitalism."[114]

If Christians are to survive in the political arena, with all its threats
to human dignity and commitment, they will not need only the discipline of intellect and will. They will need spiritual resources that enable
them to sustain hope and integrity. They will need a spirituality that is
not geared solely to the private and inward realm. What would such a
spirituality be? Roger Haight attempts to respond to the question:

> It would be a spirituality that sees the operation of grace made
> manifest precisely in a "building of the earth" in history,
> among people, in public institutions that shape human lives.
> As such this spirituality would be the very opposite of one
> that called for a withdrawal from the "world," from secular
> and profane activities. For this spirituality would see grace as
> a call to participate in history. This Christian spirituality
> would entail an immersion in the processes of history: in the
> public events and crises, large and small, that influence other
> lives in this world; in the corporate institutions and structures
> that shape and govern human existence in the world; in the
> small or local institutions or ways of life that often oppress and
> dehumanize this group or render that one powerless and pas-
> sive. In this spirituality the idea of "saintliness" would not
> consist in a "state of life" but would only apply existentially
> and concretely to some form of engaged behavior.[115]

Confronted by massive bureaucracies, computerized forms of oppression, principalities and powers that have assumed new and more sinister technological faces, Christians who are active in political struggles need more and better spiritual resources. Without such inner strength and sustaining power, they will not survive.

One of the real strengths of the Christian community is its international character, rooted in its commitment to Christ across boundaries and barriers of race and nation. Because political issues are increasingly global issues, it is essential that churches build networks across continents involving support, mutual solidarity, exchange of ideas, disciplined and informed prayer, and careful strategic thinking. To some extent this already happens through such organizations as the World Council of Churches and the various transnational church organizations. But these can easily become top-heavy, as "social action curiae" meet at high-powered conferences and make decisions on behalf of the people—an ecclesiastical replica of the governmental structures. However useful such bodies are, they are not an adequate model of international Christian political work.

Informal links need to be forged between grass roots communities at the local level through which ideas can be shared and collaborative action planned. Churches on the ground, whether in Latin America or Britain, Africa or the United States, are often closer to the realities of politics, closer to the effects of political decisions and legislation, than any other groups. They see more and they know more than the politicians, who are often remote and protected. They need to have confidence in the knowledge, credibility, and power that such closeness brings, and they need to share it both with their brothers and sisters elsewhere who are having similar experiences and with those whose consciousness and indignation need to be aroused. Out of such networks could rise genuine "communities of resistance and solidarity,"[116] rooted in detailed knowledge and sustained by prayer, that could be mobilized in effective challenge and active work for justice. Such activity calls for extremely good use of organization. Few institutions are as well organized at the local level as churches, and few use their organizational potential so ineffectively.

Though it is clearly a mistake to concern oneself with local issues to such an extent that the wider national and international concerns are neglected, my experience is that all effective Christian political witness must begin locally, with back-street issues that affect the people of the neighborhood in which one is set. From such local knowledge and local struggles, connections can, indeed must, be made with wider issues. But connections can only be made in the course of struggle. There has to be something to connect, and so the spade work has to be done at the back-street level. Christians in a neighborhood need to act cross-confessionally; indeed, if the "ecumenical movement" does not start at the level of local collaboration, it will never get off the ground. There must be locally based communities of Christian people, committed to politics and to prayer, who will take their place alongside all men and women of good will, whatever their faith or allegiance may be.

Such groups will not be "vanguards" on the Leninist model. However, Christians can learn a good deal from both the strengths and the weaknesses of traditional organizing within Marxist movements. Lenin believed strongly in a disciplined party of highly professional revolutionaries. The Leninist party was marked by directive leadership and "the most rigorous and truly iron discipline."[117] There was a strong emphasis on education. Certainly no Christian action is likely to be effective that neglects strong organization, discipline, and teaching. To that extent the "vanguard" model has its uses as a corrective to much vague and flabby Christian pseudo-organizing. The problem with much liberal Christian action is that it has not even got to this Leninist point, which it needs to reach in order to move beyond it.

There are two major problems with the Leninist model. The first, which it shares with some forms of Christian action, is a tendency to treat the words of the sacred text (Lenin, Trotsky, the Bible, or some aspect of rite or cultus) as inerrant and unalterable. Trotskyist groups in particular have tended to become sects of the pure, fundamentalist devotees of the orthodox doctrine, producing "a desert of intellectual talmudism and political ineffectiveness."[118] The second, and related, problem lies in the belief that the elect know all that needs to be known and in a consequent failure or inability to listen to the voices of the people or to learn from their experience. As a result the vanguard becomes more and more detached from contact with ordinary people, and their reentry into the mainstream of community life is as difficult as that of any addict.

Sheila Rowbotham, a British socialist feminist writer, has strongly criticized the Leninist and Trotskyist traditions as the "politics . . . of a chosen elect" in which the party becomes "a red zone from which professional revolutionaries sally forth with a superior knowledge, untouched by culture themselves, to insert, inject, imbue or saturate and drown other movements."[119] Rowbotham calls them "a small band of fanatical know-alls, trotting about raising other people up to their 'level' of consciousness, the very notion of which is necessarily elitist and invulnerable."[120] "They had," she reflects, "all those certainties as if everything was known, the whole world and its history was sewn up and neatly categorized."[121] If one alters the odd word, her account sounds suspiciously like a description of many Christian groups.

Nevertheless, recognition of the dangers of elitism and insensitivity should not lead Christians to think that there is no need for the disciplined, committed cell. The Christian movement is called to be a movement of truth, and though truth must constantly be encountered and learned afresh, the doctrinal element of the faith must not be overlooked. The "postmodern" notion that no truth can be known runs flatly contrary not only to the whole of Christian history but also to common sense. But the ascent to truth is not gradual, gentle, or free from difficulty: it involves struggle, conflict with illusion, and the encounter with darkness and doubt. A major part of the church's political task is to subject political claims to the most rigorous scrutiny. The unmasking and exposure of illusion and falsehood is central to prophetic political work, and here it is important that intellectuals, theologians and other academics, should be brought into close practical collaboration with grass roots Christian activists. The isolation of intellectuals in academia has had seriously damaging effects on their public political responsibility. It is many years since the public role of the theologian or philosopher was recognized in most parts of the Western world. Probably Reinhold Niebuhr was the last significant public theologian, and George Kennan the closest to a public philosopher, in recent American history. That vacuum will not be filled quickly, but the task of building alliances between intellectuals and the public must not be delayed.

The role of the intellectual as political critic was a constant theme of C. Wright Mills as long ago as the 1940s. In an essay of 1944 on "the role of the intellectual in society" Mills wrote,

> The independent artists and intellectuals are among the few remaining personalities equipped to resist and fight the stereotyping and consequent death of genuinely lively things. Fresh perception now involves the capacity continually to un-mask and to smash the stereotypes of vision and intellect with which modern communications swamp us. These worlds of mass art and mass thought are increasingly geared to the de-mands of politics. That is why it is in politics that intellectual solidarity and effort must be centered. If the thinker does not relate himself to the value of truth in political struggle, he cannot responsibly cope with the whole of live experi-ence.[122]

These are important and timely words for the Christian thinker in the last years of the twentieth century.

It is important that Christians do not invoke a false notion of pu-rity as an excuse for avoiding the political arena. There is the danger of compromise, of abandonment of one's principles, of betraying one's values, but these are not fragile possessions that can be hidden in a field or locked away in a sacristy for safety. Purity cannot be preserved through inactivity and evasion of responsibility. Purity survives through facing the threats to its identity, through the practical conflicts of incarnation and passion. Risks must be taken; hands and feet must be made dirty; integrity must be tested in concrete struggle.

Finally the Christian in politics must be joyful, celebrating the vic-tory over injustice and oppression in the midst of failure and trial. Politics needs songs and dances, wildness and jubilee, and the dimension of cel-ebration should be something that Christians can bring to political strug-gles. Today we need to learn afresh from Latin America, South Africa, and the countries of the East about the power of liberatory music and the importance of celebration in the midst of strife. For no vigorous political movement has ever existed or can exist without resistance music.

Nourished by the divine commitment in incarnation and passion, and inspired by the songs of the new creation, the Christian in politics must be a person of hope. Pessimism is so easy, and many people, especially middle-class people who are not used to struggle, tend to give up very easily. The literature of political movements in the West in the last fifty years is full of disillusionment and loss of hope. George Orwell's writings did much to ridicule the idealists of his generation and to instill self-distrust, pessimism, and despair in many.[123] Nor is Gramsci's famous slogan "pessimism of the intellect, optimism of the will" a very helpful one, for it leads people to believe that defeat is likely and that one must nevertheless act as if this were not so, an attitude of "resolute despair."[124] Christian engagement in politics must be rooted in an honest facing of current reality with all its gloom and hopelessness, yet nourished by the firm belief in the resurrection and in Christ's victory over all unjust powers. That Christ is risen, and has conquered not only death but the death-dealing world of political oppression, must be the driving hope of the Christian in the march from Babylon to the New Jerusalem.

4

THE DESERT IN THE CITY

Contemplation and the Back Streets

But seek the welfare of the city where I have sent you into exile, and pray to the Lord on its behalf, for in its welfare you will find your welfare.

JEREMIAH 29:7

The monasteries kept alive the image of the Heavenly City. As the new urban communities took form after the Tenth Century the monastery made an even deeper imprint on their life at first than did the market. . . . Here was the peace and order, the quietness and inwardness beloved by Christian men.

LEWIS MUMFORD, 1961

In other ages and other places the focal point of the church's program may have been the countryside or the town, but in this age and nation the focal point must be the inner city. It is there that the social ills of our society are most evident. It is there that the ministry of pastoral love is most desperately needed, and it is there that the decisions are made which affect the society in which we live. Yet it is the inner city which is the most neglected missionary front in our country today.

PAUL MOORE, 1964

I sat there overwhelmed. (Revised Standard Version)
I sat there dumbfounded. (New English Bible)
I sat there distraught. (New American Bible)
I sat there like a man stunned. (Jerusalem Bible)
I sat there astonished. (Authorized Version)

EZEKIEL 3:15

The City of London historically had four gates, four points of entry and exit: Bishopsgate to the north, Billingsgate to the south, Aldersgate to the west, and Aldgate to the east. At each gate stood a church dedicated to Saint Botolph, the patron saint of travelers. Three of them still stand; the Billingsgate church was destroyed in the Great Fire of London in 1666. Aldgate was first mentioned in the reign of King Edgar (959–975), and we know that in 1374 Chaucer lived in a house above the gate. A church has stood at Aldgate for over a thousand years; the original Saxon church was enlarged in 1418, and the present church of Saint Botolph was built in 1744.

Beyond Aldgate to the east is the area known as the East End of London, or, to give it its modern legal name, the London Borough of Tower Hamlets. This area comprises the three former boroughs of Stepney, Bethnal Green, and Poplar. The term *East End* is often used more loosely (but incorrectly) to include parts of Shoreditch and Hackney to the north.

My Context: The East End of London

The East End is one of the poorest and most deprived areas of London, indeed of Britain, and suffers a formidable range of social problems. Having grown as an urban unit from the age of Elizabeth I, the area began to decline in population after the building of the railways in the mid-nineteenth century and particularly after 1901. Between 1921 and 1971 the population fell from 529,000 to 165,000, a decline of 70 percent. The devastation of the Second World War in particular led to significant loss of population, which continued and intensified in the postwar period, partly because much of the housing was destroyed by wartime bombing. Between 1961 and 1971 the population fell by 40,000, and by the mid-1970s it was a quarter of what it had been in 1901. However, during the 1980s, and particularly since 1986, the population has begun to increase once more for two reasons. First is the growth of the Bangladeshi population and the presence within this community of a large number of women of child-bearing age; it is estimated that the Bangladeshi population in the age range 5 to 14 will grow by over 450 percent by the year 2001. Second is the development of the Docklands area, the biggest current business development project in Europe. As a result of these two factors, Tower Hamlets today is the only part of Inner London that shows vigorous population growth, reversing, in one small area, the general pattern of inner city population decline throughout the country. However, as a result of the Docklands developments and of "gentrification" in that and other parts of the area, the East End, once the cheapest part of London, is now among the most expensive, housing costs having risen by 115 percent between 1981 and 1985. At the 1981 census over 50 percent of households in the East End were below the official poverty line, and a study several years later showed 41 percent of the population claiming welfare benefits, the highest figure for any London borough.

The area has been plagued for many years by unemployment, due mainly to the collapse of manufacturing industry. Today manufacturing jobs are concentrated in the same five trades as in the mid-nineteenth century—clothing, furniture, metals and engineering, printing and paper, and precision manufacturing. A survey in 1986 showed that almost 64 percent of the population were manual workers. But there has been a general loss of job opportunities that the Docklands development has done little to alter. Between 1961 and 1971 over 30,000 jobs were lost in the area, so unemployment levels remain high, in the Spitalfields Ward reaching a figure around three times the national average.

For many years there have been severe problems of housing overcrowding, severe damp in roofs and walls, homelessness, environmental health, and physical and mental illness. Spitalfields, which adjoins the City of London, with its massive wealth and luxury, is the most overcrowded ward in the whole of the United Kingdom, with around 28 percent of households living in overcrowded conditions. The reputation of Spitalfields as a district of desperate poverty and a center for derelict and rootless people goes back many years. In 1807 it was said to be "inhabited almost entirely by poor persons" and in 1963 was described as "London's worst slum."[1] A former Chief City Planner for Chicago visiting Spitalfields in the early 1960s could not believe his eyes.[2] Since then, though there have been considerable improvements in some areas, homelessness has increased, and the number of vagrant alcoholics in the area has continued to rise. Those who do have housing often suffer from serious damp and from sewage back flow. In a recent study of two housing developments, over 72 percent reported damp rooms;[3] in another study tenants saw up to four inches of sewage in the backyard. Although the local water authority denied that there was danger, they have recently invested a million pounds to improve the drainage infrastructure in the Isle of Dogs, the heart of the Docklands development.[4]

The health problems of the East End are a classic example of the "inverse care law": the greater the need, the less adequate is the provision. At the 1971 census, Tower Hamlets had the highest perinatal mortality rate in Britain, with morbidity, mortality, and incidence of bronchial diseases at 60 percent above the national average. Alone in London, Tower Hamlets in the early 1980s was among the ten areas in Britain with the highest death rates. The Black Report on *Inequalities in Health* (1980) had a special appendix on the East End. Studies over many years have shown high rates of mental illness, one study showing the schizophrenia rate for part of the East End to be over twice the national average.[5] The numbers of children in foster care are among the highest in Britain, and truancy figures among the highest in Inner London.

The East End has provided the context for most of my adult life and pastoral ministry. Beginning in the Whitechapel area in 1958 as a student, I moved, several years later, a few miles north to Shoreditch and then, after some years in Soho in the West End, to Bethnal Green. For the last few years my work has been in the Spitalfields and Aldgate areas on the eastern edge of the City of London.

In this chapter I shall be more personal than at any other point in this book. I shall reflect on the life of prayer and action within the inner urban context, using the East End and Soho as the material base for my reflections. It is important to do this, and not to speak vaguely about prayer and action, prayer and justice, without any indication of the concrete reality within which they are pursued. The East End and Soho have been my context. As I look back on the various phases of my life and ministry, I see in each phase two processes: a negative process of disillusionment, a stripping away of illusions and falsehoods, of superficial ideas and stereotypes, of pseudoreligion; and a positive and creative process, a movement toward wholeness, integration of body and mind, flesh and spirit, personal and political. Each phase was painful, at times disintegrating, yet the overall experience has been one of liberation. Each phase involved a breaking process in which illusions were shattered and the facades of false confidence and false security were broken down. Spiritual growth is rarely a gentle, gradual ascent, but instead is a series of crises, conflicts, *kairos* moments, through which we are confronted with threats, choices, challenges, to which we respond or fail to respond. Either way these crises do not leave us unchanged.

"Not Always a Pleasant Place": Cable Street

For the experience of the holy in the midst of the common life of the back streets, the most significant and most formative period of my life was my time in Cable Street in the East End of London at the end of the 1950s and the first few years of the 1960s. Cable Street— the Cable Street that I knew in those years—has been called "a straight, classical, disgraceful, old-fashioned run-down slum."[6] It was for many years the social center of the London Docks. Since the early eighteenth century it had been a gathering place for desperate and rootless people, an early version of "skid row." Since the 1940s African and Caribbean seamen had settled there. As a young, and very naive, student, I arrived in this street in September 1958, and within a few weeks I found myself living in number 84, a Franciscan mission that had been set up in a former brothel. It was to be my home for over three years.

The people who formed the Cable Street community were immensely varied, but they had five features in common. They were all poor. They were all insignificant: in the eyes of officialdom, the police, the local authority, they didn't matter. They were despised: the neighborhood had a bad name. To live in Cable Street was a distinct disadvantage. They were sorrowful: the street was a place of great pain, sadness, and despair; many had given up hope that things might change. And they were marginal; the rest of London, and even of the East End, carried on as if they were not there.

There are few streets of London (or of any city) that have been the subject of radio programs. Patrick O'Donovan's program "The

Challenge of Cable Street," broadcast in February 1950, was one of the better attempts to communicate something of the atmosphere and tragic character of the street, "not always a pleasant place." O'Donovan described "a sense of hopelessness and of poverty that has ceased to struggle." He was horrified by the first few hundred yards of Cable Street, the district that had become my home: "I think these few hundred yards are about the most terrible in London."[7] Two years later a black American journalist, Roi Ottley, produced a less sensitive and highly sensational account of the street in his book *No Green Pastures.* Ottley wrote, "Today, down by London Dock in about a square mile of back streets, there exists a dismal Negro slum. The neighborhood, situated in the Borough of Stepney, abounds with brothels and dope pads in old tumbledown buildings. Few slums in the U.S. compare with this area's desperate character, unique racial composition, and atmosphere of crime, filth and decay." Ottley contrasted the Cable Street cafes with "the good-natured exuberance of a Negro tavern in Harlem." In Cable Street, on the other hand, "the atmosphere resembled the Casbah in Algiers—mysterious, sinister and heavily-laden with surreptitious violence."[8]

The district continued to attract hostile publicity right down to the late 1960s, when demolition work began on the old slum property. Ashley Smith, writing in 1961, called Cable Street "the filthiest, dirtiest, most repellently odored street in Christendom," though a more sympathetic observer, the seaman George Foulser, pointed out that it was a friendly neighborhood and its inhabitants were an object lesson in multiracial living for people elsewhere.[9]

Although I had been born into a poor working-class family in a run-down, deprived area, it was Cable Street that brought me face-to-face with the poverty and oppression of the classic slum, with the dehumanizing effect on its inhabitants, with the amazing resilience and survival power of people who had been crushed, broken, and written off. God was either in the midst of all this, or God was not! I went to Cable Street as a rather smug, arrogant, condescending do-gooder; I emerged as a very chastened, humbled, shaken, and, I hope, matured person who had gained more from the love and humanity of those people than they had from me.

Theologically Cable Street brought me face-to-face with the meaning of incarnation: incarnation not simply as a historic event, but as a continuing theological and pastoral principle. I discovered the truth, manifested in the history of Israel, that God is revealed and God's word is heard among the exiles, the dispossessed, the people on the margins of the world. I came to see how central is the incarnation, the Word made flesh, to all Christian pastoral ministry and spirituality. It is that truth that drives us to seek and to serve Christ in the poor, the ragged, the despised, and the broken. It is that truth which makes it impossible for Christians to opt for a spirituality that despises the flesh, fears human passion, sexuality, and warmth, and shuns the world of politics as squalid and contaminating.

It was the very ordinary life of this obscure London street that brought home to me the commonness of grace and the ordinariness of spirituality. I think I went there believing that I was bringing love, bringing intellect, bringing care, possibly bringing Christ, to the Cable Street community, a deprived community. I came to see that it was I who was deprived, that it was I who was in need of their love and care, that Christ was to be found there and did not need to be brought in from outside, and that until that fundamental truth of God's presence and activity in the midst of the oppressed and downtrodden is recognized, all pastoral ministry and all religious life will be unreal.

In the last ten years or so, the "preferential option for the poor" has become a central feature of much Christian thought and action. The American Roman Catholic Bishops' pastoral letter on the economy says that "the option for the poor is the social and ecclesiological counterpart of the emptying *(kenosis)* of Jesus in the incarnation."[10] Over this period, books have been written on such themes as "the power of the poor in history," "toward a church of the poor," "bias to the poor," and so on.[11] And this theology of the poor has coincided, in Britain, with a rediscovery of the extent and seriousness of real poverty in the midst of affluence.

Much of the rediscovery of the poor in the nineteenth century took place in the East End of London. The publication of a pamphlet entitled *The Bitter Cry of Outcast London* in 1883 led to a tremendous upsurge in pastoral work in the slum areas. However, much Christian concern about "the poor," then as now, has been very condescending and has been compassionate rather than just. It has failed to see the truth in R. H. Tawney's comment that what thoughtful rich people call the problem of poverty, thoughtful poor people call the problem of riches.[12] It has failed to see the struggle against poverty as part of a more fundamental struggle for a society based on equality.

We need to recognize two truths. First, poor people are our equals. They are not there as the objects of our care, not there in order to be "done good to" or "worked among." They are not some undifferentiated mass called "the poor" or "the underclass" about which we can hold learned international conferences, and with which we can establish an "I–it" relationship of condescending concern. Those who are not poor need to listen to and learn from the experience and struggles of poor people. Like Ezekiel among the exiles by the River Chebar, we need to sit where they sit, need to sit astonished and amazed. To be biased toward the poor involves a bias against inequality and the patronizing ethos that goes with it. Second, poor people are part of a socioeconomic context. To minister to them purely as individuals and to ignore the context in which their lives are lived is a serious lack of caring. It is a dangerous form of idealism that does not face the full reality of human life.

In Cable Street I was learning something of the meaning of a phrase that was to become very fashionable in the 1960s: the servant church. It was some years before I was to see that the servant church should not replace the prophetic church; the two must go together. The two New Testament passages that are often used in connection with the theme of the church as servant are Matthew 25, the parable of the sheep and goats, and John 13, the account of the feet washing.

Augustine said that Matthew 25 had impressed him more deeply than any other gospel passage, and it has become a key text in Latin America. It teaches us that Christ is recognized and served, or not recognized and neglected, in the sick, the naked, the hungry, and the prisoner. The symbol of the feet washing, which replaces the institution of the Eucharist in John's account, has been restored to its sacramental centrality on Maundy Thursday, though in some black Pentecostal churches it is an integral part of every Eucharist. It is a constant reminder that caring, Christological caring, is characterized by its ordinariness, by its humility, by its action rather than its words—feet washing is a silent ministry—and by its willingness to be contaminated by dirt and disease and blood.

What these passages are teaching us, and what I think I was learning in Cable Street, is that the true and living God is not encountered directly. Unlike the idols, God is not seen face-to-face, but God is known, recognized, loved, and served in lowly service of those who are made in God's image. To fail to serve the poor and lowly is to fail to recognize the face of Christ. Conversely a crucial test of our spirituality must be, How does it work out in practice? If we cannot love the sister or brother whom we have seen, how can we claim to love God whom we have not seen? The ability to see Christ, to see the image and likeness of God, in the faces of the most despised and neglected of humankind is a diagnostic test of true spirituality.

Christian spirituality is thoroughly materialistic, incarnational, earthy, and fleshly. The genuineness, the reality, of our spiritual claims has to be tested out amidst the dust and dirt of the back streets. Spirituality cannot exist in a vacuum, in some esoteric private realm. The compartmentalizing of "spirituality" and "spiritual direction" as disciplines in their own right, carefully separated from other compartments, has done considerable harm in the recent past. It is an urgent task to bring spirituality back to earth, back to the common life; only then can it be Christian.

When I look back at the Cable Street period, one of the key inspirational figures for me was Dorothy Day. Almost totally unknown in Britain, the *Catholic Worker* was banned from the Roman Catholic book shops because it was "communist" and from the anarchist book shop because it was Christian. The only source for it at the end of the 1950s was an Anglo-Catholic anarchist, Laurens Otter, who used to sell it at Speakers' Corner in Hyde Park every Sunday. Dorothy Day (about whom I shall have more to say later) was an old-fashioned Catholic radical who took seriously the obligation to perform the corporal works of mercy. But she saw that to practice mercy and compassion in a society that was merciless and cruel was a deeply subversive act. The Franciscan house in Cable Street was certainly inspired by the Catholic Worker houses of hospitality, which had become centers of care in the poorer areas of American cities, and in 1963 a new community, the Simon Community, emerged there, directly modeled on the Catholic Worker, to work alongside homeless and rootless people.

Dorothy Day—and Thomas Merton, whom I was beginning to read—brought home to me something that had been emphasized in an older phase of my own Anglican tradition: the close connection between the presence of Christ in the sacraments and his presence among the poor and lowly people of the world. Never was this truth so powerfully expressed in its relationship both to the Eucharist and to the feet washing than in the speech to the 1923 Anglo-Catholic Congress by Frank Weston, then Bishop of Zanzibar. Weston began by saying that the one great truth we need to learn is that

> Christ is found in and amid matter—spirit through matter—God in flesh, God in the sacrament. But I say to you, and I say it with all the earnestness I have, that if you are prepared to fight for the right of adoring Jesus in the Blessed Sacrament, that you have got to come out from before your tabernacles and walk, with Christ mystically present in you, out into the streets of this country and find the same Jesus in the people of your cities and villages. You cannot worship Jesus in the tabernacle if you do not pity Jesus in the slum. . . . And it is folly, it is madness, to suppose that you can worship Jesus in the sacrament and Jesus on the throne of glory when you are sweating him in the souls and bodies of his children. . . . Go out and look for Jesus in the ragged, in the naked, and in the oppressed and sweated, in those who have lost hope, in those who are struggling to make good. Look for Jesus. And when you see him, gird yourself with his towel, and try to wash his feet.[13]

The Sacraments and the Common Life: Hoxton

"Following of Jesus," says Gustavo Gutierrez, "is not along a private route, but is part of a collective enterprise."[14] Centuries earlier, John Wesley had made a similar point: "The Gospel of Christ knows of no religion but social religion, no holiness but social holiness."[15] This truth was becoming more and more important to me in these early years in East London. I was ordained as a deacon in May 1964 and went to the Church of the Most Holy Trinity, Hoxton, on the northern tip of the East End. Some years later I wrote a small book called *The Social God*, based on my experience in the area.[16] I took the title from two great Anglican pastors, Conrad Noel and Stanley Evans, who used this phrase often in their teaching and writing. They held that the whole gospel and the whole of Christian theology was social, rooted in the dogma of the Trinity, the expression of the social character of God. To speak of "the social implications of the gospel" or of "the social gospel" as if there were some other gospel would be confusing, for the entire Christian reality was social from beginning to end. It is this truth that lies at the heart of my experience of the Christian community in East London.

In the East End, neighborhoods, and their history and culture, are of crucial importance. Cable Street was perceived as a strange and alien zone by many in the mainly white neighborhoods. It was to one of these white working-class neighborhoods, Hoxton, that I moved in 1964. The three years I spent there as deacon and priest had a profound impact on my understanding of the corporate character of Christian discipleship and my understanding of the place of the Eucharist and of daily prayer in the life of the parish community. It also raised for me some disturbing questions about the nature of community itself, and about the danger of communities that become closed in on themselves.

Hoxton, part of the district called Shoreditch, is an old working-class neighborhood of London, an urban village. It was the setting for Oliver Twist, Marie Lloyd, and the Eagle from "Pop Goes the Weasel." The district had the lowest rate of population movement in Greater London; it was a tightly knit complex of families interrelated since the time of Dickens. In my time there it was almost entirely white. The district had known extreme poverty and deprivation, and some of that had survived into the 1960s. Crime rates were high, and the underworld of criminal syndicates was powerful. The pubs were the center of community life. Here was much of the traditional culture of East London—jellied eels and whelk stalls, pearly kings and queens, music halls, street markets in Club Row and Brick Lane. There was an abundance of street life still in the 1960s, but new influences were appearing—Mods and Rockers, the drug culture, the music of the Who and the Beatles—and the young people were moving away from the pubs to the discotheques and coffee bars.

The Church of the Most Holy Trinity stood at the center of the neighborhood. It was in the very strict sense a neighborhood church. Nobody worshiped there who could not walk to the church in ten minutes. The church, not surprisingly, reflected, and in some ways, reinforced, the positive and negative aspects of the local community: its amazing sense of mutual care and support, its networks of information and help, its sense of being an extended family, its tremendous sense of fun; but also its wariness of, and hostility to, strangers, its racism, and its inward-looking character.

The whole life of the parish centered upon the Parish Mass. Holy Trinity, and most of the adjoining parishes, had been built as part of the sacramental and liturgical revival associated with the "Romanizing" wing of the Oxford Movement of the nineteenth century. Here in the 1840s, 1850s, and 1860s, were built back-street baroque churches with massive altars and multitudes of lamps, lights, and statues for eucharistic worship. Historically the recovery of the centrality of the Eucharist in the Church of England coincided with the recovery of the parish unit; the Mass became the central act in these new churches of the poor. And all the pastoral and social outreach to the neighborhood was seen as flowing from, and back into, the sacramental action, for beneath the sacramental action was a sacramental view of reality: not only bread and wine but all material things, all created life, were vehicles of the divine.

I learned more than I can express both from the neighborhood life of Hoxton and from the eucharistic life of the parish there. While I was there, the Second Vatican Council was meeting. Liturgical changes were prefiguring and symbolizing fundamental theological and social changes whose full impact is only now being felt. As a young priest I felt that the new sacramental atmosphere was being created not only externally in the church but in me personally. I was being forged, often painfully and paradoxically, into a sacramental person, in Austin Farrer's phrase, a "walking sacrament."[17] The old language about carrying Christ mystically present within me, about the extension of the incarnation, was important and held deep meaning for me. I had come to see all Christian action as an extension of the incarnation and the

Eucharist. The situation in Hoxton in some respects was almost medieval: church and sacrament, pub and street market, an urban village. And yet there was something that worried me very deeply about it; it was the sense that what the church was doing was baptizing and ritually reenacting the old order, strengthening the sense of local community and solidarity, in a way that had potential for real danger. By the late 1960s the dangers became evident as Hoxton began to mobilize against the influx of black people from districts to the south and north. In 1965 one of our parliamentary candidates was Sir Oswald Mosley, whose British Union of Fascists had gained considerable support in the area in the 1930s. In 1967 the National Front, the first significant postwar fascist party, was formed, with one of its leading London strongholds in the streets around the church.

This sense of unease led me to focus on the sacraments, and particularly on the Eucharist, as embodying a fundamental question, Is the church the shrine of an old, stable order, or the sign of a new world, struggling toward transformation? Does the Eucharist sanctify the past or anticipate the future? Are there perhaps two different theologies, possibly even two different gods, one a static, cultic, settled god of the status quo—the pagan harvest festival kind of religion—one the liberating God of the Exodus who leads the community of disciples out of false securities into freedom? I had become interested in Stewart Headlam, that early precursor of liberation theology, who in the late nineteenth century saw the Eucharist as a feast of human liberation, the foretaste of a new age. Headlam's view of the Eucharist in relation to the life of the community horrified the more pietistic church people in East London in his day. For him and for me, the Eucharist and the church itself only made sense as pointers toward the Kingdom of God, the new age of God's justice. I came to see the church as a pilgrim community. Yet the Eucharist as celebrated in many churches, by its stress on correctness, order, restraint, and formality, seemed merely to recreate and sanctify the past, freezing it, protecting it against the changes and upheavals, not to point toward the new.

I began to see the real danger of a creation-centered, incarnational, sacramental religion that had no room for judgment, prophecy, redemption, or struggle. It was precisely such a religion that provided the spiritual soil for Mussolini, Franco, and Salazar, and for other oppressive regimes today. Sacramentalism is not enough. And yet the doctrine of the Body of Christ is a powerful weapon in the church's struggle against injustice. It is more than a vague sense of fellowship; it is the doctrine of a new creation, a new humanity in which there is neither Jew nor Greek, male nor female, bond nor free. In terms of modern racism, of the nation-state, of patriarchal and sexist society, this is highly explosive and seditious teaching. It was a truth that came home to me powerfully in the church, and in the streets, of Hoxton in the middle years of the 1960s, though I did not grasp many of its implications until years later. It has become more powerful as the years have progressed.

"A Long Road to Canaan":[18] Soho, Drugs, Homelessness, and Night Ministry

On 1 June 1967 the Beatles released their album *Sergeant Pepper*. In Britain that summer was the Summer of Love, a summer marked by massive consumption of LSD and the appearance of "flower children" as the San Francisco hippie culture spread to London. A little earlier a well-known London physician, Lady Isabella Frankau, had died, leaving behind her a large number of heroin addicts who had been thrown onto the street market. Lady Frankau was the best known of the "junkies' doctors," a small group of physicians who prescribed for, and tried to help, the growing number of heroin and cocaine addicts.[19] Since my time in Hoxton, pastoral care of drug users, particularly users of heroin, had taken up a good deal of my time, and it was during the summer of 1967 that I moved into the parish of Saint Anne, Soho, at that time the heart of the drug culture of London. As 1967 moved toward winter, the atmosphere became very dark and destructive as the needle culture spread to embrace young kids on the amphetamine fringe. By 1968 the earlier line between intravenous heroin and cocaine users, a small group concentrated around Piccadilly Circus, and a much larger community of oral amphetamine users all over Soho had broken down, and we were increasingly faced with drug users who would inject anything they could lay their hands on. Care of the street addict, from crisis ambulance work to long-term spiritual help, occupied much of our time in Soho.

This work, and the associated work with young homeless people, helped me to see the close and vital link between care of individuals and political struggle. Through work with the Soho Drugs Group, a loose network of local workers that I started in 1967, and with Centrepoint, our all-night center for young homeless people that began in December 1969, I saw that pastoral care of the individual in crisis could not be separated from the prophetic task of pointing to injustice within the central structures of the nation's life. It is not possible to minister to the alienated youth living on the streets without addressing oneself to the causes of that alienation. It is not possible to care for homeless people from other parts of Britain who arrive in central London without asking fundamental questions about the economy of Scotland and of the north of England, or about the lack of cheap rental housing, or about the appalling increase in the number of mentally ill patients discharged onto the streets (under the euphemism of "community care"). It is not possible to look at heroin and cocaine addiction without considering the wider context, not only deprivation and long-term hopelessness about the future, but also the heavy dependence of some Third World economies on opium and coca production. It is not possible to deal with problems raised by abuse of prescribed drugs without looking at the ethics of the pharmaceutical industry and at the whole question of our society's dependence on psychoactive chemicals to address personal needs. All care for individuals raises political and spiritual questions about the values of a society and the structures that embody them. Through close and deep involvement in specific issues at the local level—drug abuse, homelessness, prostitution, the problems of the young homosexual, and so on—many Christians have been led to the work of political analysis and theological reflection on the political realities.

Soho is a place of great exuberance, the center of London's night life, the heart of theaterland; full of clubs and restaurants, it is a place of great joy and amusement for many. But beneath the surface lies a sense of darkness, of desolation and despair. It was the symbolism of darkness that was to dominate the spiritual climate of my ministry in this district between 1967 and 1971. There was, first, the darkness of the night life itself. The night hours were of central importance in understanding Soho. People who were not around after 11:00 P.M.

could never understand the neighborhood and its significance among young people. There were a number of focal points for the night life: amusement arcades, coffee bars, street corners, all-night clubs. Much pastoral work was done during the night, using the clubs and bars as bases and contact points. Prayer at night became very important as we saw the need to surround the district with intercession and to try to articulate and express some of its need.

Then there was the darkness of anonymity. Many people came to Soho to be anonymous, to lose themselves, to disappear for a time. The district could absorb "difficult" people, and the bars in particular were filled with sad and lonely people in retreat from unhappy marriages and relationships and often on the verge of suicide. Many came to us at Saint Anne's because we did not know who they were and they did not know us. It was important not to intrude on this anonymity but to be available and to offer help, friendship, and support.

For others there was the darkness of despair. For many people, Soho was not the beginning of a journey to self-discovery so much as the end of the line. These people were known as "West End regulars." Many of them had moved from oral to intravenous drug use, usually of heroin, and their lives came more and more to revolve around the needle and the ritual of injection. The so-called British system of dealing with such hard-core addicts involved careful medical prescribing of heroin, trying to ensure that injection took place under clean conditions and at the same time providing the framework within which alternatives might be offered. It did not always work well in practice, but it was, and is, infinitely preferable to the criminalization of the addict, which leads to domination of the market by the criminal syndicates, with all the consequences that we see in the United States and that are now evident in Britain also. At Saint Anne's, we worked closely with physicians and with the staff of treatment centers, believing that "treatment" was most likely to be effective when addicts were seen as whole people and were accepted and helped within a community that transcended the boundaries of the disciplines involved and their restricted frameworks of understanding.

At the same time I was also encountering large numbers of people who were experiencing a real inner upheaval, a crisis of the spirit.

The physical darkness, the anonymity, and the proximity of despair made it possible for people to explore their own interior darkness in a way that perhaps they could not do in more comfortable, secure, and repressed surroundings. The exterior culture of darkness made it more possible to confront and explore the darkness within.

During these years my ministry began to undergo some powerful changes. Much of it was "despair work," entering into and sharing the darkness of others, not seeking to shatter that darkness with artificial light. There were many "fundamentalists" who attempted to do this in a way that was cruel and insulting to the depth of pain and the seriousness of the person's inner struggle. It was important for me, if I was to be a true pastor, to learn the place of silence and creative listening and to avoid the temptation to offer clichés and simplistic words. But this called for slowing down and for the cultivation of inner stillness, so I began to see the danger of frenzied activism, of overcrowding both my timetable and my mind, of overwork and its resultant tiredness. Many of us whose lives are taken up with social action of various kinds tend to overload ourselves, filling our weeks with too many projects and giving in to a kind of self-inflicted violence that kills inner wisdom. Yet it is wisdom and discernment, more than anything, that we desperately need in responding to crisis.

Confronted by so many people and such desperate needs, and increasingly conscious of my own impotence, the descent into hell, into the darknes of apparent abandonment, began to make sense. Only after that descent does resurrection come. Saint John of the Cross now spoke to me with great power. For the signs that one should leave meditation behind—the inability to meditate, the loss of any delight in prayer, and the sense of being bound—came home to me in an entirely new way in Soho. In that context there was often nothing one could do except wait in the dark. There was a certain powerlessness, a binding of the spirit, a sense of sharing in the darkness of passion and death. It was here that I discovered the place of contemplation in active ministry, the inwardness of priesthood, the need for spiritual direction. It was in the midst of one of the most active and demanding phases of my life and ministry that I came to see the necessity of contemplative prayer and inner reflection.

"Blood on the Streets": Fighting Racism and Fascism in Bethnal Green

The Romans tended to use the East End as a dwelling place for the dead rather than the living, and one of the earliest Roman cemeteries was at Lolesworth Field in Spitalfields. It was the breaking up of this field for brick making in 1576 that was the beginning of Brick Lane, a long and rambling thoroughfare, and of modern Bethnal Green.[20] However, while the Spitalfields district became heavily built up and later became a place of refuge for immigrants from far and near, Bethnal Green was a rustic hamlet until the eighteenth century and remained the most "English" part of London. In 1743, when a separate parish of Bethnal Green was created, the area consisted of 1,800 houses with 15,000 inhabitants. By 1847, the population had grown to 82,000, and by 1901 to 129,680. By the middle of the nineteenth century it was one of the most overcrowded districts in London.

An Act of Parliament of 1745 ruled that the building of a church dedicated to Saint Matthew should be completed. The Act began with these words: "Whereas the want of a place for public worship of Almighty God hath been a great cause of increase of dissoluteness of morals and a disregard for religion, too apparent in the younger and poorer sort . . ." The building of the church was seen as a means to moral improvement and social order. If "the younger and poorer sort" were in great need of a church, however, it does not appear that they regularly availed themselves of it, and institutional Christianity never really took root in Bethnal Green. Soon after the consecration, the vestry records show that "several hundred persons" began to gather in the adjoining field to enjoy dogfighting and bullock-hunting, and on one occasion, when a bullock was being chased through the churchyard, the terrified animal took refuge in the church followed by its raucous pursuers, much to the alarm of the small congregation! Between 1746 when the church was consecrated and the 1860s, most of the rectors did not live in the neighborhood, and it was only with the arrival of Septimus Hansard in 1862 that a truly neighborhood-based parish ministry was developed.

Shortly before Hansard's arrival, one of the curates gave the following evidence to a Select Committee of the House of Commons:

What is the general moral character of your population?

Very low indeed.

Could you mention any vice as more prevalent than any other?

I am afraid that fornication prevails to an enormous degree.

Does drunkenness prevail?

We have several gin palaces and a great deal of gin drinking.[21]

However, like Hoxton, Bethnal Green remained a very English district with a mainly local-born population. By 1901 many streets in the Spitalfields part of Brick Lane were 100 percent Jewish, inhabited by refugees from Eastern Europe. Bethnal Green remained very inhospitable, with a foreign-born population of 3.5 percent. The fearful reputation of Bethnal Green as a center of anti-Semitism dates from this period. In the 1930s Sir Oswald Mosley built on this history as he organized his fascist movement in Bethnal Green.

It was to the parish of Saint Matthew, Bethnal Green, that I moved as rector in 1974. As in Hoxton, there was still the sense of a village. Within a few minutes' walk of the church were twenty-six pubs, most of them small neighborhood centers. The regular congregation of the church was about the same size as the regular clientele of one of the pubs—about thirty or forty. There was, and is, a great devotion to and affection for the church and a sense that, in some way, it belongs to the community. The residents of the area were almost entirely working class, manual workers forming 63.7 percent of the population, and at that time almost all were white. There was a sense of separation from other parts of the East End, particularly from Whitechapel and Spitalfields, with their long history of immigration and of being multiracial communities.

Bethnal Green also had a long history of paternalism, not least the paternalism of the church. After the building of Saint Matthew's, there was virtually no more church building until the nineteenth century. But by then the industrial population had grown accustomed to life without churches. The church in East London was an afterthought of the industrial revolution. Bishop Blomfield, bishop of London in the mid-nineteenth century, had built ten churches in Bethnal Green in ten years, in the belief that the reason working-class people did not go to church was that there were not enough churches! But he soon acknowledged that his experiment had failed. Here too were the settlement houses such as Oxford House, Saint Hilda's, Saint Margaret's, and University House—all sponsored by universities or public schools. This colonizing movement had helped to sap the life and initiative from local people. By the time I came to Bethnal Green we were in a postcolonial phase in which outsiders—clergy, community workers, and others—needed to discover a humbler role, putting their insights, power, and resources at the service of local people.

I was conscious that as rector of this poor parish I was seen as an establishment figure and functionary, a symbol of power and privilege, a representative of the old order. I was not willing to accept this role, so I tried to work on principles of solidarity and cooperation. Several basic maxims were essential. Do as much as you can in groups. Find your allies. Forge alliances. Discover common ground. Create networks of support, thought, and action. Make connections between struggles. Theologically this meant that I was moving away from a deductive vanguardist theology to a more reflective approach. And here the liberation theologians were, and remain, a major influence. This was especially true in their understanding of *praxis*, in their sense of theology as the "second step," to be preceded by a commitment to justice, and in their insistence that theology starts where the pain is, among the most oppressed.

But all the inherited wealth, power, and ideology of the established church was against such an approach. Here, in a district where most people lived in flats or small houses, we were forced to live in an enormous rectory with a huge garden, impossible to maintain, yet a symbol of privilege and difference. If you were willing to play the role of the nineteenth-century "church condescending," no doubt such a mansion could be used. But for anyone who believed in equality and solidarity, it was intolerable. The whole structure of the place was a fundamental obstacle to pastoral work.

It was easier to develop work from the church building. One obvious way of displaying the fact that the church belonged to the people was to leave it open all the time. Few other churches in the area were open, and there were obvious dangers of vandalism and so on.

But we felt that a locked church was a contradiction in terms, and it was important to make it clear not only that the church was a place for prayer, silence, and peace, but also that it was a place that belonged to the community and was a center of friendship and acceptance.

A few minutes to the south of us was the largest Bangladeshi community outside Bangladesh. In 1978 the Bangladeshi community numbered around 15,000; by 1984 it had grown to 20,000. Most of the Bangladeshis were, and are, employed in clothing or in the restaurant business. Though many have done well, they are "considerably the most disadvantaged" of all the minority groups.[22] Today the Brick Lane district is the heart of the community and is secure from racial attacks. But in 1974 this was not so. The phenomenon of "Paki-bashing" seems to have begun in Bethnal Green in 1969, and the following year Derek Cox, a well-known local youth worker, reported, "The current racial problem in Spitalfields, and possibly the worst, is the growth of resentment against the Pakistani community. . . . There is considerable "Paki-baiting" and "rolling" (robbery with violence) by some of the local young people. The situation is becoming both violent and unhealthy, and is evident in the schools as well as the streets."[23] The violence increased after 1976, and during 1978 there was a series of murders, of which that of Altab Ali on 4 May was the most memorable. It was Ali's death that sparked off a whole series of protests and demonstrations against racism and led eventually to the mobilization of the community against attacks. Every year the murder is commemorated, and the scene of the murder is now named Altab Ali Park.

The escalation of violence was linked with the rise of the National Front and other racist and fascist groups. Much of my work in Bethnal Green was concerned with combating the rise of racist organizations. It was essential that the evils of racism and fascism, and their material embodiment in the National Front and similar groups, should be named, identified, and resisted. But the problem went deeper than this, and there was the more difficult task of undermining the roots of racism within the community. Why were racist explanations for their troubles plausible? How could the frustration and paralysis that had created an ideal climate for grass roots fascism be undermined and changed into hopeful struggle? How could we create an atmosphere that was more open to the development of a multiracial community?

The rise of the National Front and its satellites was in large part a response to the corruption and complacency of the Labour Party. This party had been in power for so long that it had lost its way, lost its vision, and become a reactionary and regressive force. Many people had given up all hope that real change could come through the established political channels. Also, within the area was a large number of disenchanted and restless youth, many of them the rejects of all the systems—church, probation service, youth clubs, welfare state. To them the National Front offered meaning and purpose: it helped to mobilize them into a movement. It was in fact among the rootless youth that the fascists made their most significant progress. For many of these young people, vandalism had become the last available form of social action. The coming of the National Front at one level represented the escalation of vandalism into a political movement.[24]

Since the late 1970s racial attacks have not subsided, but the geographical pattern has changed. Brick Lane, because the Bangladeshis have organized, has become more a community, a safe and secure place to be, and not an area to which organized racist groups can safely go. The violence has moved into the side streets, into mainly white housing estates, and into distant neighborhoods where Bengalis and other Asian people are thin on the ground.

In combating the growth of racism in Bethnal Green I was aware both of the Christian roots of my resistance and of the need to join hands with all people of goodwill who were committed to this struggle. I came to see the importance of not "going it alone," and of the need for solidarity; for the avoidance of zealotry and the need for humanity, tenderness, warmth, and loving friends; the need to listen to and learn from the community; the need for an open approach, to see and learn new perspectives on old issues; and the need to see God at work in strange places, including in the midst of conflict and upheaval.

Theology and the Back Streets: Some Inspirational Figures from the Past

Today my work base is at Saint Botolph's Crypt in Aldgate, at the point where the City of London ends and the East End begins. I am employed here on the staff of this inner city parish as a theologian. The

Crypt has for thirty years been the main center for homeless people in the area. My task, in communion with my comrades and coworkers, is to try to make creative and redemptive sense of the turmoil and upheaval that characterizes this part of London and to try to discern the will of God and the working out of God's activity.

In this attempt to work out a theology in the midst of social struggle, I have found many people, living and dead, of literally crucial importance to me. I choose here eight, all of them dead, whose work, writings, and influence, and, in two cases, personal friendship, have helped to give shape and direction, vision and inspiration, to my work. I believe that such reliance on and communion with other people is a necessary part of what it means to be one of the "communion of saints," and indeed of what it means to be human at all.

"All Shall Be Well": The Hopeful Mysticism of Julian of Norwich

In a highly activistic, work-dominated culture such as ours, in which people are defined by what they do rather than who they are, the very existence of solitaries and hermits presents a fundamental test of our belief in the life of prayer. Judged by the managerial professional model, that is, in terms of function and efficiency, the solitary is absurd. Julian of Norwich was a solitary in the fourteenth century. It is clear that her life of solitude was not a selfish, egocentric withdrawal, a flight of the alone to the alone, but a life of love, warmth, and care toward her "even Christians," a life of solidarity with Christ's passion that overflowed in compassion for humanity, a life nourished by a profound optimism about humanity and the world. Like Saint Anthony, the first hermit, Julian would have insisted that her life and her death was with her neighbor, and that only those committed to the common life could risk the commitment to life in solitude. No one who is enclosed within the false self, the self-absorbed self, can be a true solitary. The Christian solitary lives and has meaning only within the context of Christian solidarity, within the living organism of the Body of Christ. Julian the solitary mystic is part of this common life.

Both Julian and her context speak to me in my London context of the late twentieth century. For the fourteenth century in England, like our own time, was a period of great social upheaval and intense interior striving, an age of militancy and mysticism, of upheaval in soil and soul. Externally it was a time of distress among agricultural laborers, of exploitation of the rural peasants and the urban poor, of sickness, disease, and social violence. It was the age of the Black Death and the Peasants' Revolt. Among the peasants and others who rose up in 1381, there was a thirst for social justice and for equality, a desire to see the end of serfdom and bondage. Though many commentators blamed the rising on those heretics and "outside agitators" who were loosely lumped together as "Lollards"—a term used in a similar way to the current use of the terms *Marxists* and *anarchists* (as used, for example, by Margaret Thatcher in relation to the poll tax revolts of 1990)—historians such as Rodney Hilton suggest that the social radicalism of the period drew its impetus more from the orthodox Christian tradition and from patristic writers like Saint Basil, Saint Ambrose, and Saint John Chrysostom, whose works had been rediscovered with enthusiasm.[25]

With the revival of interest in the English mystics at the end of the 1960s, Julian has attracted much attention. Since Thomas Merton described her as one of the greatest English theologians, there has been increasing attention also to the theological direction in which Julian can guide us. Some have looked to her as a prophetic figure, "the dawn star of the truly Catholic reformation which is only now emerging over the whole world."[26] Her cell at Norwich has become a place of pilgrimage for people from all over the world, not all of them Christians, in search of mysticism and a contemplative approach that is rooted in simplicity, optimism, and earthiness. Simplicity, optimism, earthiness: these are positive, creative, and abiding contributions that Julian can make to our theological understanding and to our discipleship, and they have been a continual source of strength in my ministry. They are brought together in her powerful and unifying symbol of the "small thing the size of a hazelnut." I believe that the popularity of Julian and of what we might term her "hazelnut theology" is soundly based. She is a wise guide for those who seek a spirituality grounded in the common life.

The simplicity of Julian is central to her life and theology. To a large extent the attraction of Julian is linked to the need for a corrective to centuries of cerebral, head-dominated religion. Historically

Julian came at the end of a period in which a major cleavage between heart and head had damaged Western religion. A wedge had been driven between theology (in the head) and mysticism (in the heart). Julian is a mystical theologian, however. In her understanding of God, she returns to the older tradition of seeing God as the Ground of all reality and as intimate and knowable. God, she claims, is courteous and homely. Her dominant theme is the closeness of God. God is closer to us than we are to ourselves. "It is very greatly pleasing to him that a simple soul should come naked, openly and familiarly." Linked with this is the sense of the ordinariness of prayer and contemplation. Prayer is natural. It is sin that is unnatural. The way of prayer involves us in a return to simplicity, a return to the reality of what we in essence are.

This sense of contemplative prayer as ordinary and available to all is one of the most important insights of our era. It was of crucial significance to me in Soho. Julian saw it clearly, but the centuries have obscured it and "ladder" notions of the spiritual life gained ground. During the 1960s Archbishop Michael Ramsey emphasized that "the contemplation of God with the ground of the soul, is, as those old writers insisted, accessible to any man, woman or child who is ready to try to be obedient and to want God very much."[27] Julian is important for teaching that prayer is natural: it is what we are made for, and it is open to everyone.

A second feature of Julian that has been important to me is her optimism. Julian is optimistic, hopeful, and joyful. "Nowhere in all Christian literature are the dimensions of her optimism excelled."[28] She stands as an abiding corrective to that cosmic theological pessimism that is often associated with a high doctrine of the Fall combined with a low view of human potential and of the power of grace. This combination, which we saw in Niebuhr and many of his followers, has done great damage to Christian discipleship, eroding hope and vision, reinforcing gloom and acquiescence in evil. There are still Christians who talk and write as if the Fall and original sin were the only Christian doctrine. But Christians do not believe in the Fall in the same way as we believe in God, in the Cross, or in the power of the Holy Spirit. Christians accept the Fall but believe in the power of grace to transform and transcend it. Against the tradition of pessimism,

Julian asserts that sin is unnatural. It is "in opposition to our fair nature." Indeed "it belongs to our nature to hate sin." She goes further, insisting that "in every soul that shall be saved, there is a godly will that never consented to sin, nor ever shall."[29]

This approach to sin is at the heart of Julian's optimism. She held that we are more truly theomorphic, God-shaped, than fallen, that we are more truly in heaven than on earth. So her theology is marked by confidence and joy. In contemplating the victory of the Cross she "laughed greatly." The Christian response to the Passion of Christ, she claims, is one of cheerfulness, and she speaks of the "joy and bliss of the Passion." Though she does not deny the reality and power of sin, she asserts that all shall be well, and this is repeated with emphasis.

> I may make all things well, and I can make all things well, and
> I shall make all things well, and I will make all things well,
> and you will see yourself that every kind of thing shall be
> well.[30]

This theological optimism is in sharp contrast to what Huizinga calls the "somber melancholy" and immense sadness that marked the waning of the Middle Ages, a pessimism brought on by war, sickness, plague, and economic depression.[31] Julian offers a necessary corrective to the pessimism of her age, and to that of ours. Her theology is rooted in a belief in the image of God in humanity. She teaches that the image of God in us, that central point that does not consent to sin, is of far greater theological significance than the Fall. Sin is, in the strict sense, accidental; it is not part of what makes a human being. This is not shallow, superficial, naive optimism, but optimism it certainly is. The confidence of Julian's "All shall be well . . ." comes as a result of that encounter with the Passion which is so central to the book. It is a confidence that is rooted in the experience of transfiguration through suffering. Julian's cheerfulness and laughter is not superficial heartiness: it is passionate because it is Passion-based.

And there is an earthiness about this spirituality that has spoken to me in my ministry in London. Julian stresses the solidarity of all people in God. In the sight of God, all people constitute one humanity.

Very deliberately—and in line with the Eastern Christian tradition—
she insists that "our nature is joined to God in its creation."[32] And
this solidarity includes both the physical and nonphysical aspects of
our nature, our substance, and our sensuality. The whole of us, all of
our nature, is in God. Wherever I am, in Cable Street, Hoxton, Soho,
Bethnal Green, or Aldgate, or anywhere in the world, I am in God,
the Ground in which I stand.

Knowing by Unknowing: The Dark Night of Saint John of the Cross

Saint John of the Cross (1543–1591), the Spanish mystic, has been a
major influence on my life and understanding. On the surface this may
seem very odd. What can a Carmelite friar living four hundred years
ago have to contribute to life and work in the inner city at the end of
the twentieth century? At a superficial level there would seem to be no
connection.

Saint John of the Cross was a poet, and his writings include both
poems and more systematic texts on the inner life as a journey toward, and within, the reality of God. His best-known works are *The
Ascent of Mount Carmel* (of which *The Dark Night of the Soul* is a section)
and *The Living Flame of Love*. The phrase "the dark night of the soul"
is the sum total of most people's knowledge of John's work, and the
phrase is usually misunderstood. It is often believed to be a pathological condition of the religious life, an illness, a kind of spiritual depression. But to see it this way is to misunderstand John of the Cross
very seriously, for, in writing about the dark night, he is writing of the
very nature of faith itself.

It was in Soho that the writings of John of the Cross began to make
sense to me and to express much of what I was feeling and seeing.
Here I was encountering people who were entering a kind of darkness in which they seemed to be lost, but through which in fact they
would find themselves, a darkness that was a way of progress. People
who had found no nourishment in conventional religion were encountering, sometimes with the aid of drugs, levels of reality of which they
had been unaware. They were coming into contact with experiences
that traditionally had been seen as "mystical."

Here too I was finding that my own life was undergoing a shift from the pseudo-certainties of youth to a more obscure and interior way, a way of faith that was at home with darkness, uncertainty, and humility in the face of mystery. And this is essentially what John of the Cross is writing about. His concern is with the transition from intellectual understanding (or failure to understand), to a deeper and more obscure level of knowing that, following early Eastern theologians, he calls "unknowing" *(agnosia)*. He claims that in order to make progress in knowing and loving God, and in attaining full humanity, we need to come to the end of our conventional "certainties" and move beyond it to a new level of knowing. This new level is the way of faith, a way of knowledge through darkness. The purpose of the Christian life, and the aim of spiritual direction, is to help people enter the dark night of faith. Yet much conventional religion simply helps people to find a refuge from this darkness. It offers protection rather than encounter. Thus the mystical teaching of John of the Cross undermines, and challenges, forms of conventional religion that rely for their success on false certainties and rigid forms.

The way of faith, John insists, is necessarily obscure. We drive by night, only seeing a little of the way ahead. We make progress precisely by not understanding, by darkness. In Soho I was coming to see how important this truth is in pastoral work and in political struggle. We need to act on the basis of faith, on an insight that is nourished by darkness, a conviction that has its roots in silence, a vision that is not clear but is firmly based in that mysterious reality which is the darkness of God. If social and political action is not to decay into fanaticism, it needs those deep roots.

For John of the Cross, the dark night is not a negative and destructive experience: it is the experience of fire and light, of the living flame of the love of God, as experienced by finite beings. Faith blinds and dazzles the intellect; the sheer intensity of faith overwhelms it. And the darkness grows always deeper. For the dark night is not a phase, it is a symbol by which John speaks of the whole of reality. All our life and all our activity takes place in the context of this darkness.

The night comes upon us. We are never prepared for it, for the essence of the night is the sense of being out of control, of being bound and controlled by the mysterious working of the Spirit of God. Only later do we identify what has been going on and are able to express it. I believe that the effectiveness of our work for justice in the world is directly related to our encounter with this central core of darkness. For truthful and just action can grow only out of deep roots in truth and justice.

As I read the words of this Spanish mystic, so distant from my present life and experience, I am led into the darkness of which he speaks. I am helped to understand something of the mystery of God and of the way of faith and through this to help others who are beginning, or continuing, their own spiritual journey. For Christians who are seeking to enter into their own inner darkness and to work for justice in the light of faith, Saint John of the Cross remains a wise and perceptive guide.

Dancing to the Jubilee: The Liberating Theology of Stewart Headlam

Stewart Headlam (1847–1924), the rebellious nineteenth-century curate of Bethnal Green, was dismissed from every job he ever held in the Church of England, and eventually had his license removed by the bishop of London. Undoubtedly he was "the most bohemian priest in the Church of England,"[33] probably the most controversial clergyman of the Victorian age, and, as Edward Norman has claimed, "the first really serious socialist, in the modern sense, in the church."[34]

Headlam was in many respects a wild and reckless figure, committed to dance, drink, doubt, and revolution. He delighted in shocking respectable church people, calling the Church Catechism an egalitarian manifesto, offering the Athanasian Creed, that early defense of Trinitarian and Christological orthodoxy, as a basis for socialism, and regarding the Sunday Eucharist as "the weekly meeting of a society of rebels against a Mammon worshiping world order."[35] On the occasion of the Jubilee of Queen Victoria in 1886 he announced that "the Queen's Jubilee is good, but the people's Jubilee is better" and went on to point out that the original Jubilee, revealed by God to the liberator Moses, was a program of liberty and of land nationalization.[36] Headlam wanted nationalization of everything, including the pubs,[37] though he meant more by nationalization than state control, and his socialism was of a strongly libertarian character. He preferred the word *communist,* though there was no sign of Marxist influence. Those who assisted at Holy Communion, he claimed, are bound to be holy communists.[38] As a passionate disciple of the economist Henry George, he campaigned for the single land tax.

Yet it would be a serious mistake to dismiss Headlam as a utopian eccentric. His gospel and his political practice were rooted in theology. All his writing consisted of articles and small books, and he never wrote any substantial theological work. Yet his writing contains the seeds of much later theological reflection, and he anticipated a good deal of the liberation theology of the twentieth century. He rejected the false spirituality of those who saw redemption in purely "spiritual" terms. Jesus Christ, he held, was a "social and political emancipator . . . the preacher of a revolution."[39] He had a strong sense of the social consequences of the incarnation, the taking of the whole of humanity into God, and of the sacramental nature of the creation. "The Incarnation and the Real Presence of Jesus Christ sanctifies all human things, not excluding human passion, mirth and beauty."[40] He saw the church as "a great cooperative organized institution for human welfare and human righteousness."[41] In all his thinking, Headlam proclaimed a theology of unified grace, and in this he anticipated the Second Vatican Council. In his view of creation as a sacrament, and of the church as a body that was concerned with the transformation of the world, he helped to lay the foundations for the theology of the future.

Headlam has been a major inspiration to my spirituality and pastoral practice ever since I wrote a short piece about him at the end of the 1960s.[42] Later I was privileged to be rector of Saint Matthew's Church, Bethnal Green, from which he had been dismissed, and where his formal ecclesiastical career ended, and we celebrated the centenary of the founding of the Guild of Saint Matthew in 1977. But Headlam's importance for me lies not only in his commitment to the people of East London, but in his whole theological perspective, and in the unity he forged among theology, worship, politics, and fun. He was fiercely opposed to the churchiness that had already afflicted the Anglo-Catholic movement, and he saw the real danger of "an exotic hothouse of piety." He feared the growth of churches in which concern with the minutiae of liturgy replaced serious social concern. "I dread," he wrote, "the turning away of people's attention from the real disorders, the social and industrial disorders, to mere irregularities of worship."[43]

For Headlam, the Christian community had to be involved in far more than the practice of religion. Its aim was nothing less than salvation and peace, *shalom*, and this involved health, education, politics, beauty, and pleasure, all vital elements in that striving for fullness of life that was central to the gospel. Hence Headlam's passion for the ballet and the music hall was not a fringe interest but was at the heart of his theological enterprise. It was his lecture "Theaters and Music Halls," given in October 1877, that led to his removal from office by the bishop of London. Two years later he founded the Church and Stage Guild, the first organization for pastoral work within the theatrical world. When challenged by the bishop to defend his support of the ballet, he presented a summary of the teaching of the Athanasian Creed and concluded, "These are the theological facts on which I base my vindication of the stage."[44] Headlam's theology and life was all of a piece, and there was no trace of dualism. "It is because we are communicants," he wrote, "that we go to the theater, because we are priests that we believe in progress."[45]

Headlam was a person of deep compassion and sensitivity for the oppressed and persecuted, and he was not afraid to espouse unpopular causes. It would be an exaggeration to call him an early gay rights campaigner, but he stood bail for Oscar Wilde in 1895, and the fact that his wife was a lesbian may have made him more understanding of homosexuality than was common among clergy of the period.[46] He was one of the few clergy to stand by the Irish nationalist Charles Parnell after his affair with Kitty O'Shea. He was antimonarchist and opposed to the establishment of the Church of England. He supported indiscriminate baptism and attacked the "rigorists" as sectarian and elitist. In contrast to those who stressed reserve in communicating religious knowledge and taught laypeople to be passively obedient to the clerical caste, Headlam held that the task of the clergy was "to stir up a divine discontent."[47] Instead of passive obedience, he urged doubt and questioning: "Question everything; take nothing for granted; prove, sift, test every opinion, however reasonable, however cherished."[48]

Headlam and his disciples in the Guild of Saint Matthew, itself a model for future support networks, looked toward the Kingdom of God as "a righteous communistic society"[49] and saw the church as the herald and forerunner of that Kingdom. The church existed, therefore, "not for its own sake but for the sake of the whole human family."[50] It was this concern for humanity and for human fulfillment, human dignity, and human progress that made Headlam's thought "a seed plot of ideas the power of which is not yet exhausted."[51]

Sentinel on the World's Frontier: The Contemplative Spirituality of Thomas Merton

"The men of the twenty-fifth and fiftieth centuries," wrote one commentator, "when they read the spiritual literature of the twentieth century, will judge the age by Merton."[52] In spite of all the exaggerated claims and the growth of a cult around his memory, there is no doubt that Thomas Merton (1915–1968) was one of the most significant figures in the history of modern Christianity. A prolific author, Merton was, for most of his life, an enclosed Trappist monk. He once wrote of his vocation:

> Night is our diocese and silence is our ministry.
> Poverty our charity, and helplessness our tongue-tied sermon.
> Beyond the scope of sight and sound we dwell upon the air,
> Seeking the world's gain in an unthinkable experience.
> We are exiles at the far end of solitude, living as listeners,
> With hearts attending to the skies we cannot understand,
> Waiting upon the first far drums of Christ the Conqueror,
> Planted like sentinels on the world's frontier.[53]

Two images dominate this poem: watching and listening. They are the key elements in contemplative prayer: vision and attention, the ministry of eyes and ears. There is another image: that of helplessness, marginality, and bafflement. Together they represent the life of Thomas Merton and, in a most powerful way, the situation of Christians in the present age, the situation that he embodied and symbolized.

Merton's life was a struggle with illusion, a struggle for humanity. In all his writing he laid great emphasis on the importance of "accepting ourselves as we are in our confusion, infidelity, disruption, ferment and even desperation."[54] He had seen many examples of people who were never themselves and who wore out their minds and bodies in trying to have other people's experiences.[55] Merton was concerned with the attainment of solitude, of interior harmony and peace. His writings were taken up with such themes as the desert, conflict, and contemplation in the midst of action. In his view, contemplation was not a way of escape, an avoidance of action; it was an advance into the reality of solitude and the desert, into the confrontation with poverty and the void. Only through this process could any wholeness be achieved.

I discovered Merton in the midst of a very active ministry in Soho. He was a wise guide to me in a number of ways. He saw the danger of "do-gooders" who rushed into the work of helping others but did not deepen their own self-understanding and integrity. They could only communicate to others the contagion of their own obsessions, delusions, and prejudices.[56] Merton was a prophetic sign and warning to me as I slogged away at the problems of Soho, but he was also an illuminating symbol, a light for my path, for he spoke to me of the work of the solitary explorer, the monk who searched the existential depths of faith. The monk in Merton's vision was a marginal, restless person. The monk withdrew from "the world" in order to "deepen fundamental human experience."[57] The monk confronted humanity at the point of darkness and despair. I came to see that what Merton said about the monk was actually true of all Christians in the modern world. "The monk is essentially someone who takes up a critical attitude toward the contemporary world and its structures" (p. 329). But Merton went further than this: he held that the marginal position of the monk brought him into a solidarity with other marginal people and groups.

What drew me to Merton most of all was his sense of the holiness of the common, the immense dignity and value of ordinary life. For here was a mystic of the streets, one who saw glory in the midst of the common life. In a well-known account of one incident in his life, Merton wrote,

> In Louisville, at the corner of Fourth and Walnut, in the center of the shopping district, I was suddenly overwhelmed with the realization that I loved all these people, that they were

mine and I theirs. That we could not be alien to one another, even though we were total strangers. It was like waking from a dream of separateness, of furious self-isolation in a special world, the world of renunciation and supposed holiness.[58]

The sense of the holiness of the world, and of the dignity and God-shaped character of human beings, that comes through so strongly in these words was central to Merton's mysticism. It was through the common that one encountered the holy, through human beings in their ordinariness and common life that one encountered the divine. Merton's spirituality was utterly incarnational and worldly. For it was into this world that Christ had come, and it was here, and only here, that he could be discovered, known, served, and loved.

Into this world, this demented inn, in which there is absolutely no room for him at all, Christ has come uninvited. But because he cannot be at home in it, because he is out of place in it, and yet he must be in it, his place is with those others for whom there is no room. His place is with those who do not belong, who are rejected by power because they are regarded as weak, those who are discredited, who are denied the status of persons, tortured, excommunicated. With those for whom there is no room, Christ is present in this world.[59]

Merton helped me to see that all of what is called "social ministry" is in fact a discovery of Christ, a revelation and epiphany of God's presence, a working out of the truth of the incarnation in terms of human relationships.

But Merton was a social critic as well as a servant. Or rather he was servant not to the false values of the world but to the prophetic Christ, the challenger and disturber of human illusion. He spoke words of truth to a world that existed in "the womb of collective illusion."[60] Much of Merton's later writing was of a prophetic kind, an expression of his disturbing ministry of interrogation directed toward conventional notions of reality and sanity. Merton saw real dangers in sanity, dangers that are brought out most clearly in his "Devout Meditation on the Death of Adolf Eichmann." Eichmann had been pronounced perfectly sane by a psychiatrist at his trial. How much easier it would have been for us all had he, and other key figures within the Nazi terror, been treated as psychotic, deeply deranged, mad. Yet he was quite sane, without doubt or inner turmoil. Merton sees his sanity as the central problem because, though we equate sanity with justice, humanity, prudence, and the capacity to love and we rely on the sane people to preserve the world from barbarism, in fact it is the sane people who are the most dangerous. In a world where spiritual values have no meaning, the whole concept of sanity has become meaningless.[61] Merton believed that the 1960s in the United States were comparable to the 1930s in Nazi Germany,[62] and it was symbolic that he died on the same day as Karl Barth. Both of them had been theologians of resistance, spiritual figures of great power in confrontation with evil.

Because of his knowledge of the Christian resistance to Nazism, and because of his deep perception into the contemporary religious climate in North America, Merton saw the danger of false spirituality, specifically of that turning in on the self that led to narcissism and self-absorption.[63] There could be no abiding support for the life of prayer in a false supernaturalism that was not rooted in real life. So a major part of Merton's writing was devoted to the attack on unreality in religious life. In Henri Nouwen's words, "Merton understood that the unmasking of illusion belonged to the essence of the contemplative life."[64] Yet Merton remained hopeful about human potential and about the power of grace. Like Julian of Norwich, he believed in the reality of the image of God in humankind. That image was indestructible. It had been disfigured, but it could never be destroyed. Like Julian, Merton believed that there was a point within every person that was untouched by sin.[65]

Merton embodied in himself the trends, crises, spiritual currents, and polarizations of his age in a unique way. Though his early writing was addressed to the world of pre–Vatican II Roman Catholicism, his later work reflected, and helped to develop, a new age: the age of the counterculture, of Vatican II, of the East-West dialogue, of the struggle for racial justice, of the recovery of the contemplative spirit, of resistance to nuclear weapons, of post-Constantinian Christianity. His book *The Sign of Jonas* (1952) was a significant turning point in his work, and by 1958 we were seeing "a vastly expanded social consciousness."[66] His writings from 1963 until his death in 1968 were the most important and most influential of his life. In these writings there was the concern to unite contemplation and action, the mystical and the prophetic, the revolution of the spirit and political revolution. These are among the key issues that will determine the shape of the Christianity of the future. They were the key issues of Merton's spiritual quest.

More than any other single individual, it was Merton who shaped my understanding of priesthood. I recall very vividly, at the height of struggles about drug policy in London in 1968, arriving back at Saint Anne's Chapel in the early hours and reading with renewed meaning, some words from *The Sign of Jonas*:

> You just lie there, inert, helpless, alone, in the dark, and let yourself be crushed by the inscrutable tyranny of time. The plank bed becomes an altar and you lie there without trying to understand any longer in what sense you can be called a sacrifice. Outside in the world, where it is night, perhaps there is someone who suddenly sees that something he has done is terrible. He is most unexpectedly sorry and finds himself able to pray.[67]

More than any other words at that time, they helped me to see what I was up to.

Storefront Catholicism: The Subversive Ministry of Dorothy Day

Dorothy Day (1897–1981) is best known as the founder of the *Catholic Worker*, both a newspaper and a movement. Since her death, campaigns for her canonization have been supported by both radical and conservative sections of the Catholic community, though it is interesting that much "mainstream" church literature about her has ignored, or played down, the anarchism that was so central to her life and work. Dorothy Day was both a traditional Catholic and a revolutionary anarchist. She took the papal encyclicals with great seriousness and continually embarrassed the American hierarchy with her nonviolent civil disobedience campaigns, always supported by quotations from sources of impeccable orthodoxy. Her style, it has been said, was mystical, liturgical, sacramental, and orthodox.

The *Catholic Worker* newspaper began on 1 May 1933. Its original audience was the people of the streets of New York. For many years it was impossible to obtain it in "respectable" Catholic circles. In London at the end of the 1950s, when the Catholic book shops refused to stock it on the grounds that it was "communist," and the anarchist book shops because it was Christian, the only source was the Anglo-Catholic anarchist Laurens Otter, who used to sell it at Speakers' Corner in Hyde Park every Sunday. Today, still selling at one cent, the paper is read all over the Christian world and is a source of strength and inspiration to thousands of people.

At one level the paper and the movement is deeply conservative, steeped in the papal encyclicals, the liturgy, the lives and sayings of the saints, and the words of Jesus. It has been a radical grass roots prophetic witness within Catholic orthodoxy, seeking to recall the church to its true vocation and to the roots of its commitment, and it has been interesting—and in some respects disturbing—to note that since Dorothy Day's death the importance of her witness has been recognized by many members of the hierarchy. Not that she was totally without recognition during her life: on her eightieth birthday she was greeted by Pope Paul VI. But since her death a devotional cult has grown up, many of the devotees being people who would have opposed—and, if they understood it, would still oppose—all that the Catholic Worker movement stands for. On the other hand, many individuals, including many non-Christians, owe their social awareness on the issues of poverty and urban deprivation to their experience with the Catholic Worker. One prominent figure who began his study of urban poverty through working as a volunteer in the Worker houses was Michael Harrington, whose book *The Other America* (1962) was the most important single influence on the "war on poverty" of the mid-1960s.

The Catholic Worker remains a countercultural phenomenon within American religion. From its origins, many years before the appearance of "postmodernism" and the critique of modernity, it has represented a fundamental rejection of the foundations of the modern world—government, bureaucracy, and industry. In terms of the history of Christian social movements, it combines the traditions of ethical separatism and of prophetic transformation, with its constant insistence on the need for change from below. As one statement put it, the Catholic Worker witnesses to

> a complete rejection of the present social order and a nonviolent revolution to establish an order more in accord with Christian values. This can only be done by direct action, since political means have failed as a method for bringing about this society. Therefore we advocate a personalism which takes on ourselves responsibility for changing conditions to the extent we are able to do so.[68]

One central feature of the Catholic Worker has been the fact that its social witness arises out of its solidarity with the very poor and its identity as a "community of need," a community of wounded people. The philosophy of the movement arises from the life of its houses, located in the heart of the disintegration of inner urban decay. They contain and manifest structural sin.

> That ingrained structural sin is most visible in the dirt and disorder of the houses and the brokenness of all who live there. The closer we get to a Worker community, the more glaring that sin becomes. We celebrate the values of community in contrast to the egoism of bourgeois society. Can we ignore the daily evidence that broken people living together are as likely to deepen wounds as to heal them? . . . It seems that it is in the moments of our failure that God finds room to touch us . . . but while we are confident that the Catholic Worker movement looks toward the reign of God, we cannot postulate a relation of cause and effect, but only one of cross and resurrection.[69]

There is nothing romantic or idealized about the Worker houses: only desperate and painful, yet caring, reality.

And here the nonviolence of the movement emerges clearly as a nonviolence that is constantly tested and purified in daily struggle. It is nonviolence rooted in the life of the streets. Dorothy Day challenged her critics to come and share that life.

> Let those who talk of softness, of sentimentality, come to live with us in cold unheated houses in the slums. Let them come

to live with the criminal, the unbalanced, the drunken, the degraded, the perverted. . . . Let their flesh be mortified by cold, by dirt, by vermin. . . . Let their noses be mortified by the smells of sewage, decay and rotten flesh. Yes, and by the smell of blood, sweat and tears spoken of by Mr. Churchill, and so widely and bravely quoted by comfortable people.[70]

For Dorothy Day, this sharing of life was at the very heart of Christian living, because it was in sharing the life of poor and lowly people that Christ was known and loved.

> We felt a respect for the poor and destitute, as those nearest to God, as those chosen by God for his compassion. Christ lived among men, the great mystery of the Incarnation, which meant that God became man so that men might become God, was a joy that made us want to kiss the earth in worship because his feet once trod that same earth.[71]

There was nothing of the "trendy" elitist radical about Dorothy Day: unlike some Catholic radicals, she always attended the humble and very conventional working-class churches of the Lower East Side.[72]

The spirituality of the Catholic Worker is rooted in the daily experience of the incarnation and passion of Christ in the lives of men and women. In a letter of 1972 that speaks of "Christ's continuous crucifixion on Skid Row," some members of the Worker house in Los Angeles wrote,

> The blasphemy that we know as Skid Row is a modern-day Golgotha wherein greed and oppression have daily erected a new cross, and the tortured body of Christ comes to us under the appearance of so-called winos and bums. Here on a daily basis is the reenactment of that ancient tragedy on Calvary. . . . On the fringes of society where Christ lives a marginal existence with his poor brothers and sisters, suffering and brutality is the price one pays for walking the streets. Lives are lost over an extra piece of meat or bread. A stolen pair of shoes makes the difference between surviving or not. And alcohol is the only anesthetic to dull the sharp cutting edge of reality.[73]

The Catholic Worker, rooted in "the daily practice of the works of mercy" and committed to "creating a new society within the shell of the old,"[74] has been for me and for many others an inspiration and a testimony to the social power of the small-scale Christian community. The works of mercy, nonviolence, and simple solidarity with the poor have been central to its life. Dorothy Day was its key figure, mother and guide. She saw that it was necessary to incorporate social thinking into the works of mercy. More than any other individual, she helped to earth the social encyclicals of the popes by putting them to practice in the life of New York City. Without her work and witness, "Catholic social doctrine" might have remained a cerebral and remote thing. Without her commitment, there might never have been a Catholic peace movement, a fact that was implicitly recognized in the American bishops' pastoral letter *The Challenge of Peace* (1983). With Peter Maurin, who coined the term *green revolution*, she helped to launch the modern ecological movement, and much of Schumacher's early work was first published in the *Catholic Worker*.

In the little house in Cable Street, inspired by Dorothy Day, I found that combination of prayer, care, and witness to the new order that lay at the heart of all her work. In her writings I found a powerful fusion of orthodoxy and daring, of rootedness in the tradition and wildness in the spirit, of solidarity both with the saints and the liturgy and with the poorest of God's creatures. Her storefront Catholicism continues to inspire and shape my ministry.

Troublemaker Extraordinary: The Urban Radicalism of Saul Alinsky

"Radical is teaching ministers tactics of social revolution," announced *The New York Times* on 2 August 1965. A few weeks later, on 13 September 1965, *Newsweek* described this same radical as the "gadfly of the poverty war." Saul Alinsky (1909–1972) was at various times accused of being a communist, a Trotskyist, and an agent of the Vatican. The best-known community organizer in the United States, he brought together insights and methods of work from the Roman Catholic Church, the Al Capone gang, the department of sociology at the University of Chicago, and union organizing. As a sociology student in Chicago under E. W. Burgess and R. E. Park, the founders of the "Chicago School" of urban sociology, Alinsky devoted his post-graduate work to the Al Capone gang, and it was from these early experiences of urban conflict that his community work began.

Alinsky was never in the strict sense a revolutionary, rather an American radical (as he called himself) in the tradition of Thomas Jefferson and James Madison rather than Marx or Engels. There is no hint of Marxist influence anywhere in his work.[75] His only two books, *Reveille for Radicals* (1945) and *Rules for Radicals* (1972), became best-sellers and continue to influence urban activists all over the world. His name became legendary, and he was feared by the powerful. "Wherever I go," he once remarked, "there is trouble." Beginning with the "Back of the Yards" community in Chicago's meat-packing district, Alinsky moved on to found the Organization for a South West Community, the North West Community Organization, and the Woodlawn Organization on the South Side, the first major black neighborhood movement in Chicago. He was described by *The Economist* in 1967 as "the only radical who has succeeded in organizing the Negro communities."[76]

Alinsky was one of the first people in the modern period of urban life to recognize the organizational potential of the churches, especially of the Roman Catholic church, with its solid working-class and immigrant base. Although he was a Jewish agnostic, much of his work was with churches. Yet it was from the churches that much of the opposition to him came. In 1959 the Lutheran theologian Dr. Walter Kloetzli attacked him, accusing him of a "hidden purpose" and hinting at racism and subversion. The *Christian Century*, the influential liberal Christian journal, pursued a vendetta against him from 1959 to 1964. Editorials in the *Century* accused him of "exploiting urban decay" and of "Marxist class war."[77] "Alinsky denounces reconciliation," announced another editorial.[78] In one issue, on 3 August 1963, he was described as part of a Roman Catholic conspiracy, though the editor, Harold Fey, saw him as a Marxist. In fact it was Fey who "pinned a Marxist label on Alinsky,"[79] a label that remains to this day among the ignorant and ill-informed sections of the media.[80]

Certainly there was much support for Alinsky from the Roman Catholic community. In the 1950s Monsignor Jack Egan, himself a legendary figure in Chicago community action, introduced Alinsky to

Cardinal Stritch, and he was very close both to Stritch and to his successors, Cardinals Meyer and Cody. It was during the 1950s also that the French philosopher Jacques Maritain asked Alinsky to meet with Cardinal Montini (later Pope Paul VI) to advise him on trade union work in Milan. Maritain was one of Alinsky's greatest admirers. He saw him as one of the few really gifted men of the twentieth century and "the greatest man of action in our modern age." He described *Reveille for Radicals* as "epoch making."[81] Alinsky in his turn saw Maritain as his "spiritual father,"[82] and often quoted one of his sayings: "The fear of soiling ourselves by entering the context of history is not virtue but a way of escaping virtue."[83]

Though I have some serious doubts about the way Alinsky's methods have been developed by his successors, the figure of Saul Alinsky himself has been a constant source of strength to me and continues to influence my work. Though he himself was not a Christian, many of his insights offer important contributions to Christian social action at the neighborhood and community level. An obvious example is his emphasis on the need for effective organizing. He was first and foremost an organizer. "To hell with charity," he wrote. "The only thing you get is what you are strong enough to get. So you had better organize."[84] On the other hand, he was a great believer in keeping his opponents in the dark about his plans and his power base. He held the view that "power is not only what you have but what the enemy thinks you have,"[85] and many of his most effective tactics were based on threats. The occupation of the urinals at O'Hare Airport in 1964 has become part of Chicago mythology, even though it never actually took place. The threat was enough.

Another characteristic of Alinsky that attracted me to him was his tremendous sense of humor. Not for him the serious, unrelaxed intensity of so many activists. He was a brilliant practitioner of ridicule and an exponent of the social power of fun. "The establishment," he wrote, "can accept being screwed, but not being laughed at. What bugs them about me is that, unlike humorless radicals, I have a hell of a time doing what I'm doing."[86] He saw ridicule as his most potent weapon and believed that a good tactic was one that people actually enjoyed. And this was part of a much deeper aspect of Alinsky's faith: his deep trust in the ability of ordinary people to think and to act. He saw how vital it was that radical organizers should not lose touch with the sense and the style of the common people. "Never go outside the experience of your people," he advised, adding that one should, "whenever possible, go outside the experience of the enemy."[87] Alinsky was a great listener, and his stress on listening to the people has been a major influence on my ministry in East London. He was committed to help and support, not paternalism.

> You prove to people they can do something, show them how to have a way of life where they can make their own decisions—and then you get out. They don't need a father who stands over them.[88]

Most of all, Alinsky saw that real change could not take place without conflict, and it was this conviction that brought him into dispute with the liberal wing of the churches, which sought change without conflict. The Roman Catholic church accepted his methods more easily than did the Protestant groups; it would be valuable to explore the reasons for this. In 1965 the Episcopal Diocese of West Missouri set up a committee to examine Alinsky's approach and, though they were on the whole favorable, they found some of his methods "alarming and highly inflammatory."[89] And they were correct, for Alinsky believed strongly that conflicts and divisions had to be brought to the surface so that they could be dealt with. In the words of one of his most quoted maxims: "Rub raw the resentment of the people to the point of overt expression."[90] Dissatisfaction and discontent needed to be stirred up.

So Alinsky became, in the eyes of many commentators, the epitome of the "outside agitator." It was an image that he was happy to welcome.

> My critics are right when they call me an outside agitator. When a community, any kind of community, is hopeless and helpless, it requires somebody from outside to come in and stir things up. That's my job—to unsettle them, to make them start asking questions, to teach them to stop talking and start acting.[91]

Alinsky was direct and confrontational. He did not believe in politeness, "going through the proper channels," or any of the niceties of bureaucracy.

> When you want something, don't bother with official city machinery. Go to the man who can give you what you want, and make him hurt until he gives in.[92]

His methods were totally opposed to those of the gentle pressure groups, those who sought to win friends and influence people in the corridors of power. On the contrary, Alinsky argued,

> The only way to upset the power structure in your communities is to goad them, confuse them, irritate them, and, most of all, make them live by their own rules.[93]

He was critical of liberal welfare policies and antipoverty programs, which he termed "welfare colonialism." Such programs "served" people from above and tried to buy off militant leaders. Alinsky was a believer in power from below. Though he believed that the middle class was a potential catalyst of change, he held that if it did not move in a radical direction, it would move toward a "native American fascism." He had no time for liberals. "A liberal is a guy who walks out of the room when a discussion turns into a fight."[94]

Alinsky believed that his function was to disturb. He was a troublemaker, an unmasker of illusion, an agitator who posed disturbing questions.

> If I had to put up a religious symbol the way some people have crucifixes or Stars of David, my symbol would be the question mark. A question mark is a plowshare turned upside down. It plows your mind so that thought and ideas grow.[95]

In raising questions and creating discontent and tumult, he opened up the areas of potential change. And he did this with his typical fusion of cool-headed planning and irreverent attack. Maritain wrote of Alinsky that "the soul of his tactic was a healthy, vocal and aggressive irreverence. He loved to tweak the noses and pluck the beards of the establishment."[96] And *The Economist* said of him, "It requires little imagination to discover why he is so disliked by his opponents: he cannot be bought; he cannot be intimidated; and he breaks all the rules."[97]

Back-Street Pastor: The Eucharistic Politics of Stanley Evans

Stanley Evans (1912–1965) spent the whole of his ministry in inner London. Ordained in 1935, he threw himself, as a young deacon, into the antifascist movement during the years of the Spanish Civil War. He was active in the peace movement during these years, and became secretary of Islington Peace Council in 1937. Within a short time he was in demand in Europe as a speaker on issues of socialism, fascism, and East-West relations. His activity in Europe increased after the Second World War, so much so that on 23 December 1946, the bishop of London wrote and asked him not to say that he had come from the Diocese of London![98] Evans was a key figure in building relations with the Soviet Union during the Stalin years and was leading parties of clergy both to Russia and to Eastern countries long before it was fashionable or safe to do so. He chaired the British Soviet Friendship Society during the 1950s, and on 13 March 1953 he preached a sermon at the memorial service for Stalin in London. Although Evans followed the Communist Party line closely until 1956, in his later years he was a more independent socialist. His pamphlet *Russia Reviewed* (1956) expressed a critical yet still supportive view of Soviet society. Unlike many former communists or Soviet sympathizers, he remained on the left. He was vice-chairman of the Campaign for Nuclear Disarmament during its early years and heavily involved in campaigns for human rights in many countries.

Because of his socialist convictions, Evans was not offered a post as a parish priest until 1955, twenty years after his ordination, and he had no job at all between 1946 and 1955. During these years, he spent much of his time debating critics of the socialist societies—or attempting to do so, for many were wary of entering into debate with so well informed and so formidable an opponent. The secretary of the Oxford University Socialist Club, writing in 1953 to cancel a planned debate, told Evans that he "could find no one willing to debate with you."[99] Many found Evans difficult, uncompromising, and intransigent, and the Church of England, then as now, found turbulent priests difficult to handle. The Bishop of London said that he was "his own worst enemy,"[100] and even when he was finally appointed to a parish, there were sixty letters of objection. However, on 6 January 1955 he was instituted as parish priest of Holy Trinity, Dalston, a run-down district of Hackney, and his ministry there was remarkable, controversial, and prophetic, anticipating much that was to transform the shape of Christian worship and ministry in the coming years.

Evans, though a man of brilliant intellect, never sought to work full time within the academic world but was committed to the work of neighborhood ministry. He had a clear view of the role of the parish church in its relation to the local community.

> In the first place, the parish church, the focal point of local worship, must also become the focal point of local community. In this it must in no way seek to oust the pub which is its only rival for this function in most localities (political parties, it must be noted, are inevitably sectional and sectarian in approach and outlook) but be the center in which the separate families of many pubs or other centers can find a common home.[101]

He was strongly opposed both to clericalism and to sectarianism, holding that the church was the church of the whole nation. He saw the back-street church as a force for social righteousness and as a center for common life in the district. But, as he said, its one rival as a focus of community was the pub, and no one had a more exalted view of the social role of the pub than Stanley Evans. He seemed to know every pub in London and could describe its history and its role in the life of the area. The pub was a place of relaxation, friendship, and common life. As such, it was an important site for pastoral ministry. When, on 7 July 1960, Bill Sargent was instituted as Evans's successor at Holy Trinity, it is significant that his institution in church was followed the next day by his imbibulation at the Prince Arthur pub, where he was also instituted into the possession of the Vicar's Beer Mug. A parish memo noted, "The form of imbibulation, though modern, is in keeping with the Catholic practice and traditions of the parish."[102]

This strong sense of the value of the common life, in which church and pub should relate and learn from each other, was one of the features of Evans's thought that drew me to him. He held a strongly sacramental view of the world and was swift to respond to developments within the culture. As rock and roll began its transformation of youth culture, he opened "Old Dick's Dive" in the church as a center for young people. The hostility was fierce to this invitation to the young to gather on Sunday nights without any attempt at instant conversion. Harold Legerton, secretary of the Lord's Day Observance Society, commented, "Young people introduced to the church through rock and roll are not worth having. I think they would be better off on the streets than in the church."[103] But Evans believed that the role of the church was to reach out to people on its fringes. He was an early exponent of the "bias to the poor." The church, he said in 1962, had "a bias toward the underdog, a bias toward the hungry, the homeless, the illiterate, the persecuted."[104]

Evans's sense of the parish as the center of social righteousness and the local cell of the Kingdom was expressed in the liturgical life of Holy Trinity Church. Here, in the 1950s, there was a "general communion" as the central weekly act of worship, and it was always followed by breakfast and discussion of the sermon. As a disciple of Conrad Noel, Evans had a strong sense of the power of beauty and drama in worship, and this was visibly manifested in the joyous celebration of festivals. Thus at Rogationtide in 1956 the procession included the carrying of the three black flags of peace, the banner of the Dragon (representing greed and power), and the banner of the Lion of Judah. On Saint Barnabas Day, there was Cypriot singing and dancing. In all this there was a view of liturgy as a celebration of life involving splendor and enjoyment, a prefiguring of a new world. In his liturgical celebrations, Evans was way ahead of his time, anticipating the liturgical renewal of the 1960s.

At the heart of Stanley Evans's ministry was the doctrine of the incarnation, the truth that God had taken human flesh and had, by that act, sanctified all human life. He expressed his belief in an account of why he was not keen to go to the Holy Land on a pilgrimage.

> The fact that I have never had any deep desire to go to Palestine and kneel at the site of the manger at Bethlehem, or rejoice at Cana where the water was turned into wine, or tread the bitter road to Calvary, is simply a reflection of the fact

that I have been brought up to realize that Bethlehem could be the outhouse of any pub, that all water can be made wine, and there are Calvaries enough and to spare in London and New York. The essential theological point of the early councils of the Church was their declaration of the universality of Christ, and for all that anybody can say to the contrary, we have so been brought up to accept this that it never crosses our mind to doubt it.[105]

For Evans, all social ministry was rooted in social doctrine, in the social nature of God. He was already using the phrase "the social God" in his notes for 1935. It was his understanding of the centrality of sound doctrine that led him to see how important were the early debates about the nature and person of Christ. In a talk given in 1952, he observed,

It is not an accident that Arianism achieved its major success among the Goths to whose tribal system it was well suited, for it did two things: it made God a supreme and absolute potentate like the Emperor or a Gothic king, alone in glory; and, because it made Christ a creature, it created the possibility that his teaching could be overthrown—there might be no Kingdom! Indeed, reference to Athanasius' *Defence Against the Arians* shows his adversaries maintaining the doctrine that Christ's Kingdom would have an end. It was because they were protagonists of this Kingdom that Athanasius and his comrades fought.[106]

For Stanley Evans, orthodox Christology was at the heart of pastoral and political practice. It was because God took flesh in Jesus Christ that the church was deeply and irrevocably committed to the social struggle.

It was because Evans's pastoral and political practice was so rooted in theology that he was fiercely opposed to superficial "trendiness." As he wrote in 1959,

It is not just a question, as all too many may think, of the church "modernizing itself." Young people may prefer snappier music, but they will not for long be fooled by it. Not snappier music, nor shorter psalms, nor basic Bibles; not cushioned pews, nor rocking parsons, nor jiving in the aisles; nothing but sincerity and truth will do.[107]

The commitment to sincerity and truth lay at the heart of his work. He saw that a church that did not have its foundations in the gospel and in commitment to the truth would die.

Evans saw himself and the movement that grew up around him as standing within a historical tradition of Christian faith and struggle. In January 1958 he began *The Junction* (named after Dalston Junction railway station) as "a journal of Anglican realism." He defined Anglican realism as a tradition that took seriously the realities of the material world and the struggles and advances of modern society; a tradition that rejected dualism, and that saw matter and spirit as different aspects of the same reality. He believed that evangelicalism, liberalism, and Anglo-Catholicism had "played their part and had their day." Anglican realism, he claimed, was a tradition that had deep roots within the Christian history of Britain.

> It looks back to leaders like Theobald who brought learning and order to a divided land.
>
> It looks back to saints like Botolph who combined land development with prayer and gave food to the poor.
>
> It looks back to bishops like the Saxon Wulfstan who stamped out the slave trade at the time of the Norman Conquest.
>
> It looks back to inspired leaders like Becket who defied kings in the interest of the people.[108]

Evans had a realistic and visionary awareness of the historical tradition as alive and empowering, a constant source of renewal.

The dominating symbol of Stanley Evans's life was that of the Kingdom of God. He saw theology as dynamic and complained that many theologians were seeking "an impossible stability." Faith was a handmaid to life, to navigation. It was only in the course of movement that one came to any understanding of truth.[109] All human history was movement. He looked beyond the historical confines of the past to the hope of the future. A relentless critic of the theology of the sixteenth-century Reformation, he wished to move beyond its conceptual limits and argued in 1961 that "it is time for a new reformation."[110] Earlier, in a symposium of 1954, he had stressed the centrality of Kingdom theology to any renewal of the faith:

> It is around this one basic concept that Christianity arose. "The Kingdom of God," wrote Canon Widdrington, "is the regulative principle of theology." This teaching has been betrayed, side-tracked, forgotten, in one Christian generation after another. But its roots are firmly planted in the official documents of the church, especially in its Holy Scriptures. Constantly it arises to trouble the waters, and to challenge the defeatism of those who, in the name of Christianity, refuse to confront reality.[111]

Three years later, in a parish lecture at Dalston, he predicted the shape of future divisions and future convergence:

> If we turn to the churches we find a two-dimensional split. On the one hand the historic split between east and west has been followed, particularly in the west, by a denominational fragmentation which is today sustained by reference to historic formulae the real meaning of which has been obscured by the passage of centuries. On the other hand, running right across these splits, is the other one which, stated simply, divides Christians into those who believe in the coming of some kind of Kingdom of God upon earth, and those who do not.[112]

Today, as we look across the wastes of "Christian civilization" and the poverty and individualism of the churches, we see how accurate was Stanley Evans's assessment of our condition.

Among the features of his life and witness that influenced my own ministry, a number stand out as being of particular importance: his rootedness in a living tradition of faith and life, his sense of standing within a history and of that history as the seedbed of dynamic and liberating truth; his emphasis on the corporate worship of the Christian community and of its common life of sharing expressed in the Eucharist; and his conviction that intellectual gifts had to be put at the service of communities of people in struggle. He was a true theologian of the back-street church, committed to the search for truth and for the Kingdom as it manifested itself in those streets, yet committed equally to the struggle for peace and justice for all peoples.

In Evans's only major work, *The Social Hope of the Christian Church*, published just before his death in 1965, he quoted words from a hymn of Saint Ambrose: *Laeti bibamus sobriam Ebrietatem spiritus.* "Let us joyfully drink of the sober drunkenness of the Spirit." "To be a Christian," he commented, "is to be a controlled drunk, purposively intoxicated with the joy of the life which is perpetually created by God himself."[113] It was this life and joy that Evans proclaimed and lived.

Conflict and Comprehension: The Urban Vision of Ruth Glass

Ruth Glass (1912–1990) belonged to Weimar Germany, where she was born into a family of rich rabbinical traditions. She herself was an atheist and an unfaltering Marxist, though the fiery humanism of the Jewish prophetic tradition was in her blood. She began her literary career as a teenage journalist on a radical weekly in Berlin, and one of her earliest essays, recently reprinted, describes the condition of unemployed youth in the year before Hitler came to power:

> A vast nationwide epidemic has already broken out: the neglect and subsequent demoralization of the young unemployed. . . . The process of disintegration has already radically attacked body, mind and spirit. They roam around as living examples of the state that people fall into when they live a life devoid of human dignity.[114]

The account, as disturbing in its passion as in its precision, could well be mistaken for an account of the position of the urban "underclass" in American or British cities in the 1990s.

After escaping from Berlin, she came to London (via Prague and Geneva) and began her career as a social scientist. Though she spent several years during the Second World War as a research officer with the Bureau of Applied Social Research at Columbia University in New York, most of her academic life was spent in London, with periodic visits to India and other developing countries. She was the pioneer of urban sociology in Britain, and through her Centre for Urban Studies, which she established at University College, London, in 1954, passed most of the future urban planners of the Third World. A principal area of her expertise was social statistics, and she was the first academic in Britain to make use of the sophisticated data of the 1961 census to combat popular myths about black minorities and housing. Her academic work was meticulous, thorough, and, at times, devastating in its attack on established assumptions. She was a constant critic of the planning dogma that, since the 1940s, had led to the decline of the urban economy and to social and racial segregation in the inner city. She was one of the first to call attention to the problem of land exploitation as a result of the denationalizing of land development rights and values through the Town and Country Planning Act of 1959. It was this Act that led to the massive spiral in profiteering, symbolized in central London by the commercial building called Centrepoint—"this insolent building" as she described it in 1973.[115] Empty since 1964, the building had been receiving supplies of heating oil throughout the oil financial crisis of the mid-1970s.

Ruth Glass was no ordinary academic. Her entire life and work was dominated by a passionate concern for the downtrodden and the oppressed. From 1960, when she published *Newcomers*, the first detailed study of the West Indian immigrants in London, much of her work was concerned with the position of minorities in the urban areas. *Newcomers* began, "It would not occur to anyone who writes a book on criminology to state in the preface that he is opposed to murder,"[116] but because the ethics and etiquette of race were different, the book had to begin before the beginning with a statement of her own strong moral opposition to all forms of racism. She saw that racism still generated vast destructive forces, and she believed that one of the most destructive of current beliefs was the assumption that "racial prejudice is immutable." She was a leading critic of what she termed "the number theory of prejudice," the view that prejudice increased in direct proportion to the numbers of black people in a society.[117] It was this view that was to form the basis of British immigration control policy. She saw, and warned of, the increase in scapegoating of minority groups in Britain in the early 1960s. She was totally opposed to immigration controls based on color, describing the theory behind the controls as "a new doctrine of original sin combined with a new faulty political arithmetic."[118] But she was equally critical of apparently liberal devices that, in the current climate, could be misused. Thus she denounced the question about parents' country of birth in the 1971 census and the "inflated highly elastic pseudo-statistics" that it produced, leading to the reinforcement of stereotypes.[119]

Much of Ruth Glass's work was concerned with the contradiction between labor needs and social provision. She pointed out that while immigrants were recruited from the Caribbean to service the labor market, there was no housing provision for them and considerable discrimination in the private rented sector. "The very people who are wanted on the labor market are regarded as expendable on the housing market."[120] More and more she saw racist stereotypes reproduced and used as the basis of policy. In a letter to *The Times* that was not published—itself an indication of the changed political climate, for almost all Ruth Glass's letters to that paper had been published from the 1940s until the early 1980s—she responded to an American professor who had "roamed the streets of Brixton" in search of Britain's race problem. Why had he insisted on the emotive word "roamed," and not simply walked, asked Ruth Glass, and she went on to describe the four principal ingredients of a racialist stew, all contained in his article. First, you create racial stereotypes, writing about groups in the unisex singular—the black, the Jew—while we (plural), white people, relate to this phenomenon in a We–It relationship. Second, the stereotype is then reinforced by depicting "it" as alien, the carrier of problems. Third, the stereotype is aided by the use of verbal fog and an obtuse lingo. Finally, it is heated up by the use of the language of violence and terror, the portrayal of racial minorities as a threatening presence.[121]

Ruth Glass was one of the first researchers to examine the "twilight zones" of London and to warn of the deterioration of conditions in areas such as North Kensington, scene of the race riots of 1958 and of the housing racketeering associated with Perec Rachman that came to public attention during the Profumo scandal of 1963. She was there during the years of Rachman, the most notorious slum landlord for the black community, and she stressed that he was only the best-known representative of a whole system of profiteering. But in the hysteria and horror around the Rachman revelations, the underlying issues were not dealt with.

> If anyone was censured, it was those who were exploited, not the exploiters. Since then the Commonwealth Immigrants Act has been passed—hardly an obstacle against real estate profiteering. But no significant measures have been taken to stop the spiral of urban land values and rent. Are memories so short? Apparently they are: and it is that which points to the moral of the Rachman story. It is one of many recent examples of delayed reaction, of inertia and apathy, in matters of social policy.[122]

She saw the danger that the divisions between the wealthy and the poor districts of London would become increasingly sharp, that the poor districts would become more concentrated districts of "marginal people," and that they might become more divided from the wealthier districts along racial as well as class lines. All her warnings have proved valid during the 1980s. She coined the term *gentrification* during the early 1960s, warning that the poor would be squeezed out of the inner areas by the very wealthy, leading to "upper class ghettos": in this too, what she predicted has come to pass.[123]

Though she was a distinguished researcher, Ruth Glass was strongly opposed to research for its own sake, particularly where the political will and the commitment to change were lacking. She attacked the international Habitat conference of 1976 as "a costly pretentious exercise in obfuscation" and suggested that the planners should abandon their conferences and use the money to supply water taps in Third World cities.[124] She was scathing about those who called for more research when the data was already available, seeing such calls as excuses for further inaction. North Kensington's housing problems, she pointed out, had been "known and documented well before the Milner Holland report [a government report of 1965] was published."[125] Of housing research, she wrote in 1965, "It is curious that the very examples of gaps in information which are usually quoted in the housing field refer to matters which have been quite well known for a considerable time." She went on,

In the housing sphere especially, there are all sorts of perennial fables which still flourish, though they have long been disproved. The idea that lack of essential information is responsible for the law's delay and the muddle of social policies is one of these fables. Of course, more systematic intelligence is needed. And its production would be well worthwhile—provided that it were utilized. There has been no want of facts to prevent the most patent mistakes in housing programs. Even so, such mistakes have been, and are still being, perpetuated. Indeed scarcity of information is a poor alibi for the vagaries of social administration. It is not social policy that is held up by inadequate research. In British housing, as in other fields, the difficulty has been the other way round. Social research has been obstructed by lack of system and vigor in social policy.[126]

Her words are still applicable: urgent needs are still "met" by calls for more research, almost always as a way of delaying or avoiding effective action.

Of all the influences on my ministry, my friendship with Ruth Glass is perhaps the most extraordinary. As far as I know, I was her only close Christian friend (though she had a deep respect for Helmut Gollwitzer, whom she knew slightly). As a parish priest in the East End of London and in Soho, I constantly drew on the resources of this atheist and used her in seminars and training sessions with clergy, youth, and community workers, and others concerned with urban problems. She helped us all to place our work in the context of accurate knowledge. She helped us to see that our pastoral ministry and our political action needed to have this solid basis in sound research and unassailable factual information. Moreover, she strongly believed, as a social researcher, that research and struggle must be closely related, and from her home, close to Notting Hill Gate, she kept a very close eye on events in North Kensington and other districts of potential crisis, offering support to deprived and struggling communities. She anticipated the urban uprisings in British cities long before they occurred. In an essay of 1964 she predicted that "there will be turmoil in and around many cities of the world even before 1984";[127] two years later, she warned that "aloofness from conflicts . . . does not lead to their comprehension."[128]

Prayer, Silence, and Struggle: The Contemplative Life in the Inner City

I feel that I have lived through much of that turmoil of which Ruth Glass wrote so powerfully and prophetically. Arriving in London as a student just after the race riots in North Kensington in 1958, I was a curate during the conflicts between Mods and Rockers in 1964, a priest in Soho during the late 1960s when needle use in the West End rose to epidemic proportions, a parish priest in Bethnal Green at the peak period of organized racist violence from 1976 to 1978, and a field officer for race relations at the time of the urban rebellions in British cities in 1980, 1981, and 1985. Yet these external and often dramatic occurrences are merely the surface features of an underlying and more deeply pervasive climate of turbulence and restlessness, a climate of injustice and inequality. It is within this climate that prayer and silence must become the nourishing power of struggle and resistance.

How am I, as an urban pastor, to find spiritual resources that will enable that struggle for justice and that resistance to the oppressive powers to be sustained and to flourish in what is often unpromising ground? How am I to make creative and redemptive sense of all this anger, despair, and pain that surrounds me and all who work in the inner cities? If theological reflection, spiritual renewal, pastoral ministry all occur within a specific context, then this square mile, east of Aldgate, is my context. It is here, not elsewhere, that I have to discern the activity of God, the signs of the times, the distortions and tragedies—and the potential—of human history. Most of what is called theology takes place in universities, within a very particular kind of cultural milieu, quite different from that in which most people live and work. Even what is termed practical theology or urban pastoral training often goes on within academia. In making a conscious and deliberate choice not to be part of that world but to be a theologian on the staff of an East End parish, I am choosing a path that diverges from what is taken to be normative in Western Christianity.

Yet I believe this path marks a return to an earlier tradition in which theology was seen as a reflective process, rooted in prayer, the practice of silence, and involvement in the struggles and aspirations of humankind and of specific human communities. I have come to see, as an activist, the central place of silence in my life and in the lives of all who would work for peace and justice at a more than surface level. There is a sense in which silent waiting on God is the heart of prayer, a simple abiding in emptiness, weakness, and attention, a recognition that it is the Spirit who prays within us in inarticulate groanings (Rom. 8:26). For Jesus, the very early dawn was a key time for prayer (Mark 1:35), and so it has been for me and for many others for whom the day becomes busier as it progresses. I would not recommend this time of prayer as a rule for everyone, and it is important that we do not become slaves of time; our prayer rhythms and patterns need to be very flexible. But there is something very special about the early morning, when in many places there is physical stillness and a reduction of external activity, which can be conducive to the prayer of attention. To spend an hour in waiting on God in the early stillness is a valuable preparation for the hectic and often frenzied activity of the day.

It is equally important, however, that the inner stillness that comes from the practice of silent attention to God is allowed to spill over into the activity itself, so that it is not all tense and in danger of becoming manic. Saint Anthony, the first Christian hermit, advised, "If we push ourselves beyond measure, we will break: it is right for us from time to time to relax our efforts."[129] This remains sound advice, for there is a real danger of burnout, that affliction which leads many activist Christians to the point of collapse and subsequent withdrawal from the active life. But burnout is not simply a problem of personal survival or personal health; it has effects on the community who are the recipients, often the victims, of social action or pastoral care. The hyperactive person, whether community worker or pastor, who has not given time to inner stillness (*hesychia*) will soon communicate to others nothing more than his or her inner tiredness and exhaustion of spirit—not a very kind thing to do to people who have enough problems of their own.

Silence is an integral part of ministry and of effective Christian action. In silence we open ourselves up to the activity of God and to the movements of history. If it is important to listen to the voice of God, to try to discern and distinguish the voice of God amid the conflicting voices around and within us, it is also important to listen to the voices of the world, particularly the hidden, neglected voices. It is important to listen carefully to the language of silence, the silence of crushed, broken, battered people. A contemplative, reflective approach is a necessary part of any sustained social action, and without that base social action is bound to become superficial and to lack both depth and staying power. Silence helps to create stillness and the ability to hear. It also creates a climate of discernment and scrutiny, of persistent interrogation, of inner struggle to discern the signs. Truth is rarely revealed in a straightforward or unproblematic way. Often it is only in the context of darkness, whether the external darkness of tumult or war or the internal darkness of confusion and uncertainty, that some profound truths become clear. As Alan Ecclestone has written, "There are things that can only be seen in darkened skies, questions only heard in the silence of utter dismay. Such a time is ours."[130]

Linked with the silence is the prayerful and meditative use of the Bible. Like William Stringfellow, himself a consistent social and political activist, I find myself more and more needing to stress both the place of Scripture in the life of prayer and action and the importance of a biblical spirituality.[131] The origins of what we call meditation within the Christian tradition lie in the practice among the early Egyptian monks of prayerfully repeating biblical texts. The Greek word *melete* signified a concerned brooding, pondering, upon these texts. Within the Benedictine tradition there grew up the practice of what has been called "totally involved reading."[132]

Such prayerful reading is very different from the way we read when we are desperate to finish something or from the casual reading that often accompanies train journeys. It is a way of reading that is akin to prayer—indeed the Jesuit Jean Grou saw such reading as "half a prayer."[133] In the use of the Bible, it is a persistent, quiet yet firm, pursuit of the truth, a struggle for the Word for our time as it reveals itself in the subversive memory of ancient revelation. It is part of the spiritual discipline of becoming a people of the Word, a biblical people.

There is one aspect of brooding on the Scriptures that is particularly important in times of upheaval and crisis, and this is the use of prayer as lament. The whole notion of lament has almost vanished from our liturgical consciousness. In ancient Israel, lament was a spiritual genre that focused on distress and tragedy in the life of the nation or of individuals, and that was a vehicle for the articulation of grief and anger. The Psalms and the Lamentations of Jeremiah are the classic examples of this type of literature. The "cursing" psalms, which so embarrass modern churchgoers that they are normally omitted from the recitation of the Divine Office, are pleas for justice, cries from the heart of pain and grief. They belong to the category of lament, and they represent a vital part of prayer. Walter Brueggemann has shown how necessary is the expression of grief within a community,[134] and it is something that we have lost. In the midst of frustration, sorrow, and hopelessness, we find no way to express how we feel at the heart of our life of prayer.

One of the most vital aspects of a spirituality for struggle is the building up of resources to live with darkness and desolation. We could say that the whole work of contemplation in the midst of action is a sharing in darkness and desolation, a sharing in the dying and rising of Christ. Christianity had its roots in the darkness of cross and contradiction, and those who follow Christ today in the troubled world of injustice and oppression need to live daily with the reality of death and destruction. Lamentation is a necessary part of the spirituality of justice making. It is the flip side of resistance. Today the sense of lament is caught more by poets and novelists than by theologians. Thus Toni Morrison writes of the barrenness of ghetto existence, "The soil is bad for certain kinds of flowers. Certain seeds it will not nurture, certain fruit it will not bear, and when the land kills of its own volition, we acquiesce and say the victim had no right to live. We are wrong, of course, but it doesn't matter. At least on the edge of my town, among the garbage and the sunflowers of my town, it's much, much, much too late."[135] Such recognition of the stark reality of life can lead easily to despair, and it is important to be able to carry a certain amount of despair with us if we are to share the pain and grief of those who have lost hope. The desert tradition spoke of the need for *penthos*, inner grief, a quality of life that can come only through sharing pain, sharing something of the descent into hell. What distinguishes it from absolute despair is the deep and subversive faith in the resurrection, a faith that may be, and often is, contradicted by the evidence of the present. Yet it remains a cherished inner light that shines in the midst of the prevailing darkness.

Contemplation is an experience of both darkness and light. Contemplative vision is a kind of seeing by not seeing, an obscure knowledge, an insight from within shadows and shades. The ground on which we sit and pray is sometimes hard and dry; sometimes it crumbles and cracks. Yet we need to stay there while we can, stay with the perplexity and the lack of clarity, for the clarity we seek comes only out of the heart of the darkness. It cannot be negotiated or administered. It is a result of a *metanoia*, a profound upheaval of spirit in which systems crack and language is stretched beyond its limits. There, in the resulting chaos, lives the possibility of a new vision. It is out of such contemplative upheaval that prophetic voices may sometimes be heard.

It is in part because of the intolerable pressure that such prayerful solidarity with oppression puts on individuals, and in part because of the danger of self-deception, that what is traditionally called spiritual direction has become a vital necessity for those involved in social action. The more I find myself involved in campaigning, in protest, and in political struggle, the more necessary is that relationship of sharing, of guidance, and of mutual support that is the core of the relationship of direction. "God the Creator," wrote Saint Basil, "arranged things so that we need each other."[136] Many people dislike the term *spiritual direction*, with its undertones both of authoritarianism and of a compartmentalizing of the "spiritual," and there is nothing sacrosanct about it. The term is of sixteenth-century origin, and it may be less misleading to speak of guidance or to go back to the term favored by Aelred of Rievaulx in the twelfth century—*spiritual friendship*.[137] Many also, and rightly, see the danger of developing spiritual elites, and this too needs to be watched. Yet what is essential to this ministry is the nurture of Christian character and consciousness, the provision of support and companionship in struggle, and the gentle guiding of a person toward fuller understanding of the truth. The spiritual director or guide is before all else a companion, a comrade, a fellow pilgrim.

After many years, and even centuries, of neglect of this personal ministry, many people are misusing it—through excess use and overdependence, through confusion with counseling and therapy, and so on[138]—and it is important to emphasize that it is a very humble relationship. The late Gilbert Shaw, who at one period is said to have been director to over two thousand people—"something surely without parallel in the Church of England" or, indeed, anywhere else!—put it very simply: "I'm a pilgrim sitting at the roadside on the way to Jerusalem and as the other pilgrims pass by I like to be able to give them a little word of encouragement to put them en route again."[139] The director's role is a lowly and limited one. Today much spiritual support and guidance is given and received through the medium of small supportive groups or cells within which there is prayer, silence, mutual respect and trust, and a courageous testimony to truth. Critical support is particularly important for activists, for, as two recent writers have warned, "Individual champions of sacred causes who feel the need to leave behind the critical support of the people of God are particularly vulnerable to self-deception."[140]

In this chapter I have deliberately drawn on my experience in a small part of one British city. I have done so because it is the part of the world that I know best, and it is always better to write of what one knows; because it is only through the concrete and particular that we can come to any appreciation and understanding of the wider issues; because I passionately believe that all theological reflection and all soundly based social and political action must begin with an analysis of and response to the local situation before it can move beyond it; but most of all, because it is through our outer journeys, with their pitfalls and false paths as well as their discoveries and achievements, that we grow deeper in our response to and love of the God who is the beginning and the ending, and who remains the Ground in which we stand.

5

Beyond the New Dark Age

Tradition, Prophecy, and the Future

I know: the paths of the soul, overgrown, often know only the night, a very vast, very barren night, without landscapes. And yet I tell you: we'll get out. The most glorious works of man are born of that night.

ELIE WIESEL

It has lately come to pass that America has entered upon a dark age.

WILLIAM STRINGFELLOW

A crucial turning point in that earlier history occurred when men and women of good will turned aside from the task of shoring up the Roman *imperium* and ceased to identify the continuation of civility and moral community with the maintenance of that *imperium*. What they set themselves to achieve instead—often not recognizing fully what they were doing—was the construction of new forms of community within which the moral life could be sustained so that both morality and civility might survive the coming ages of barbarism and darkness. If my account of our moral condition is correct, we ought also to conclude that for some time now we too have reached that turning point. What matters at this stage is the construction of local forms of community within which civility and the intellectual and moral life can be sustained through the new dark ages which are already upon us. And if the tradition of the virtues was able to survive the horrors of the last dark ages, we are not entirely without

grounds for hope. This time however the barbarians are not waiting beyond the frontiers; they have already been governing us
for quite some time. And it is our lack of consciousness of this
that constitutes part of our predicament. We are waiting not for
a Godot, but for another—doubtless very different—Saint
Benedict.

ALASDAIR MACINTYRE

The theme of a new dark age is a familiar one, though there has
been considerable variation in how this is understood—from the
predictions of early Trotskyists that a "new barbarism" would characterize the death throes of late capitalism to the present claims by moral
philosophers and others that the postmodern world is one without
any coherent moral shape. The term *post-Christian* entered the vocabulary many years before *postmodern,* though the accuracy of both has
been questioned. Today the optimism of an earlier epoch has given
way to the language of diversity, fragmentation, and uncertainty. Predictions of doom have both increased and changed in character. Alongside warnings of environmental collapse have come warnings of
cultural collapse, of moral and spiritual disintegration, of the decline
and decay of values. The center cannot hold, we are told on all sides,
and the spiritual and moral foundations of the culture of the West
have been eroded. Yet such speculation is not associated purely with
a sense of doom and fatalism. For some years now a range of thinkers
have seen the latter years of the twentieth century as a "leap epoch" in
which human consciousness is passing to a new level. We are, so these
thinkers argue, in a confused transitional period. A new world is struggling to be born.

Such reflection reached a particular kind of peak during the counterculture of the 1960s. The dawning of the Age of Aquarius on
5 February 1962—when Jupiter came into alignment with Mars, Mer-
cury, Venus, Saturn, the sun, and the moon—was seen by many as the
dawn of a new era of spiritual awakening. The rediscovery of the East,
the resurgence of occult and magical notions, the concern for the earth
as well as for the world within, were all part of this sense of a new era.
There was a mingling of despair and eschatological vision. Much of the
spirituality of the counterculture was not unlike the millennialism of

earlier ages. Theodore Roszak, whose writings reflected the changing character of the new sensibility, saw the age as one of Kali Yuga, an age of tragic darkness. Roszak was concerned at what he saw as the diminished mode of consciousness of urban-industrial society, a one-dimensional consciousness dominated by the scientific and technological, excluding the visionary and imaginative dimensions. Yet in the quest for a new synthesis of the religious and the political, a new politics generated by the energy of spiritual renewal, he saw the ending of the wasteland. In order to move toward this new phase, there was a need for disaffiliation and internal restructuring so that a new society could be shaped and tested within the shell of the old. In the counterculture Roszak saw the beginnings of a new saving vision, the possibility of a new age of spirit.[1] In similar vein spoke Herbert Marcuse, R. D. Laing, and others. In Britain, Glastonbury became a focal point for new age reflection as William Blake's vision of the "reawakening of Albion" struck chords in many hearts. Much of the thinking of the present "new age" movements was born in that decade; holistic medicine, for example, with its theme of a fundamental shift in planetary consciousness, is well within the mainstream of counterculture thinking. What was central to the decade was a sense of spiritual struggle, of striving toward the new. While some spoke of darkness and of a new dark age, others spoke of a new reformation.[2]

Today's climate, on a superficial analysis, seems frighteningly different. Though much of the spirituality of the 1960s has returned in the form of new age movements, and though many of the spiritual currents of the present, like those of the 1960s, show affinities with Gnosticism, millennialism, and the occult, these are by no means the only features of our period. More striking and more disturbing has been the resurgence of what is commonly termed fundamentalism.

The Danger of Fundamentalism

The term *fundamentalism* was originally applied to a growth within the evangelical wing of American Christianity that, in the period before the First World War, was concerned to reaffirm "the fundamentals" of Christian faith against the alleged betrayals of liberalism. The early fundamentalists were as concerned with the threats from liberal theology, socialism, communism, and the evolutionary theories of Darwin as they were with restating the inerrancy of the biblical text in the face of the "higher criticism."[3] Since those days, Christian fundamentalism has gone through many phases, and the term has often been used to describe a range of evangelical groups and positions that differ one from another. Yet, in spite of a history of slipshod and imprecise usage (a history that it shares with many other "isms"), the term is a useful one. It can, of course, mean—as no doubt its original proponents intended—a commitment to fundamentals, to the foundational beliefs, principles, and values of a tradition, and in this sense it is a term that many would be proud to claim. But to define the term in this way is to ignore its history. I shall use it here to describe a constellation of attitudes within religious traditions that show certain common features. Though our primary interest here is in fundamentalism in its Christian form, concern is currently being expressed at its appearance in, for example, Islamic and Jewish traditions. Thus, although in the limited sense of textual inerrancy Islam is fundamentalist *per se* in a way that Christianity is not, this is not the only feature, or indeed the most important feature, of fundamentalist movements.

Belief in the inerrancy of the sacred text, be it Koran, Torah, or Christian Scriptures, is only one aspect of a wider phenomenon that, in its historical manifestations, shows a number of characteristics. First is an unwavering belief in the certainty of its position and a deliberate exclusion of doubt or uncertainty. This is associated with a refusal, and after a time an inability, to listen to alternative or contrary positions and with the acquisition of a style of rhetoric marked by cliché, repetition, and irrationality. Second is a desire to impose its moral and ideological position on the rest of the community. Within their own boundaries, fundamentalist groups tend to be narrow, rigid, oppressive, and authoritarian, and they may at times veer toward a form of totalitarianism. Third is a culture of bigotry and intolerance that historically has been associated with racial exclusionism, repressive attitudes to women, and an extreme right-wing political position. Although fundamentalism within the Christian tradition has tended to be identified with evangelical movements, there has existed for many years a Catholic fundamentalism that has at times provided support for fascist or reactionary regimes. Like its Protestant equivalent, Catholic fundamentalism is marked by a strongly authoritarian and repressive moral position. The use of violence by fundamentalist groups is common, whether it be the violence of the state (as in Franco's Spain or Salazar's Portugal) or of the lynch mob (as in the history of the Ku Klux Klan and similar religious movements in the "Bible Belt" of the United States). Historically, fundamentalism goes hand in hand with bigotry, intolerance, and violence. It is a pathological form of Christianity that is spiritually and socially extremely dangerous.

One of the facets of fundamentalism (and one that has also affected Christian traditions of a different hue) has been the identification of the Christian tradition with a particular culture. T. S. Eliot, an Anglo-Catholic with marked authoritarian leanings, believed that Christianity was so inseparable from European culture that, if Christianity disappeared, so would the culture. Yet Eliot, in his analysis of a Christian society, curiously—and disastrously—ignored the experience of the holocaust and its roots in the European Christian tradition.[4] One finds the same kind of uncritical attitude to the dominant culture in such recent movements as the Moral Majority, Christian Voice, and other groups in which the "American way of life" is seen as a kind of embodiment of Christian civilization. What is missing in these positions is any sense of conflict between gospel and culture or any sense of the need for repentance or self-scrutiny within a culture.

One could say that one aspect of fundamentalism, its belief in biblical inerrancy, was inseparable from the beginnings of the United States. Had Columbus not believed, on the basis of 2 Esdras 6:42, that the land surface of the earth was equal to seven times the area of the seas and oceans, he might not have believed that he could reach India by the western route! Fundamentalism grew out of the American evangelical and revivalist movements. From its beginnings it was opposed to the theory of evolution, and, though concerned to counteract the influence of heretical adventist groups such as Millennial Dawn (later renamed Jehovah's Witnesses), it held a strong belief in the return of Christ to earth. Most fundamentalists are adventists and believe in the millennial reign of Christ. In the 1920s the movement became closely linked to anticommunism, a linkage that was revived in the 1950s and in some circles continues to this day. It has also been linked with a fierce hostility to the papacy (a hostility that reaches its most destructive and deranged form in Northern Ireland), though newer forms of biblical literalism have involved Roman Catholics under the influence of charismatic renewal. In recent years there has been a massive resurgence of Christian fundamentalism in the Sunbelt region, that stretch of territory that runs from Charleston, Savannah, and Jacksonville to the urban south of California. Much of this new technological fundamentalism, with its electronic church and its massive mailing lists, represents an onslaught on the entire culture of modernity, which emphasizes individual rights, pluralism, toleration of dissent, democracy, and so on. Ironically the rejection of modernity has come from groups who have learned to use the technology and methodology of the modern age to an unparalleled degree.

With the growth of modern communications, especially satellite television, and the influence of American cultural norms on Europe, the new electronic fundamentalism is finding a hold in Britain also. One leading evangelical, Michael Saward, has compared some aspects of its style to the culture of fascism.[5] And there is a good deal of evidence that a new religious fascism is a factor in our current climate.[6] Yet fundamentalism remains a danger to authentic spirituality even when it is not allied to the extreme right politically. In all its forms, fundamentalism represents a narrowing of vision, a closing of doors, a diminishing of human beings, and a backward force in human history.

The Need for Roots

For many people, however, this age is characterized not so much by the pseudocertainty of the fundamentalists or the exciting variety and cultural pluralism of the postmodernists as by a pervasive loss of faith and hope in anything, an emptiness at the heart of our social and cultural life. The narrowness of vision, the reduction of consciousness to the level of technical expertise, has given way in the lives of many people to a culture of despair, a loss of meaning and overall significance, and particularly a loss of belief in the possibility of real social transformation. In part, no doubt, this is linked to the collapse of "grand narratives," of any sense of belonging to a movement or tradition with a clear purpose and goal. And this collapse finds its expression in much writing that adopts the style of lament for a lost age. A book like Allan Bloom's *The Closing of the American Mind* (1987),[7] though it can be justly criticized for simplistic analysis, clearly spoke to the gut feelings of millions of people. There has been a loss of rootedness in a living tradition, and this has led to a sense of spiritual and moral deprivation and loneliness. The "existential emptiness" of which Viktor Frankl spoke many years ago seems now to characterize entire communities and even nations.[8]

Such a state of deprivation and loneliness, often leading to despair and desolation of spirit, cannot be banished by sermons, positive thinking, or effective counseling. It is in fact a perfectly rational response both to widespread confusion and to the barrenness of much cultural life. The disintegration that is born of despair is a necessary part of that turbulence which provides the basis of a shift toward the new. Within the classical mystical tradition, a major part of the work of spiritual direction consists in helping people to move out of their false security to the point of disintegration and entry into the dark night and in guiding them through the subsequent upheaval and turmoil. Yet this is a far cry from the aim and practice of conventional religion, which offers a safe neutrality in the face of chaos and horror. Much of the religion that has flourished in recent years in the "Christian" West is of this neutral type. It offers inner and often corporate security and warmth. It is a religion of comfort and reassurance. It offers no vision, no challenge, no striving toward the new.

Against this background, and in the face of these ominous and dangerous signs, there is an urgent need to recover and renew the tradition that Martin Luther King once called "creative maladjustment" and that I have referred to as "subversive orthodoxy."[9] This is a tradition that seeks to combine fidelity to the past, to the subversive memory of the people of Israel and of Jesus of Nazareth, and openness to the future toward which God is leading us. Any dynamic and growing life needs to engage with the past, for, as evolutionary theory shows, if a break with the past is too radical and lacks continuity, then things fall apart, and coherence and solidarity are threatened. Similarly, in the renewal of spiritual life there must be a mingling of old and new, a recovery of lost traditions, insights, memories, and truths, combined with an openness to the future and a willingness to grasp the vision of the new reality that is just beyond our grasp. This striving for newness, for change that is beyond the limits of present concepts of the possible, is a vital part of any true and vibrant spirituality. This is why Augustine insists that the new humanity must sing a new song.[10]

We are seeking a tradition that is open to the disturbing challenges from which renewal of life can come. Spiritual life stands always in need of interrogation by the Word of God, of self-scrutiny and perpetual *metanoia*. It is a tradition that is never "at ease in Zion" but always restless, always struggling. It is a tradition of pilgrims and sojourners who are never fully at home in this world, never adjusted to the values and norms of any given order, but always seeking to be a community of contradiction and dissent, of scandal and prophetic testimony. It is a rebel tradition, a tradition of faithful and truth-seeking nonconformity, a tradition of sojourners in quest of a better city.

It is a living tradition within which exploration and yearning can be integrated into, and be subjected to the critique of, wider networks of thought and understanding. Faith and spiritual life cannot exist in a vacuum, so our struggle is for a way of faith that will hold together the wisdom of the past and the turmoil of the present as it moves toward an uncertain future. It is a tradition that seeks to offer a middle way between what the Indian philosopher Bhikhu Parekh has termed the polarities of sacred text and moral void.[11] It is a tradition that refuses to accept the choice between the false certainty of the fundamentalists and the emptiness of the relativists. And there is considerable evidence that many are seeking a faith that does not despise reason, that is both faithful to revealed truth and open to the leadings of the Spirit into new paths, a faith that has room for doubt and darkness. Such a living faith can flourish only within a community with a pattern of belief, life, and values. It is within such a community that tradition is preserved and passed on from one generation to another.

Such a tradition of critical and subversive orthodoxy is very different from fundamentalism in either its Catholic or its evangelical forms. Fundamentalism represents a failure or an inability to reinterpret inherited norms and positions, and, because of this, it is at the mercy of powerful interest groups in any given society. The quest for spiritual roots cannot be satisfied by the narrowness of fundamentalism, nor can the quest for a dynamic and living faith be satisfied by its captivity to the past. And yet no renewal that is not in some sense faithful to the past, that has not in some way "returned to source," can hope to sustain those who seek depth and stability as well as vision and hope.

To return to the source is to return to a living stream, not to a stagnant pool. It is to a liberating tradition that we return, not to a source of bondage. And much depends on our motives for return. Are we seeking security, safety, a vantage point from which we can stand above the movements and struggles of our age, stand against the currents and tides? Or are we seeking resources of vision and of hope for our own struggles and movements toward a new humanity? In the last resort it is a question of movement. If we are standing still, determined to stay where we are, we will look to the Scriptures and the tradition for reinforcement of our rigid positions. And undoubtedly we will find enough to reinforce those positions. But the Scriptures are a liberating word, a word of deliverance. They describe, and are rooted in, an exodus tradition, a death and resurrection journey. If they are to convey their liberating power, they must be read by pilgrims on the move. Only the person who is running can read this word (Hab. 2:2), for it is the story of a people in pilgrimage, the story of a journey from slavery to liberation.

It is important that we try to avoid seeing faith in terms of intellectual content ("the faith"), and spirituality in terms of devotional attitudes and feelings. Faith is the way of the spirit, the "spiritual life" is simply the life of faith nourished by the powerful wind (*ruach*, spirit) of grace. These are not two worlds, two levels, but one. If we hold on to the word *spirituality*, it should only be because we recognize that we all stand under the guidance, and often under the devastating judgment, of the divine *ruach*, the wind of God, which is the framework within which faith can blossom and grow. Spirituality is life-giving movement, life driven and energized by God. Spirituality is life in Christ: to be "spiritual" is to be in Christ, to know Christ and the power of his resurrection, sharing his sufferings and death (Phil 3:10). Spirituality is life within the love and continual life-renewing power of God. In the words of Emily Brontë's poem,

> With wide embracing love
> Thy spirit animates eternal years,
> Pervades and broods above,
> Changes, sustains, dissolves, creates and rears.[12]

Spirituality is about life. "We beg you," implored the Eucharistic Prayer of the ancient liturgy of Serapion of Thmuis, "make us truly alive."

I concluded my book *Experiencing God* (1985) with a proposed manifesto for a renewed spirituality.[13] That book was a reflection on the tradition of the Christian past, an attempt to make prayerful and theological sense of the experience of God, using the symbols for that experience that the great Christian teachers used. I want to conclude this book by returning to that manifesto, looking at it as a guide to the future and to the characteristics of spiritual life as we enter the twenty-first century.

Toward a Renewed Spirituality: Reflections on a Manifesto

1. A renewed Christian spirituality will be concerned with the recovery of the vision of God in the contemporary world. It will seek to speak of God and the deep things of the spirit in ways that are meaningful in the present climate. It will seek, humbly and carefully, to take account of the insights presented by Marxism, by depth psychology, and by the secular quest for enriched consciousness, while seeking also to remain faithful to the Christian spiritual tradition.

It may seem obvious, but in the present climate it needs to be emphasized, that there can be no spirituality within a Christian framework of understanding that is not rooted and grounded in God and in the quest for the vision of God. But this quest does not take place within a private esoteric world, cut off from the common life of humankind: it can only occur within the rough-and-tumble, the complexities and ambiguities, the stresses and strains, of contemporary living. There must be a holding together of vision and context. Similarly, though the vision of God is shrouded in mystery, the attempt to speak of it in some way is an important, if limited, part of the Christian tradition. To recognize that all cannot be said is not to say that nothing can be said. The constant struggle to express profound truths in the language of the age is one that must not be abandoned. It involves much more than the mere reassertion of propositions from the past.

When I first wrote the words above, the collapse of "Marxist" societies in Eastern Europe had not occurred; today, for many, Marxism is as dead as God was once thought to be. Yet it would be wrong to confuse the fate of the post-1917 regimes with the total disappearance of Marxism as a body of thought. Though incomplete, it contains insights and approaches that must be appropriated by serious Christians in the approach to the twenty-first century. Christian spirituality must take serious, prayerful, and thoughtful account of Marxism and of the movements in thought and action that have been inspired by Marxist faith and ideology. As Marx himself saw clearly, new history can only be made out of the old.

The encounter between the Christian tradition and schools of psychology, and other approaches to human consciousness, must be an encounter marked by humble learning in the context of critical debate. Of course, Christians can learn much from these recently developed disciplines. Yet the various schools of psychiatry, psychotherapy, and counseling are all less than a hundred years old and need the wisdom of the older currents of reflection. The Christian tradition of spiritual guidance and spiritual discernment has a great deal to give to the newer secular movements. Recent writing on pastoral care has been marked by a sense of the need to recover ancient values and insights and by a discontent with excessive dependence on current secular trends.[14]

2. A renewed Christian spirituality will be rooted in the experience of God in the life of the Jewish people. In the study of the Old Testament, it will bear witness to the revelation of God in the desert to a people of pilgrimage. It will speak of God's holiness and God's justice and will seek holiness and justice in personal and social life.

Christian spirituality is rooted in the spiritual history of Israel, and specifically in the Jewish understanding of God acting in the upheavals of history. Among those upheavals the Exodus from Egypt holds a crucially important place. The Exodus is more than a historical event: it became for Israel an ever-present reality, a paradigm of salvation history. To the individual Jew, the regular celebration of the Passover was an enactment of "what Yahweh did for *me* when *I* came out of Egypt" (Exod. 13:8). Joshua addressed the people of a later generation, reminding them that "your eyes saw what I did to Egypt, and you lived in the wilderness a long time" (Josh. 24:7). The Exodus is the account of a divinely guided journey. In the ancient world, only Virgil's *Aeneid* is in any way comparable to it. Through this journey a fearful and disorganized mob of slaves is molded into a people—the phrase "people of Israel" is first used in the Exodus story. It undermined slavery within the new covenant community, for those who had been liberated from Egypt must never again be enslaved (Lev. 25:39, 42). The events recalled here are events of spiritual and political transformation.

The wilderness experience was to remain central to Israel's faith experience. God is a wilderness God (Jer. 2:6 f.), and it is from the early Sinai revelation that the call "Set my people free" is heard. The Exodus, that great movement of liberation, grew from the encounter with God in the cloud and thick darkness. That which began in mysticism ended in politics: contemplation led to liberation. And any spirituality that is formed by Jewish and Christian understandings must be a spirituality of movement, movement motivated by the encounter with mystery. It will be a spirituality of the liberating journey. In chapter 2, I argued that liberation from oppression is central to the gospel. The spirituality that will service and nurture the Christians of the twenty-first century will be a spirituality that recognizes God's liberating work in human history, in the upheaval and turmoil of nations, communities, and individuals. The spirituality of Exodus is not a spirituality of comfort and security; it calls us out of security into an encounter with God in the wastes of uncertainty and wilderness. Such pilgrimage is of the very stuff of faith.

If the symbol of liberation in the Mosaic tradition is the Exodus, the symbol of equality within the liberated territory is that of the Jubilee. The principle of the Jubilee is that of equitable distribution of the land among the tribes (Lev. 25), and as such it is the "cornerstone of Israel's ethical practice."[15] Behind it lies a more fundamental principle: the land belongs to God. It is part of the redemptive process, part of the covenant. There is no absolute right of ownership of land. Human beings hold the land on lease until the redistribution in the Fiftieth Year. The theme of "release," encompassing both the land and individuals, has its origins in Leviticus 25, the proclamation of liberty in the Jubilee Year. The theme is taken up again in Isaiah 61, a further proclamation of liberty, in which "prisoners" probably means those who are the victims of poverty and economic oppression.[16] The excavations at Qumran in 1956 showed the way in which the Jubilee theme was used in eschatological reflection and imagery, where it becomes a symbol of the restoration of humankind and of nature to their original state of dignity and equality, a new spiritual beginning, and the reversal of material forms of oppression. The Jubilee manifesto in Isaiah 61, including its reference to "the day of vengeance" (Isa. 61:2), was in use by a number of revolutionary leaders around the time of Jesus. As used on the Day of Atonement, this passage launched the Jubilee Year.

Jesus came to fulfill the law and the prophets, and a major aspect of his teaching was his emphasis on "the weightier matters of the law, justice and mercy and faith" (Matt. 23:23). Recent writers on the ministry of Jesus have stressed how central is the theme of Jubilee to his message. In his use of the passage from Isaiah he omits the reference to the day of vengeance, substituting the phrase "to set at liberty those who are oppressed" from Isaiah 58:6 (Luke 4:16–30). Debt was a major problem in Galilee because of Herod's oppressive taxes, and the theme of debt was a recurring one in Jesus' teaching. A spirituality that is faithful to this part of Jewish teaching as reinforced and expanded by Jesus will be a spirituality that places the liberation of the earth and its oppressed and captive peoples at the center of its understanding and discipleship.

Another key feature of the spiritual history of Israel is the prophetic movement. The Hebrew Scriptures are marked by the presence of colorful, solitary, prophetic figures. A good example of the solitary prophet is Amos, who appeared at the Bethel sanctuary and prophesied its destruction. He was ordered away from the seat of power and instructed never again to disturb that sacred place (Amos 7:12–13). Amos was concerned with problems of affluence, exploitation, and profit. The rich owned several houses (3:15) and much expensive furniture (6:4) but sold the righteous for silver and the needy for a pair of shoes and trampled the poor into the dust (2:6–7). Amos condemns those who trample on the poor (5:11) and turn aside the needy (5:12).

These condemnations are repeated elsewhere and are at the heart of prophetic spirituality and action. Thus Jeremiah praises those who do not oppress the alien or shed innocent blood. This is a condition of inhabiting the land (Jer. 7:5–6). Those who are greedy for unjust gain are condemned (6:13). Jeremiah looks for one who does justice and seeks the truth (Jer. 5:1) and condemns the neglect of justice for the fatherless and needy (Jer. 5:28). He warns against false harmony, attacking those who heal the wounds of the people lightly and cry, "Peace! Peace!" when there is no peace (Jer. 6:14). Jeremiah, in common with the prophetic movement as a whole, recognizes that religion can be an escape from God. In his time the religious centers were full (Jer. 4:4; 5:5, 21–23; 8:3, 10), but there seems to have been little interest in God (7:12–16). Yet though he points to the danger of shrines (5:4, 5) and of a clinging to religion (3:14), he still looks back to the past, to the "ancient paths" (Jer. 6:16), the paths of justice and mercy. The prophets appeal beyond the law to justice and mercy. Justice is really central and has been called "the organizing principle of their message."[17] So Amos proclaims, "Let justice roll down like waters, and righteousness like an overflowing stream" (Amos 5:24).

The prophets look forward as well as back, however. They are essentially people of vision: "The words of Amos . . . which he saw" (Amos 1:1, RV). "The prophets," it has been claimed, "are frequently called 'seers,' never 'hearers.' "[18] They are watchers (Hos. 9:8; Jer. 6:17; Ezek. 3:16–21), and any failure to watch is denounced (Isa. 56:10). For without such attention, there can be no vision, thus no prophetic voice. There is too a sense of compulsion. "The Lord God has spoken; who can but prophesy?" (Amos 3:8). The words of the true prophet are like fire (Jer. 5:14). Alongside this sense of the prophetic fire is a recognition of the existence of false prophets whose words are empty and who are the stooges of the powerful. In Jeremiah they are seen as "windbags," people with wind and no word in them, a play on *ruach*, "spirit" or "breath" (Jer. 5:13).

Many years ago the Russian philosopher Nikolay Berdyayev claimed that the entire future of Christianity and the possibility of its renaissance depended on the recovery of the prophetic spirituality of transfiguration.[19] Walter Brueggemann sees the prophetic role as that of a destabilizing presence within society making sure that the prevailing system is not equated with reality and that alternatives are imaginable. He sees the task of prophetic ministry to be one of nurturing, nourishing, and evoking a consciousness and perception alternative to those of the dominant culture.[20]

Prophecy involves an engagement with tradition, and can only arise out of a living tradition. Prophecy cannot be taught, though it is linked with teaching. Hence an important part of the background out of which prophetic voices may rise is an informed and committed community. The very existence of such a corporate commitment can be a significant turning point in the history of any society. The ancient Christian witness that solidarity is a necessary element in the ascent to truth assumes a new importance in our contemporary wasteland. There is an urgent need for communities of resistance and of truthful action. It is only out of such communities that the prophetic voice will be rediscovered.

I have shown earlier that we are in a period marked by the resurgence of anti-Semitism. Such a resurgence cannot be countered by a purely negative reaction but only by a rebuilding of the foundations of that pursuit of justice and mercy, that fidelity to the covenant community, that was at the heart of the ancient faith of Israel. It is of the greatest urgency that Christians recognize and affirm their Jewish origins, and this involves returning to the faith of the Hebrew Scriptures, the faith of Exodus and of Jubilee, the faith of the ancient prophets, the faith that can nourish the prophetic vision for today. As Alan Ecclestone wrote in his study of Christian spirituality in the aftermath of the holocaust,

> Today when the nations lurch in uncertain fashion toward the one world that their many achievements make possible, we must turn to the basic suggestion of Israel's faith with new force. It is the faith of a people for ever marching, a people of tents rather than a temple, a people learning to read God's law in their hearts, a people committed to giving the stranger welcome, facing a new world with a deep trust in God. Our task today is the recovery of what is essentially a Jewish concept of man's destiny.[21]

3. A renewed Christian spirituality will find its center in Jesus Christ, seeing in him the fullness of the Godhead dwelling bodily. It will seek to be faithful to his proclamation of the Kingdom of God. It

will see in Jesus both God incarnate and a human comrade, the divine revealed and the human raised up.

In Christian revelation God is known within the framework of human relationships, and specifically within the framework of the life, death, and resurrection of Jesus. Any faith that is called Christian must take seriously the ministry and teaching of Jesus as well as the claims made about him. Any spirituality that claims the name of Christian therefore must be a spirituality that seeks to follow Jesus. Such a following is known as discipleship, and is inseparable from Jesus' own proclamation of the Kingdom of God.

In 1923 the English priest Percy Widdrington claimed that the recovery of the good news of the Kingdom of God as the heart of the gospel and the "regulative principle of theology" would lead to a reformation in the church that would make the Reformation of the sixteenth century seem a very small event in comparison.[22] Widdrington was making a threefold claim: first, that the Kingdom of God was the heart of the gospel, a claim that is now accepted by virtually all New Testament scholars; second, that its recovery would lead to a new Reformation, that is, a radical theological and cultural shift, involving both division and renewal; and third, that the church's task was not to promote itself but to promote the Kingdom. This third claim is still not widely accepted, and there are signs that we may be entering a period when church membership rather than witness to the Kingdom comes to be central to the church's concern. That would mark a serious break with the teaching of Jesus.

Since Widdrington's day there has been considerable scholarly work on the Kingdom that has confirmed his view that it is at the heart of the New Testament. The truth that we have been delivered from the dominion of darkness into the Kingdom (Col. 1:13) is part of the conviction that Christ is to restore all things—the phrase *ta panta* is repeated six times in Colossians chapter 1. The phrase "Kingdom of God" or "Kingdom of Heaven" occurs 122 times in the Gospels, in ninety of them from the lips of Jesus himself. If one takes away the references to the coming of the Kingdom, there is virtually nothing left of the gospel.

It was one of the strengths of the Social Gospel movement that it did recover the centrality of the Kingdom. These thinkers saw the Kingdom as "a redeemed social order under the reign of the Christ-like

God,"[23] and they were right to do so. Walter Rauschenbusch saw the damaging results of the neglect of this central theme. "When the doctrine of the Kingdom of God shriveled to an underdeveloped and pathetic remnant in Christian thought, this loss was bound to have far reaching consequences."[24] Sadly many of these consequences are still with us. The misuse of the statement by Jesus that his Kingdom was "not of this world" (John 18:36) to mean that it had nothing to do with this world has reinforced a false otherworldliness in spirituality and practice. The statement in Luke 17:20 that the Kingdom is *entos humon* has been wrongly translated "within you," though it clearly means "in the midst of you" or "within your grasp"; the wrong translation has strengthened a wrong kind of interiority and split between the inner life and the outer. Nor is there any basis for the "gradual permeation of society" theology so beloved of liberal Christians. In the Gospels the Kingdom is compared to mustard seed and leaven, and the emphasis is on surprise, on crisis and struggle, on nearness, immediacy, suddenness.

Though the theme of God's transforming work in history is central, the actual phrase "Kingdom of God" is rare in the Hebrew Scriptures. There are, however, nine references to the sphere of Yahweh's rule, and Yahweh is described as King on forty-one occasions. It was from this sense of Yahweh as King that the idea of the Kingdom of God arose. Salvation is seen as the coming of the dominion of the Lord, and the history of the theme is linked with the transformation of this world. In its origin the idea of the Day of the Lord was associated with political upheaval and turmoil. It involved a revelation within history, and a cleansing. It would transform the physical order (Isa. 11:6–9; 65:17; 66:27). The phrase itself *(Malkuth Shamayim)* only occurs in apocalyptic writings like Enoch, the Psalms of Solomon, and the Assumption of Moses, where it is a kind of euphemism for God. Apocalyptic writers portrayed the Kingdom as a transformed creation (1 Enoch 37–71), as the end of the age of corruption and the beginning of incorruption (2 Baruch 74:2). In the language of the Qumran sect it appears that the Kingdom is entirely earthly. It is this language that Jesus picks up and makes into the heart of his message.

For Christians, the Kingdom is a way of symbolizing the whole work of God in Christ, a work of transformation in the midst of the historical order. The Kingdom, as Norman Perrin stressed, is a symbol, not a concept.[25] It is a mystery (Mark 4:11), and it is characteristic of mystery that it absorbs and swallows up its devotees. To be a Christian at all is to be absorbed and swallowed up by the mysterious reality of God's Kingdom. "Biblical spirituality is Kingdom spirituality. To be moved and motivated by the spirituality of Jesus is to be moved and motivated by an all-absorbing concern for the coming of God's Kingdom."[26] In its total and extreme demands, the Kingdom of God is the heart of all Christian discipleship.

One crucial feature of Jesus' teaching is that the Kingdom has come and that it has brought hope for the poor and lowly. This use of "come" in relation to the Kingdom is unique to the Gospels. Elsewhere the "age to come" is in the future. For Jesus, however, there is a sense of the Kingdom as present, and this present reality is to be welcomed by feast and festivity. Unlike the Pharisees, he seems not to have adopted a rigid and detailed moral code, and he seems to have gone out of his way to enjoy "bad company." The theme of the party, the celebration, is basic to his teaching. Indeed, we can see in his style a rejection of both the militaristic and the pietistic traditions in favor of an emphasis on festival. And it was this stress on the present reality of the Kingdom and its message of liberation and joy for the outcast and the dispossessed that made his message so threatening. "Jesus' proclamation of the Kingdom was unacceptable to most of his hearers *not* because they thought it could not happen, but because they feared it might, and that it would bring down judgment on them."[27] The response to the Kingdom was a combination of joy in the present and hope for the future. And it was this fusion of present experience and future hope that gave birth to what we now call eschatology, the vision of God's work in the future .

In the New Testament it is in the Book of Revelation that we find this future vision expressed most powerfully. The whole book is a vision and has, throughout history, been "a tool for those who are discontented with the reality which confronts them."[28] Eschatology was a dominant force in shaping early Christian spirituality, and the belief that Christ would reign on earth for a thousand years was an accepted part of early Christian orthodoxy. Though it was denounced by Archbishop Cranmer in the Forty-two Articles as "Jewish dotage," the millennial hope has provided a focus for Christian visionaries in all ages. However crudely interpreted and distorted, it has represented a form of the belief that Christ's Kingdom was a reality. The proliferation of strange and bizarre forms of millenarianism has been a reaction to the church's failure to take this Kingdom vision with real seriousness, a failure to recognize the truth that, in the struggle for and hope of the Kingdom, we are fellow workers with God, who has already initiated the process in the life, death, and resurrection of Jesus Christ.

The spirituality that will nourish Christians in the future must be a Kingdom spirituality, a spirituality of the fulfillment of God's transforming work in human history. In this spirituality, the figure of Jesus will be central, and there will be a constant attempt to follow his teachings and to enter into his vision.

4. A renewed Christian spirituality will look to the faith of the Apostolic Church as exhibited in the New Testament: the faith in God who brings unity to the human race, and who has wrought salvation and reconciliation through Christ; a God of light and love; a God whose spirit brings freedom; a God who nourishes and builds up the Body of Christ. In the New Testament, as in the Old, it will seek to deepen knowledge of the living and true God.

In the New Testament letters, the work of Christ is described in terms of the breaking down of the walls of division, the establishment of a new creation, a new humanity. Christian spirituality must be deeply involved with the struggle to make this new creation and this new humanity a reality. It is a life of solidarity in Christ, a life of working with Christ toward this new reality. It is a social spirituality, a spirituality of the body.

Paul's teaching about the body is of fundamental importance in understanding the essentially social character of New Testament spirituality. It calls into question the entire notion of "spirituality" as a separate area of Christian activity and reflection.

What is so striking about the New Testament letters is the virtual absence of any real interest in the area of personal devotion or personal spiritual growth. The emphasis rather is on the body, the community, the household of God. It is through incorporation into the body that we become Christians, and through growth in the body that we progress toward the fullness of Christ. The body grows with a growth that is from God (Col. 2:19).

The body, *soma,* is in fact Christ himself, incarnate, crucified, and risen. In him there is a new creation, a new humanity. The language is startling, and there is a real novelty in the Christian use of this word. The theme of the body has been called "the keystone of Pauline theology."[29] Here is no division between material and spiritual, but rather a spiritual materialism, a stress on the physical and the material as the vehicle of the divine. "It is almost impossible to exaggerate the materialism and crudity of Paul's doctrine of the church as literally now the resurrection body of Christ."[30] Christian spirituality, then, is materialistic and corporate. It is materially embodied in a visible community that shares and expresses the life of the resurrection. Apart from this community there is no gospel and no Christianity. "No 'naked' kerygma ever existed."[31] "The visible church is a part of the gospel."[32] This sense of the church as the context and spiritual heart of the Christian life is assumed and constantly stressed in the patristic writings. So John Chrysostom sees the church as the complement of Christ, as does Augustine when he speaks of it as the *totus Christus.*[33]

Perhaps the most important lesson of the early Christian fathers is that spirituality is about communion, about solidarity, and cannot exist apart from that solidarity. Their writings and their emphases can alert us to

> the danger of being too competent in our spirituality, too sure of the geography of the higher realms. We do not know what we are to be, but we believe, as Christians, that it is in the church that we stand the best chance of receiving whatever the final gift will be. The way of life which is shown to us in the church is not nearly as well defined as some alternatives that we might fancy, but we remain on the way, not by knowing exactly what it involves but by remaining in the church in tolerant communion with our fellow Christians, even if they are not as brilliant and mystical as some other people.[34]

5. A renewed Christian spirituality will be a spirituality of the desert. From the desert experience it will cherish and seek to strengthen

the contemplative life of the church. It will seek both solitude and communion as equally important aspects of the life of the spirit.

Today Christians of all traditions are rediscovering the place of the desert in their lives. Christians of the future who seek to follow Christ in the way of the Kingdom will need also to follow Christ in his desert prayer, in his solitude and his attention to God. We will see a new approach to community that will emphasize both solitude and solidarity, recognizing that the inner life of individual persons is necessary if humankind is to become a true communion.

The spirituality of the future must be a contemplative spirituality. It must lay stress on stillness, silence, and attention to God. If this contemplative spirit is missing, religion is bound to become another form of restless activity, an appendage to the life of power, business, and competition. We are in a period when a mutant of spirituality itself, a spirituality of a private and conformist type, is being used by big business for its own purposes. The times are indeed upon us, as Daniel Berrigan predicted years ago, when the pursuit of contemplation is liable to become a subversive activity.[35] Only a contemplative church, a praying church, a church that attends to the skies, to the hidden voice of God in the movements of history, can hope to respond to the deepest needs of humankind in this terrible phase of its history.

Closely related to contemplation is solitude, that deep encounter with the self and with God that is so threatened by the present dominance of technology and by the noise that seeks to enforce superficiality and conformity. Against such demonic distortions of human destiny, only the recovery of solitude can prevail. Solitude is not opposed to solidarity but is its necessary counterpart and complement. There will be no spiritual renewal unless Christian people recognize that their quest for union with God in the ground of their being is a vital part of their discipleship. And such a recognition is of crucial importance in pastoral work, for only those who have discovered themselves in solitude can hope to be of service to others.

6. A renewed Christian spirituality will be a spirituality of cloud and darkness. It will bear witness to the mystery at the heart of God, and to the mystery at the heart of the human encounter with the

divine. It will seek to lead people away from a religion of easy answers into the dark night of faith. It will be a contemplative spirituality.

A spirituality that takes the symbolism of cloud and darkness seriously will be a mystical spirituality—not in the sense that it will be elitist or separate from the common life, reserved for a group of initiates, a refuge from the hurly-burly of life, but mystical in the sense that it will seek to enter into the deep and dark mystery at the heart of God. The Eastern Christians of the early centuries spoke of this spirituality of the cloud as *agnosia*, unknowing, a knowledge beyond conceptual limits. It is this tradition of unknowing that we need to recover and reaffirm. Rejecting the pseudocertainty of the false lights, it will be ready to stay within the cloud, within the darkness and obscurity that is the very stuff of faith.

In an age of false certainties, of rigid fundamentalisms of various kinds, the renewal of mystical theology, rooted in the *agnosia*, the unknowing, of the negative tradition, is of the greatest importance. Only a renewal of the mystical spirit can overcome the gulf between fundamentalism and the emptiness that is pervasive in our culture. The Christian of the future will, as Karl Rahner observed, either be a mystic, or will not be at all.

7. A renewed Christian spirituality will be a spirituality of water and of fire, of cleansing and purifying, of renewal and spiritual warmth. In the symbols of the water of baptism and the fire of the spirit, it will see the call to continual rebirth and the daily challenge of the God whose nature is consuming fire. It will be a charismatic spirituality.

Incorporation into Christ is through the crucial and dramatic act of baptism. All spiritual life originates in the baptismal action. In this event, we died with Christ (Col. 3:3), put off the old nature—a possible reference to the liturgical stripping of the candidate—and put on the new nature (Col. 3:9–ll). Baptism is seen in the New Testament as a burial (Rom. 6:4), a sharing in the resurrection (Col. 2:12), a putting on of Christ himself (Gal. 3:27). The body of the resurrection begins at baptism (1 Cor. 6:17; Gal. 3:27). Baptism "begins the substitution of the solidarity of one body by another."[36] The early fathers develop this symbolism of baptism as a process of death and renewal:

as the head is plunged into the water, says Chrysostom, the old humanity is buried and the new person appears.

The liturgy of baptism is a microcosm of the Christian life. It consists of four actions: the renunciation of the realm of evil; the turning to Christ as the source of light and new life; the immersion in, or pouring of, water; and the anointing with the chrism, the oil of Christ. The renunciation is crucial. It is an act of disaffiliation in which we "drop out of line." Only after this vital act can we turn to Christ and enter into newness of life in him.

Baptism is a radical moment, an act of disengagement and of transformation. Any renewal of spirituality must involve a renewal and reinterpretation of the place and meaning of baptism in the life of the Christian community. It must involve a break with the trivializing and conventionalizing of this mystery that have robbed it of its significance and contributed to the decadence and weakness of Christian life.

However, all Christian life is a manifestation of the grace of baptism, and is not complete unless such a manifestation takes place. Such a manifestation may be accompanied by dramatic signs, and this is often spoken of as a "second blessing" or as the "baptism in the Holy Spirit," though in fact it is the revealing, the surfacing, of grace that is already present. Pentecostal and charismatic movements of renewal are always associated with such manifestations, often in very physical forms—speaking in tongues, healings, prophetic utterances, and so on. It is unwise to place too much emphasis on the specific forms. What is important is that all Christian life is charismatic, graced by the Spirit, and without some manifestation of this grace, no Christian life can flourish and grow. There has to be a point at which the Spirit is ignited. Hence the term *baptism of fire* is applied to the manifestation of the Spirit in dramatic and powerful forms. At such moments individuals become "aflame for Christ."

The water of purification and the fire of sanctifying power are equally vital components of a spirituality that is faithful to the Christian tradition.

8. A renewed Christian spirituality will be rooted in the Word made flesh. It will hold to the truth of God incarnate, and will seek to

find and serve God in the flesh and blood of God's children. It will rejoice in the divine gifts of matter and of sexuality, seeing in the human the gateway to the divine. It will be a materialistic spirituality.

"The Word was made flesh." The incarnation is central both to Christian spiritual life and to Christian social action. Here, in the material crudity of Bethlehem and Calvary, of resurrection and Eucharist, the mystery of God is recognized and worshiped in the life of a human person. The flesh of Christ becomes the path to union with God. For Christians, the incarnation is more than an assertion about God's action in history: it is an assertion that humankind is made in the image of God, that human beings are God-shaped, made for God, open to God, and that it is through the human that we encounter the divine. It is an assertion that the mystery at the heart of God has its corresponding mystery in human personality and human community. Christian spirituality is not antihuman; it reverences the human mystery, approaching people with awe and with an awareness that we are on holy ground. It is a spirituality of compassion and of respect for the sacred as encountered in the flesh of men and women who are made in God's image and share in God's light.

The truth that "the Word was made flesh" and that through the incarnation there has been a "taking of manhood [humanity] into God" is so fundamental to Christian life that there can be no Christianity without it. It is the heart of all Christian mysticism, all Christian action, all Christian theology. Without it everything falls to the ground.

9. A renewed Christian spirituality will be a eucharistic spirituality. At its heart will be the celebration of the Eucharist, the sacrament of Christ's body and blood. It will recognize Christ both in the Eucharist and in those who share his nature. It will seek to manifest the eucharistic life of sharing and equality in the world. It will therefore be a spirituality of the common life, of holy communion.

In the Christian sacrament of the Eucharist, bread and wine are the vehicles of the divine presence. Christian spirituality is sacramental from beginning to end: it sees matter as the vehicle of spirit, and it values the visible signs taken from the material creation—water, bread, wine, oil—the world itself being the primal sacrament. It is through these common material things that we encounter God. All sacramental theology is based on the goodness of matter. But much bad sacramentalism makes the sacraments a world apart from the world of reality. It believes in "the sacraments" without understanding or accepting the sacramental principle, so sacraments become an escape from material reality instead of a means toward its transformation and redemption.

Bad sacramentalism makes a sharp contrast between the Eucharist and worldly bread. Such a distortion is reflected in the sad account of the European missionaries in Africa who deliberately broke and trampled on some ordinary bread in order to contrast it with the consecrated bread of the Eucharist. The Africans were shocked; they understood that according to the sacramental principle ordinary bread and ordinary wine are good, and their use in ritual worship reinforces, rather than negates, that goodness. The Eucharist presupposes the goodness of creation and of the products of human labor. If these are not good, Irenaeus wrote, then it is insulting to offer them to God at the offertory as firstfruits.[37] Because some bread and wine are offered and consecrated, all bread and all wine are potentially vehicles of the divine presence and action.

It is this sacramental principle, the truth that spiritual realities are communicated through common material things, that is basic to the ministry of Jesus. His approach to people was based on the sharing of a meal, and the activity of eating and drinking has a central place in the Gospel accounts. There is, for example, no chapter of Luke's Gospel in which food is not mentioned. It is perhaps only a slight exaggeration to say that "Jesus got himself crucified by the way he ate."[38] These meals with sinners, with the outcast and rejected, along with the postresurrection meals, are an important part of the background to the emergence of the Christian Eucharist.

In the New Testament, according to Norman Perrin, the Eucharist was "a table fellowship which celebrated the present joy and anticipated the future consummation; a table fellowship of such joy and gladness that it survived the crucifixion and provided the focal point for the community life of the earliest Christians, and was the most direct link between that community life and the pre-Easter fellowship of Jesus and his disciples."[39] Since those days this table fellowship of joy has been the living heart of Christian worship, and the spirituality of the future also must place the eucharistic celebration at the center of its life.

The recent recovery of the social significance of the Eucharist and its relationship with justice is of far-reaching significance for the future of Christian spirituality and Christian action. Wolfhart Pannenberg has suggested that this "new eucharistic sensibility . . . may prove to be the most important event in Christian spirituality in our time, of more revolutionary importance than even the liturgical renewal may realize."[40] Of course, this sensibility is not new. Early Christian thinkers saw a close link between the sacrament and the poor. There are two altars, wrote Saint John Chrysostom, the altar of stone, and the altar that is the poor. In the nineteenth century the revival of the centrality of the Eucharist coincided with the growth of the Christian socialist movement. We have seen how, for Stewart Headlam, those who assisted at Holy Communion were bound to be holy communists. And this emphasis was continued throughout the movement of the "sacramental socialists." Thus the Manifesto of the Catholic Crusade (1918) refers to the Eucharist as a foretaste of the world to come by which God is present "under the form of nourishing bread and merry wine, the symbol of the world's resurrection from its dead self and the common life of the World to Come, of the common production and distribution of bread and pleasure in the International Commonwealth of God and of his Righteousness."[41] The Manifesto goes on to stress that the God of the sacrament is an all-pervading God, not an absent God who is brought down into alien matter.

The American theologian Frederick Hastings Smyth, writing in the 1940s and 1950s, brings out the transforming power of the Eucharist. "The political watchword of the New Reformation will be the reaffirmation of Transubstantiation," claimed Smyth, and by this he meant, not a resuscitation of medieval Scholastic philosophy, but a renewal of the transformative power of a eucharistic materialism. Smyth saw that "bread and wine emerge out of a social history . . . [and] form the material basis of the church's sacrifice."[42] The social significance of the eucharistic action was brought out powerfully also in the writing of the Anglican theologian John A. T. Robinson, particularly in his book *On Being the Church in the World*. In a remarkable chapter entitled "Matter, Power and Liturgy," Robinson claimed that "a truer understanding of what liturgy is about and a more complete earthing of our religion in the consecration of bread may in fact point the way through from prayer to politics, from the holy to the common, from the world of spirit to the world of matter." The Eucharist, he goes on, is not just an action, but is *the* Christian action from which all other forms of Christian action flow. It is in fact "the basis for the whole of the church's social action."[43]

The whole idea of Holy Communion is about the unity of holy and common. The distinction between holy and common, sacred and secular, may remain in the world outside eucharistic relations, but within the Eucharist these distinctions are abolished. Robinson was a pioneer of the use of kitchen tables for the celebration of the Eucharist and promoted the house church movement of the early 1960s. He saw the way in which the Eucharist was a microcosm of all Christian action and of human society. "Just as this eucharistic action is the pattern of all Christian action, the sharing of this bread the sign for the sharing of all bread, so this fellowship is the germ of all society renewed in Christ."[44]

The Eucharist is an anticipation of a renewed society. This is an aspect that is particularly emphasized in Eastern Orthodox thought, where the liturgy is seen as "the firstfruits of the sanctification of all creation" and as "one transforming act and one ascending movement."[45] As one Western theologian has expressed it,

> The eucharistic rite, which is the source and center of the church's life, is both a symbol and a foretaste of the gathering of the human race into Christ and the transformation of the material world in him. The conversion of the bread and wine into the body and blood of Christ is the symbol and the foretaste of the transformation of the material world; the feeding of Christ's body the church with the eucharistic gifts is the symbol and the foretaste of the gathering of the human race into Christ, for in communion, as Saint Augustine says, we *are* what we *receive*.[46]

10. A renewed Christian spirituality will be a spirituality of pain, seeing in the passion and death of Jesus the heart of the gospel. It will preach Christ crucified and will seek to follow the way of the cross.

Christian faith is faith in Christ crucified. It is faith in the God who took upon himself human pain and suffering. "We preach Christ crucified" is at the heart of the Christian proclamation. There can be no Christian spirituality that does not place the cross at its very center. If it is not central, then spiritual life is in danger of being split off from the gospel itself. The cross is more than a message; it is also a way of life, it is a state of solidarity with Christ in his dying and rising. This is the inner reality of baptism and of priesthood. For Christians do not only hear the word of the cross: they enter into it, are baptized into it. "I have been crucified with Christ; it is no longer I who live, but Christ who lives in me" (Gal. 2:20). There is, in the very process of becoming a Christian, an incorporation into Christ crucified. Paul speaks of carrying the marks of Jesus in his body (Gal. 6:17) and of being conformed to Jesus in his death (Phil. 3:10). The spirituality of the cross is therefore not adequately expressed in terms either of hearing the word or of "the imitation of Christ" but rather in terms of incorporation, of solidarity, of a new creation brought about through Christ's dying and rising.

In the cross Christ is set forth as our victim who is also our hope, as the accursed one in whom we find our liberation, as the murdered one who is the source of new life. There is victory, conquest, glory, at the heart of the church's liturgy of the passion. The spirituality of the future must recover this sense of victory and glory if Christ is to be proclaimed as conqueror of sin and death.

It is essential that such solidarity with the cross is distinguished from mere acquiescence and passive endurance in the face of suffering, and from the kind of masochism that often masquerades as devotion. A major task for Christians in the future will be to recover the theme of the cross as strength, as nourishment, as source of power and life. The history of cross-centered devotion among slaves is living proof that such devotion can act other than as a reinforcement of oppression. In Latin America today the celebration of the Stations of the Cross has come to be a powerful element in intensifying social awareness, so much so that in several places its practice has been banned.

A spirituality of the cross and passion will be a spirituality that stays close to the weak and powerless, to those who, like Jesus, are marginalized and pushed outside the gate. For, as Rosemary Ruether has written, "A church that opts for the poor is one that must learn anew what it means to be baptized into the death and resurrection of Christ. For this church, the cross has ceased to be a golden and jeweled decoration on a church wall, and has become the living reality that Christians bear in their bodies."[47] The message of the cross shows us that God is never identified with the oppressor, always with the victim. A church identified with the Crucified will be a church that stands in critical distance from its dominant culture, seeing that God is revealed not at the heart of power but on its edge.

In any Christian spirituality based on the cross there is an inescapable dimension of folly. The cross, according to Paul, is the expression of the foolishness of God, and it is only those who become fools for Christ who can enter into its absurd meaning. We need therefore to create a climate in which folly and recklessness can flourish. A spirituality rooted in the cross cannot be sustained by worldly rationality, but demands a process of reversal, of *metanoia*.

Christian spirituality is a sharing in the Paschal mystery, it is a spirituality of alleluia. The mystery into which the Christian community is drawn at the Paschal feast is a mystery of dying and rising that cannot be divided. To isolate the cross from the resurrection is to distort the meaning of the mystery. Only through dying and descending into the place of the dead can we share the resurrection glory. The chant of the Orthodox liturgy of Easter must become our own continual cry of triumph: "Christ is risen from the dead, trampling down death by death, and upon those in the tombs bestowing life."

11. A renewed Christian spirituality will learn from the mystical writers to see God as the ground of all reality and of our own beings. It will seek to recover and promote a true Christian mysticism as an integral element in Christian theology. It will seek to discover and promote the ministry of spiritual guidance and deepening of the inner life and to hold together the mystical and political dimensions of the life of faith.

The spirituality of the future must encounter the depths, the inner life of which the mystics speak, and lead individuals into those depths. It will not be content with superficial notions of growth, but will seek to grow downward, inward, to grow in depth and in inner wisdom and love. In this insistence it will find itself in constant conflict with managerial and statistical notions of "church growth" that have uncritically accepted current secular models. In contrast to such notions, it will maintain its commitment to growth in spiritual depth, growth in holiness, and will see such growth as an integral part of the corporate and active life of Christian discipleship.

Such a commitment will have important consequences for the renewal of theological life. For the theology of the future must be a mystical theology. It is vital that we work to end the gulf between academia and the life of prayer, between head and heart, between "rational" discourse and devotional life, and restore theological discipline to its essential context of contemplation and worship. In the same way the spirituality of the future must be one that unites mystical and political dimensions of faith and overcomes the false cleavage that has grown up between them.

The place of spiritual direction or guidance will become more important as these struggles proceed, yet at the same time this discipline will become more and more open to distortion, misuse, and trivialization. Already many charlatans and bogus specialists have begun to exploit the spiritual hunger of the times. Discernment of true from false mysticism, true from false spirituality, will be a vital task for the Christian communities of the future. As in other ages, many false spirits and false teachers will arise, and there will be a flowering of Gnostic and other distortions of spiritual life.

12. A renewed Christian spirituality will take seriously the experience of God in women's history: the feminine namings of God in Scripture and tradition and the forgotten or neglected insights of writers who have experienced and described God in a feminine way. It will seek to listen to, and learn from, the critique of Christian tradition offered by the contemporary women's movement.

The question of the place of women and of women's experience in the Christian tradition and community may well be the issue that determines the future of the movement as a viable community of human fulfillment. Many women feel marginalized and made invisible within the mainstream churches, and male hierarchies' lack of sensitivity to this has become both a scandal and a serious disorder. Whether the gulf can be bridged within the framework of orthodoxy is by no means clear. As positions become more polarized and inflexible, increasing numbers of women are concluding that Christianity is irredeemable and incapable of reform. That debate will not be resolved quickly. Certainly no Christian spirituality can claim to be socially responsible that ignores or fails to take seriously the contribution of the women's movement in its struggles and its thinking.

A major contribution of the women's movement, and of feminist reflection on the concrete experiences within that movement, has been the emphasis on the nature of power and domination and the way in which experience is distorted and diminished by the operation of unjust power relations. Christian spirituality fails in integrity if it evades these questions of power and domination, but much of the time it seeks to do so. If it serves merely to reinforce the status quo, thoughtful women and men whose concern is to seek justice and correct oppression will cease to find in such spirituality any resource for their struggles.

13. A renewed Christian spirituality will be a spirituality of justice and of peace. It will seek to know and follow God in the pursuit of justice for all people, in the struggle against racism and other forms of domination, in the movement for world peace and for nuclear disarmament, and in the campaign against poverty and inequality. In the struggles for a more human world, a renewed spirituality will come to discern the face of God, the holy and just One, and to share the peace of God which passes all understanding.

The whole purpose of this book has been to make this point— yet more than to make a point. Certainly we need to realize that the storm in which we find ourselves is the result both of spiritual hunger and of social injustice. As Martin Luther King said so prophetically, "The storm is rising against the privileged minority of the earth, from which there is no shelter in isolation and armament. The storm will not abate until a just distribution of the fruits of the earth enables man everywhere to live in dignity and human decency."[48] We are seeking a spirituality for that struggle.

If the Christian community of the future is to develop spiritual resources for that struggle, resources that will strengthen and guide those who work for justice and peace in their communities and in the world, it will need to shed much of its inherited and accumulated baggage and learn to see itself as a community of pilgrims, a community on the move. There is nothing quite like the experience of walking to promote comradeship. The church is meant to be a people on the march, moving forward in solidarity, a pilgrim people. Sadly it often becomes a static, backward-looking people. The church of the future has to choose between a settler mentality and a pioneer mentality.[49] To stand still in the spiritual life is to go backward. The pilgrim community is oriented toward the future, a community marked and motivated by a divinely inspired restlessness. As the Jewish Passover was to be eaten in haste by people ready to move on, so the pilgrim community must always be moving forward. Lot's wife looked backward and became one of God's frozen people.

Our spiritual pilgrimage is not within an artificial religious world, but within the real world in which coal is mined and lemon meringue pie is made, the world in which companies are taken over and homeless people die in the streets, the world in which wars are declared and millions long for peace and for justice. Many Christians have been encouraged by a distorted spirituality to see this world as no more than a "vale of tears and woe." But the gospel calls us to proclaim that God loves the world, and that salvation is about its transformation. We need, therefore, in the future more worldly Christians, Christians who will renounce the false values of "the world" in the biblical sense of the fallen world order but who will love and cherish the world in the sense of the material creation, the work of God and the sphere of his redeeming activity.

The pilgrim community will often travel in the dark. One of the most serious accusations leveled against religious people is that they think they have God taped. They are too cocksure, they have all the answers. We need, as a pilgrim community, to accept that we do not have all the answers, that we will often be marching into the darkness and will be puzzled and confused as to the direction we should take. A pilgrim community will often travel in half-light, in uncertainty and bewilderment. We need to be at home in this night of faith if we are to progress.

The pilgrim community of the future, like its predecessors, will be confronted by monsters, by forces of evil and oppression. Confronted by such monsters, we will need all of our spiritual resources. This is not the time for spiritual striptease; we will need more adequate resources and a richer and deeper interior life. For we are called to a spirituality of combat. It is no accident that the march is often a symbol of protest. The Christian pilgrimage is a march against oppression, a march from the oppressive realm of Babylon to the new Jerusalem, the home of peace and justice. There is no way to escape this conflict with the forces of evil within the fallen world order.

The pilgrim community will often be limping and wounded. Jacob wrestled with God all night, and at the end of the night he still did not know the name of God. He emerged from that struggle wounded. Jesus showed his wounds to his disciples; Paul spoke of carrying those wounds in his body. A pilgrim church is a church of the wounded. The best pastors, the best spiritual guides, are those who have experienced wounding, pain, dereliction, and suffering. As we are healed by Christ's wounds, so will others be healed by our wounds—or rather, by our sharing in the wounds of Christ. We are called to be wounded healers.

A community of pilgrims needs to abandon clutter and to recover fundamentals. It needs to be set free from the obsession with trivia, to discriminate between things that abide and passing fashions and fads. The sacraments of the pilgrim church deal with basic things—bread, water, oil, the clasp of our sister's and our brother's hand. They are the food, provisions, and resources for a people on the move.

A community of pilgrims who are rooted and grounded in Christ's resurrection will be characterized by joy—not the bogus cheeriness of the hearty, jolly, back-slapping Christians, but the deep joy of those who have attained an inner assurance, a confidence and trust in the power of the risen Christ. A pilgrim church must be a joyful, confident church, which sings the songs of freedom in the midst of its bondage. "Sing Alleluia and keep on walking," says Augustine in one of his most memorable sermons.[50] As we move into the heart of the storm we will sing, but we will keep on walking.

NOTES

Chapter 1. The Soul and the Social Order

Chapter epigraphs: Jeremy Seabrook, *New Society*, 28 February 1980, p. 440.

From a Hasidic tale cited in Joan Chittister, *Women, Ministry and the Church* (New York: Paulist Press, 1983), p. 8.

Matthew Fox, *On Becoming a Musical Mystical Bear* (New York: Paulist Press, 1976), pp. xi, xii.

Editor's Note: All spelling in quotations has been Americanized.

1. G. A. Studdert Kennedy, in *Report of the Anglo-Catholic Congress* (London: Society of SS Peter and Paul, 1923).

2. Langdon Gilkey, *Society and the Sacred* (New York: Crossroad, 1981), p. 42. Cf. also his "The Political Dimensions of Theology," in *The Challenge of Liberation Theology: A First World Response*, ed. Brian Mahan and L. Dale Richesin (Maryknoll, NY: Orbis, 1981), pp. 113–26.

3. William Stringfellow, *The Politics of Spirituality* (Philadelphia: Westminster Press, 1984), p. 19.

4. Grace Jantzen, "Spirituality and the Status Quo," *King's Theological Review* 13:1 (Spring 1990), pp. 6–10.

5. Margaret R. Miles, *The Image and Practice of Holiness* (London: SCM Press, 1988).

6. Dick Westley, *Redemptive Intimacy: A New Perspective for the Journey to Adult Faith* (Mystic, CT: Twenty-third Publications, 1981), p. 103.

7. Thomas Merton, *Disputed Questions* (New York: Farrar, Straus and Cudahy, 1960), p. x.

8. For the lengthy debate on religion and capitalism, see R. H. Tawney, *Religion and the Rise of Capitalism* (London: John Murray, 1926); V. A. Demant, *Religion and the Decline of Capitalism* (London: Faber and Faber, 1952); R. H. Preston, *Religion and the Persistence of Capitalism* (London: SCM Press, 1979; Philadelphia: Trinity Press International, 1979). As I write, an international conference is taking place in Lancaster, England, "Religion and the Resurgence of Capitalism." For a useful short account

of the debate, see Christopher Hill, "Protestantism and the Rise of Capitalism," in his *Change and Continuity in Seventeenth-Century England* (London: Weidenfeld and Nicolson, 1974), pp. 81–102.

9. A. M. Ramsey, *The Gospel and the Catholic Church* (London: Longmans, 1956; Boston: Cowley, 1990), p. 38.

10. John D. Zizioulas, in *Christian Spirituality: Origins to the Twelfth Century*, ed. B. McGinn and J. Meyendorff, *World Spirituality*, vol. 16 (London: Routledge and Kegan Paul, 1986), p. 27.

11. Maurice B. Reckitt, *Religion and Social Purpose* (London: SPCK, 1935), p. 12.

12. Simon Tugwell, *Ways of Imperfection* (London: Darton, Longman and Todd, 1984; Springfield, IL: Templegate, 1985), pp. 8–9.

13. Aldous Huxley, *Grey Eminence: A Study in Religion and Politics* (New York: Harper & Row, 1941), pp. 103–4.

14. Aldous Huxley, *Heaven and Hell* (Harmondsworth: Penguin, 1956), p. 63.

15. Thomas Merton, "Is Mysticism Normal?" *Commonweal* 51 (1949–50), p. 98. Cf. Merton's *What Is Contemplation?* (London: Burns Oates, 1950), p. 6.

16. For the developments in the Haight-Ashbury, see Kenneth Leech, "The Natural History of Two Drug Cultures," *New Society*, 1 June 1972, pp. 464–66, and *Youthquake: Spirituality and the Growth of a Counter-culture* (London: Abacus, 1976), pp. 37–49.

17. Peter Parish, in *Drugs and Society* 7:1 (April 1972), p. 12. See also Peter Parish, "The Prescribing of Psychotropic Drugs in General Practice," *Journal of the Royal College of General Practitioners*, vol. 21, supp. 4 (1971).

18. Theodore Roszak, *The Making of a Counter Culture* (London: Faber and Faber, 1971), p. 177.

19. See R. A. Sandison, A. M. Spencer, and J. D. A. Whitlaw, *Journal of Mental Science* 100 (1954) p. 498.

20. Baba Ram Dass [Richard Alpert], *Doing Your Own Being* (1973), p. 33.

21. See Kenneth Leech, *Youthquake*.

22. R. D. Laing, *The Politics of Experience and the Bird of Paradise* (Harmondsworth: Penguin, 1971), p. 118.

23. These issues are discussed in many of Laing's books and papers. One little known essay that is particularly interesting for his perspective on spirituality is his "Religious Experience and the Role of Organised Religion," in *The Role of Religion in Mental Health* (London: National Association for Mental Health, 1967), pp. 51–58.

24. Theodore Roszak, *Where the Wasteland Ends* (London: Faber and Faber, 1972; New York: Doubleday, 1973), p. xxii.

25. Marshall McLuhan, discussion with Malcolm Muggeridge and Norman Mailer, *The Realist*, October 1968.

26. V. E. Frankl, *The Doctor and the Soul* (Harmondsworth: Penguin 1973), p. 9.

27. E. F. Schumacher, *Small Is Beautiful* (London: Blond and Briggs, 1974), p. 250.

28. Charles Reich, *The Greening of America* (New York: Random House, 1971), pp. 395, 4.

29. Jacob Needleman, *The New Religions* (Allen Lane, London: Penguin Press, 1972; New York: Crossroad, 1984), p. xii.

30. Laurie Taylor, *New Society*, 4 October 1973.

31. Christopher Lasch, *The Culture of Narcissism* (New York: W. W. Norton, 1978), p. 5.

32. Reich, *The Greening of America*, p. 395.

33. For a discussion of Roszak's thought, see Philip J. Mueller, "Theodore Roszak's Social Criticism," *Eglise et Theologie* 5 (1974), pp. 375–94.

34. Roszak, *The Making of a Counter Culture*, p. 67. For the later development of his thinking in this area, see his *Person/Planet: The Creative Disintegration of Industrial Society* (London: Granada, 1981).

35. *Comment éviter le Purgatoire*, cited in Gustavo Gutierrez, *We Drink from Our Own Wells: The Spiritual Journey of a People* (London: SCM Press, 1984; Maryknoll, NY: Orbis, 1984), p. 142.

36. Viv Broughton, in *Seeds of Liberation: Spiritual Dimensions to Political Struggle*, ed. Alistair Kee (London, SCM Press, 1973), p. vii.

37. Kee, in *Seeds of Liberation*, p. 3.

38. Christopher Lasch, "Narcissist America," *New York Review of Books*, 30 September 1976, p. 8.

39. Kaiser Wilhelm II, letter of 1896, cited in James Bentley, *Between Marx and Christ: The Dialogue in German-speaking Europe 1870–1970* (London: Verso, 1982), p. 28.

40. Canon R. O. Hutchinson, letter, *Church Times*, 21 January 1910.

41. Charles Gore, *The Body of Christ* (London: John Murray, 1901), p. 36.

42. Bishop of Kensington (UK), cited in *Sunday Telegraph*, 15 November 1987.

43. Richard N. Ostling, "Opting for the Browning Version: The Episcopal Church Picks an Activist Liberal as Its Leader," *Time*, 23 September 1985.

44. Jim Wallis, ed., *The Rise of Christian Conscience* (San Francisco: Harper & Row, 1987), p. 15.

45. See Melvyn Matthews, "The Director's Dilemma," *The Tablet*, 9 September 1989, p. 1024.

46. Thomas Merton, cited in James Finley, *Merton's Palace of Nowhere* (Notre Dame, IN: Ave Maria Press, 1978), p. 104.

47. Richard Woods, "Spiritual Growth, Social Action, One," *National Catholic Reporter*, 5 November 1982, p. 7.

48. Karl Rahner, *The Practice of Faith: A Handbook of Contemporary Spirituality* (London: SCM Press, 1985), p. 22.

49. Paul Tillich, *Systematic Theology*, 3 vols. (Chicago: Univ. of Chicago Press, 1951–63). For a study of Tillich's approach to this area, see Sebastian Painadath, *Dynamics of Prayer: Towards a Theology of Prayer in the Light of Paul Tillich's Theology of the Spirit* (Bangalore: Asian Trading Corporation, 1980).

50. J. L. Houlden, *Connections: The Integration of Theology and Faith* (London: SCM Press, 1986; Philadelphia: Trinity Press International, 1986), pp. 21–37.

51. The Amanecida Collective, *Revolutionary Forgiveness: Feminist Reflections on Nicaragua* (Maryknoll, NY: Orbis, 1987), p. 129.

52. For liberal Protestantism and notions of progress, see Robert Handy, ed., *The Social Gospel in America* (New York: Oxford Univ. Press, 1966); Charles Hopkins, *The Rise of the Social Gospel in American Protestantism* (New Haven, CT: Yale Univ. Press, 1940); David Nicholls, *Deity and Domination*, vol. 1 (London: Routledge, 1989).

53. Walter Rauschenbusch, *Christianity and the Social Crisis* (New York: Harper & Row, 1972), p. 29.

54. See Hopkins, *The Rise of the Social Gospel*, p. 235. For a recent assessment of Rauschenbusch, see Gary J. Dorrien, *Reconstructing the Common Good* (Maryknoll, NY: Orbis, 1990), chapter 2: "Walter Rauschenbusch and the Legacy of the Social Gospel," pp. 16–47.

55. Rauschenbusch, *Christianity and the Social Crisis* (New York: Macmillan, 1907), p. xxii.

56. Rauschenbusch, *Christianising the Social Order* (New York: Macmillan, 1912), pp. 147–48.

57. Washington Gladden, *The Nation and the Kingdom* (Boston: American Board of Commissioners for Foreign Missions, 1909), p. 4.

58. Rauschenbusch, *A Theology for the Social Gospel* (New York: Abingdon Press, 1917), p. 1.

59. Rauschenbusch, *Christianising the Social Order*, pp. 93–94.

60. Rauschenbusch, cited in *New Theology* 6, ed. Martin E. Marty and D. Peerman (New York: Macmillan, 1969), p. 87.

61. Washington Gladden, *The Christian Way*, in *An Anthology of Devotional Literature*, ed. Thomas Kepler (Grand Rapids: Baker Book House, 1947), pp. 577–78.

62. Rauschenbusch insisted that Jesus was not "a social reformer of the modern type," *Christianity and the Social Crisis* (New York: Macmillan, 1907), pp. 47, 160. See also *Walter Rauschenbusch: Selected Writings*, ed. Winthrop Hudson (New York: Paulist, 1984).

63. F. W. Bushell, *Christian Theology and Social Progress* (1907), p. 331.

64. A. M. Ramsey, "Faith and Society," *Church Quarterly Review* (1955), pp. 360–66.

65. Stanley G. Evans, ed., *Return to Reality* (London: Zeno, 1954), pp. 9–33.

66. Lord Soper, House of Lords, 28 October 1965, col. 702.

67. See John Milbank, *Nuclear Realism and Christian Reality: The Poverty of Niebuhrianism* (London: Jubilee Group, 1986).

68. Reinhold Niebuhr, *Moral Man and Immoral Society* (New York: Charles Scribners Sons, 1932), p. 81.

69. Reinhold Niebuhr, *Reflections on the End of an Era* (New York: Charles Scribners Sons, 1934), pp. ix–x.

70. On Barth, see James Bentley, "The Socialism of Karl Barth," in his *Between Marx and Christ* (see note 39), pp. 60–78; and George Hunsinger, ed., *Karl Barth and Radical Politics* (Philadelphia: Westminster Press, 1976).

71. Karl Barth, cited in John Deschner, "Karl Barth as Political Activist," *Union Seminary Quarterly Review* 28 (Fall 1972), p. 55.

72. David Marquardt, in Hunsinger, *Karl Barth and Radical Politics*, p. 59.

73. Karl Barth, *The Word of God and the Word of Man* (New York: Harper & Row, 1957), p. 295.

74. Karl Barth, *Church Dogmatics*, vol. 1, part 1 (Edinburgh: T. and T. Clark, 1957), p. 386.

75. See Niebuhr's comments in *Christian Century*, 11 February 1959, pp. 167–68, and 11 May 1960, p. 579. But in the issue of 31 December 1969 he retracted much of his critique of Barth.

76. Paul Tillich, "What Is Wrong with Dialectical Theology?" *Journal of Religion* 15 (April 1935), p. 135.

77. Reinhold Niebuhr, *Christianity and Power Politics* (New York: 1940), p. 58.

78. See Charles Villa-Vicenzio, ed., *On Reading Karl Barth in South Africa* (Grand Rapids: Eerdmans, 1988).

79. H. Richard Niebuhr, *The Kingdom of God in America* (New York: Harper Torchbooks, 1959), p. 193.

80. A. H. Halsey, *Annals of European Sociology* 23 (1982), p. 160.

81. Alasdair MacIntyre, *Whose Justice? Which Rationality?* (Notre Dame, IN: Univ. of Notre Dame Press, 1988; London: Duckworth, 1988), p. 367.

82. *The Poetical Works of John and Charles Wesley*, vol. 1 (London: Wesleyan Methodist Conference Office, 1868), p. xxii. Cf. *The Works of John Wesley*, vol. 5 (Grand Rapids: Zondervan, 1958), p. 296. On the Wesleyan social tradition in dialogue with current movements, see Theodore Runyon, ed., *Sanctification and Liberation* (Nashville: Abingdon Press, 1981).

83. M. P. Hornsby-Smith and Raymond M. Lee, *Roman Catholic Opinion: A Study of Roman Catholics in England and Wales in the 1970s*, First Report, Dept. of Sociology, Univ. of Surrey, 1979.

84. Wallis, *The Rise of Christian Conscience* (see note 44), p. xxvi.

85. Jeff Dietrich in *Sojourners*, January 1988, p. 10.

86. Philip Sheldrake, *Images of Holiness* (London: Darton, Longman and Todd, 1987; Notre Dame, IN: Ave Maria, 1988), p. 5.

87. John A. Coleman, "Is There a Catholic Moment in American Culture?" *Listening* 25:1 (Winter 1990), pp. 9–26.

88. See Michael J. Schultheir, Edward P. De Berri, and Peter J. Henriot, *Our Best Kept Secret: The Rich Heritage of Catholic Social Teaching* (London: CAFOD, 1988).

89. Richard P. McBrien, in *American Catholics*, ed. Joseph F. Kelly (Wilmington, DE: Michael Glazier, 1989), p. 10.

90. See Galilea's article "Liberation as an Encounter with Politics and Contemplation," in *The Mystical and Political Dimensions of the Christian Faith*, ed. C. Geffre and G. Gutierrez (New York: Concilium, 1974). I have also drawn on notes from a seminar in which I took part with Galilea at Saint Stephen's House in Chicago on 27 April 1982.

91. J. P. Miranda, *Communism in the Bible* (London: SCM Press, 1981; Maryknoll, NY: Orbis, 1982), p. 4; U.S. edition trans. by Robert Barr.

92. J. H. Cone, *Speaking the Truth* (Grand Rapids; Eerdmans, 1986), p. 37.

93. Cornel West, *Prophesy Deliverance! An Afro-American Revolutionary Christianity* (Philadelphia: Westminster Press, 1982), p. 15.

94. See James S. Tinney, "Black Origins of the Pentecostal Movement," *Christianity Today*, 8 October 1971, pp. 4–6; Ian MacRobert, *The Black Roots and White Racism of Early Pentecostalism in the USA* (London: Macmillan, 1988; New York: St. Martin, 1988).

95. See David O. Moberg, *The Great Reversal* (Philadelphia: Lippincott, 1972; London: Scripture Union, 1972). The term was originally used in 1957 by Timothy L. Smith, *Revivalism and Social Reform*. Reprint. (Baltimore: Johns Hopkins Univ. Press, 1982).

96. Paul Henry, *Politics for Evangelicals* (Valley Forge, PA: Judson Press, 1974), p. 29.

97. Richard Lovelace, *Dynamics of Spiritual Life* (Downers Grove, IL: Inter Varsity Press, 1979), p. 392.

98. Ronald J. Sider, ed., *The Chicago Declaration* (Carol Stream, IL: Creation House, 1974); "Social Transformation: The Church in Response to Human Need: Wheaton '83 Statement," *Transformation* 1:1 (January–March 1984), pp. 23–26; Rene Padilla and Chris Sugden, *How Evangelicals Endorsed Social Responsibility: Texts on Evangelical Ethics 1974–83* (Nottingham: Grove Booklets on Ethics 59, 1985).

99. Stephen C. Mott, *Biblical Ethics and Social Change* (London: Oxford Univ. Press, 1982), p. 20.

100. Robert M. Price, "A Fundamentalist Social Gospel?" *Christian Century*, 28 November 1979.

101. Robert Booth Fowler, *Unconventional Partners: Religion and Liberal Culture in the United States* (Grand Rapids: Eerdmans, 1989), p. 130.

102. Jim Wallis, *Agenda for Biblical People* (San Francisco: Harper & Row, 1976), pp. 6, 10, 12. Cited hereafter as *Agenda*.

103. *Sojourners*, May 1986, p. 22.

104. *The Post American*, June–July 1974, p. 3.

105. Wallis, *Agenda*, p. 61.

106. John Howard Yoder, *The Politics of Jesus* (Grand Rapids: Eerdmans, 1972), p. 157.

107. Stanley Hauerwas, *A Community of Character* (Notre Dame, IN: Univ. of Notre Dame Press, 1981), p. 6. See also his *Vision and Virtue* (Notre Dame, IN: Fides, 1974); and *The Peaceable Kingdom* (South Bend, IN: Univ. of Notre Dame Press, 1983).

108. Enoch Powell, *Wrestling with the Angel* (London: Sheldon Press, 1977), p. 28.

109. A. M. Ramsey, *From Gore to Temple* (London: Longmans, 1960).

110. See W. G. Peck, *The Social Implications of the Oxford Movement* (New York, 1933); and P. E. T. Widdrington, *The Social Teaching of the Oxford Movement*, Anglo-Catholic Congress Books, no. 5 (London: Catholic Literature Association, 1925).

111. W. G. Ward, *The Ideal of a Christian Church* (London: John Tovey, 1844; New York: AMS Press, n.d.), p. 50.

112. Valerie Pitt, in *Essays Catholic and Radical*, ed. Kenneth Leech and Rowan Williams (London: Bowerdean Press, 1983), p. 210.

113. Henry Scott Holland, *Sacramental Values* (1917), p. 143.

114. Robert Dolling, *Ten Years in a Portsmouth Slum* (1896), p. 198.

115. There are many studies of Maurice. Useful ones include Torben Christensen, *The Divine Order: A Study in F. D. Maurice's Theology*, Acta Theologica Danica, vol. 11 (Leiden: E. J. Brill, 1973), and *Origin and History of Christian Socialism 1848–54* (Aarhus: Universitetsforlaget, 1962); A. M. Ramsey, *F. D. Maurice and the Conflicts of Modern Theology* (Cambridge: Cambridge Univ. Press, 1951); M. B. Reckitt, *Faith and Society* (London: Longmans, 1932).

116. B. F. Westcott, *Socialism*, paper read at the Church Congress in Hull, October 1890. Published by the Guild of Saint Matthew, 1890. Conrad Noel called this paper "perhaps the finest exposition of the philosophic basis of socialism as contrasted with individualism," *The Optimist*, July 1908.

117. See David Nicholls, "William Temple and the Welfare State," *Crucible*, October–December 1984.

118. William Temple, *Christianity and Social Order* (Harmondsworth: Penguin, 1942), p. 7.

119. William Temple, *Nature, Man and God* (London: Macmillan, 1934), p. 478.

120. On Headlam, see Peter d'A. Jones, *The Christian Socialist Revival 1877–1941* (Princeton, NJ: Princeton Univ. Press, 1968); Kenneth Leech, in *For Christ and the People*, ed. M. B. Reckitt (London: SPCK, 1968), pp. 61–88. But the most detailed study of Headlam is John R.

Orens, "The Mass, the Masses and the Music Hall: Stewart Headlam's Radical Anglicanism" (Ph.D. diss., Columbia University, 1972). A small pamphlet by Orens with the same title is available from the Jubilee Group, 48 Northampton Road, Croydon CRO 7HT, UK, price 50p.

121. S. D. Headlam, in *The Optimist* 11:1 (15 April 1916), p. 49.

122. The term *social God* appeared in J. R. Illingworth, *Personality Human and Divine* (1894), pp. 75, 192. It was used by Noel in *The Manifesto of the Catholic Crusade* and in most of his writings. For later use, see Stanley G. Evans, *The Social Hope of the Christian Church* (London: Hodder and Stoughton, 1965), chap. 10, "The Social God," pp. 245–56; and Kenneth Leech, *The Social God* (London: Sheldon Press, 1981).

123. Reg Groves, *Conrad Noel and the Thaxted Movement* (London: Merlin Press, 1968; New York: Kelley, 1968), p. 190.

124. Conrad Noel, *Jesus the Heretic* (London: Religious Book Club, 1940), p. 221.

125. *The Order of the Church Militant*, leaflet, n.d.

126. Conrad Noel, *Socialism in Church History* (London: Frank Palmer, 1910), pp. 7–8.

127. Groves, *Conrad Noel and the Thaxted Movement*, p. 37.

128. *The Church Militant* 14 (December 1937), p. 3.

129. P. E. T. Widdrington, in *The Return of Christendom* (London: Allen and Unwin, 1922), p. 108.

130. Francis Underhill, in *Towards a Catholic Standard of Life*, Report of the First Anglo-Catholic Summer School of Sociology, Oxford, July 1925 (London: Catholic Literature Association, 1926), p. 12.

131. Evelyn Underhill, "The Spiritual and the Secular," reprinted in *Politics and the Faith*, ed. M. B. Reckitt (London: Church Literature Association, n.d.), pp. 11–24.

132. D. G. Peck, *Catholic Design for Society* (London: Dacre Press, 1940), p. 13.

133. J. A. T. Robinson, *On Being the Church in the World* (London: SCM Press, 1964), p. 34.

134. John Davies, in *Essays Catholic and Radical* (see note 112), pp. 188f.

135. Geoffrey Ahern and Grace Davie, *Inner City God* (London: Hodder and Stoughton, 1987; North Pomfret, VT: Trafalgar Square, 1989), p. 119.

136. John W. de Gruchy, in *A Call for an End to Unjust Rule*, ed. Allan Boesak and Charles Villa-Vicenzio (Edinburgh: St. Andrew Press, 1986), p. 104; John W. de Gruchy, *Cry Justice!* (London: Collins, 1986; Maryknoll, NY: Orbis, 1986).

137. See John W. de Gruchy, *Bonhoeffer and South Africa* (Grand Rapids: Eerdmans, 1984); Charles Villa-Vicenzio, ed., *On Reading Karl Barth in South Africa* (see note 78).

138. M. M. Thomas, *Towards a Theology of People*, in *Urban Rural Mission*, vol. 1, (Kowloon, Hong Kong: Christian Conference of Asia, 1977), p. 11.

Chapter 2. "Let the Oppressed Go Free"

Chapter epigraphs: Gustavo Gutierrez, *A Theology of Liberation* (Maryknoll, NY: Orbis, 1974), p. 208.

"The Gospel and Revolution," Letter of Sixteen Bishops of the Third World, printed in *The Catholic Worker* (April 1968), pp. 4, 6.

All scriptural citations, unless otherwise indicated, are from the Revised Standard Version, copyright © 1952, 1971 by the Division of Christian Education of the National Council of the Churches of Christ.

1. Cited in Charles Jones, *The Religious Instruction of Negroes in the United States* (Savannah, GA: T. Purse, 1842), p. 20.

2. Desmond Tutu, cited in *Network* (London: USPG, Autumn 1981), p. 30.

3. See Wendy Doniger O'Flaherty, ed., *Karma and Rebirth in Classical Indian Traditions* (Berkeley and Los Angeles: Univ. of California Press, 1980).

4. See *Oxford English Dictionary*, 2d ed., s.v. "liberation."

5. The term seems first to have been used by Gutierrez in a talk at Chimbote, Peru, in 1968. See Philip H. Berryman, *Liberation Theology* (Oak Park, IL: Meyer Stone, 1987), p. 24.

6. *New Encyclopaedia Britannica*, 15th ed., 1989. The Micropaedia does, however, have an article on liberation theology.

7. David J. Bosch, "Currents and Cross Currents in South African Black Theology," *Journal of Religion in Africa* 6:1 (1974).

8. Gayraud S. Wilmore, *Black Religion and Black Radicalism* (New York: Doubleday, 1973), pp. 53–54.

9. Wilmore, *Black Religion and Black Radicalism*, p. 75.

10. Levi Coppin, cited in J. H. Cone, *Speaking the Truth* (Grand Rapids; Eerdmans, 1986), p. 95.

11. Wilmore, *Black Religion and Black Radicalism*, p. 14.

12. *Gospel Pearls Hymn Book*, ed. Willa A. Townsend (Nashville: NBC Public Board, 1921), p. 106.

13. I have drawn on the valuable unpublished dissertation by my friend Pastor Rose Jackson, "The Nature and Role of Black Gospel Music in the Black Pentecostal Worship Service" (D. Min diss., University of Chicago, 1986).

14. Nicholas von Hoffman, cited in *Chicago Reporter* 14:12 (December 1985).

15. Linton Kwesi Johnson, "Jamaican Rebel Music," *Race and Class* 17:4 (Spring 1976), p. 397.

16. Geddes Hanson, "Black Theology and Protestant Thought," *Social Progress* (September–October 1969), p. 6.

17. James Cone, "The Social Context of Theology," in *Doing Theology Today*, ed. Choan Seng Song (Madras: Christian Literature Society, 1976), p. 34.

18. J. H. Cone, *God of the Oppressed* (New York: Seabury Press, 1975), p. 136.

19. Elaine Foster, "Thoughts on the Black Religious Experience in Britain" (Paper given at the conference History of Black People in London, University of London, 27–29 November 1984), p. 21.

20. Linton Kwesi Johnson, "Jamaican Rebel Music," p. 407.

21. John Rex and Sally Tomlinson, *Colonial Immigrants in a British City* (London: Routledge, 1979), p. 245.

22. *The Times*, 23 February 1981; John Brown, *Shades of Grey* (Cranfield Police Studies, 1977).

23. Cited in Horace Campbell, *Rasta and Resistance* (London: Hansib, 1985; Trenton, NJ: Africa World, 1987), p. 60.

24. Ruth Glass, "Ashes of Discontent," *The Listener*, 1 February 1962, pp. 207–9. Also included in Ruth Glass, *Clichés of Urban Doom and Other Essays* (Oxford: Blackwell, 1989), pp. 210–16.

25. Cornel West, "Subversive Joy and Revolutionary Patience in Black Christianity," in *Prophetic Fragments* (Grand Rapids: Eerdmans, 1988), pp. 161–65.

26. Cone, *God of the Oppressed*, p. 9.

27. Rowan Williams, *Resurrection* (London: Darton, Longman and Todd, 1987; New York: Pilgrim, 1985), pp. 12, 16.

28. Dennis Altman, *The Homosexualization of America* (Boston, Beacon Press, 1982), p. 4.

29. The term is often attributed to Audre Lorde in 1978, but was used by George Weinberg, *Society and the Healthy Homosexual* (New York: Doubleday, 1973).

30. Constance L. Hays, "Anti-gay Attacks Increase and Some Fight Back," *The New York Times*, 3 September 1990; New York, *Gay Men's Health Crisis*

Newsletter, October 1986; Carl Siciliano, "An Epidemic of Violence Against Homosexuals," *Catholic Worker*, May 1987, p. 3.

31. Evan Drake Howard, "Extremism on Campus: Symbols of Hate, Symbols of Hope," *Christian Century*, 15–22 July 1987, pp. 625–28.

32. See references above and *The Independent*, 14 May 1990.

33. Cited in *Catholic Worker*, May 1987.

34. See Sara Diamond, *Spiritual Warfare: The Politics of the Christian Right* (London: Pluto Press, 1989; Boston: South End Press, 1989).

35. Simon Watney, "The Wrong Ideas That Are Plaguing AIDS," *The Guardian*, 16 October 1987.

36. See articles in *Church Times*, 8 January, 11 March, 20 May, and 3 June 1988.

37. *Church Times*, 3 June 1988.

38. Diamond, *Spiritual Warfare*, p. vi.

39. Edward Norman, "A Place for Gay Christians?," *The Times*, 7 May 1988. See also his article "AIDS and Compassion," *LGCM Journal* 46 (1988), pp. 10–13.

40. "Intrinsically disordered" is the phrase used in official Vatican statements. Cf., *Declaration on Certain Questions Concerning Sexual Ethics* (1975) and *Educational Guidance for Human Love* (1 December 1983). For "symbolic confusion," see Ruth Tiffany Barnhouse, *Homosexuality: A Symbolic Confusion* (New York: Seabury Press, 1979).

41. *National Catholic Reporter*, 7 November 1986.

42. Kittredge Cherry and James Mitulski, "We Are the Church Alive, the Church with AIDS," *Christian Century*, 27 January 1988, pp. 85–88.

43. David Randall, "Reflections on a Pastoral Journey" (Unpublished manuscript, 1988).

44. Audre Lorde, *Sister Outsider* (Trumansburg, NY: Crossings Press, 1984).

45. *Sexuality: A Divine Gift*, Education for Mission and Ministry Unit, Episcopal Church, 1987, p. 1.

46. Rowan Williams, "John Wesley: A Fool for Christ," *Fairacres Chronicle* 21:1 (Spring 1988), pp. 8–12.

47. Robert Lambourne in *Contact*, Spring 1974, p. 38.

48. Margaret R. Miles, *The Image and Practice of Holiness* (London: SCM Press, 1988), p. 160.

49. Carter Heyward, *Touching Our Strength: The Erotic as Power and the Love of God* (San Francisco: Harper & Row, 1989), p. 125.

50. Heyward, *Touching Our Strength*, p. 7.

51. Sam Keen, *To a Dancing God* (London: Fontana, 1970; San Francisco: Harper, 1990), p. 142.

52. Rowan Williams, "The Body's Grace" (Lesbian and Gay Christian Movement Tenth Michael Harding Memorial Lecture, 2 July 1989). The phrase is taken from Paul Scott's novel *The Day of the Scorpion*.

53. Irenaeus, *Adv. Haer.* 5:2.

54. Gregory of Nazianzen, *Ep. 101*.

55. John Chrysostom, *Homily 5 on Romans;* John Climacus, *Ladder of Divine Ascent* 3:1; 27:14. See John Chryssavgis, "The Notion of 'Divine Eros' in *The Ladder* of St. John Climacus," *St. Vladimir's Theological Quarterly* 29:3 (1985), pp. 191–200.

56. Gregory Palamas, *Hagioritic Tome*, in *Patrologia Graeca*, ed. J. P. Migne (Evanston, IL: Adler's Foreign Books, 1965–71), 150:1233B.

57. See Dennis Meadows et al., *The Limits to Growth* (Washington D. C.: Potomac Association, 1972); "Blueprint for Survival" in *The Ecologist* 2:1 (January 1972); Barbara Ward and Rene Dubos, *Only One Earth* (New York: Norton, 1972); E. F. Schumacher, *Small Is Beautiful* (London: Blond and Briggs, 1973; New York: Harper Collins, 1989); Satish Kumar, in *The Green Fuse*, ed. John Button (London: Quartet Books, 1990), p. xv.

58. Theodore Roszak, *Person/Planet: The Creative Disintegration of Industrial Society* (St. Albans, England: Granada, 1981).

59. Paul Ehrlich, cited in Philip Shabecoff, "Action Is Urged to Save Our Planet," *The New York Times*, 28 September 1986.

60. Jonathon Porritt, *Seeing Green: The Politics of Ecology Explained* (Oxford: Blackwell, 1987), pp. 93–111.

61. Fritjof Capra, *Green Politics* (New York: Dutton, 1984), p. 55.

62. Lynn White, "The Religious Roots of Our Ecological Crisis," *Science* 15 (1967), pp. 1203–7.

63. See James Barr, "Man and Nature: The Ecological Controversy and the Old Testament," *Bulletin of the John Rylands Library* 55 (1972–73), pp. 9–32; John Austin Baker, "Biblical Views of Nature," in *Liberating Life: Contemporary Approaches to Ecological Theology*, ed. Charles Birch, William Eakin, and Jay B. McDaniel (Maryknoll, NY: Orbis, 1990), pp. 9–26; Jonathan Gorsky, "Judaism and the Environment," *The Month* (February 1991), pp. 78–83.

64. Gerrard Winstanley, cited in Christopher Hill, *The World Turned Upside Down: Radical Ideas During the English Revolution* (London: Maurice Temple Smith, 1972; New York: Viking Penguin, 1984), p. 104.

65. Thomas Traherne, *Poems, Centuries and Three Thanksgivings*, ed. Anne Ridler (1966), p. 177.

66. J. M. Plunket (1887–1916), cited in Robert Faricy, *Wind and Sea Obey Him: Approaches to a Theology of Nature* (London: SCM Press, 1982; Westminster, MD: Christian Classics, 1988), pp. 73–74.

67. Conrad Noel, *Socialism in Church History* (London: Frank Palmer, 1910), p. 143.

68. See Matthew Fox, *Original Blessing* (Santa Fe, NM: Bear, 1983), and *The Coming of the Cosmic Christ* (San Francisco: Harper & Row, 1988); Thomas Berry, "The Spirituality of the Earth," *Riverdale Papers: On the Earth Community* (New York: Riverdale Center for Religious Research, n.d.); Peter Medawar, *Pluto's Republic* (Oxford and New York: Oxford Univ. Press, 1984), pp. 20–23, 242–51, 329.

69. John A. T. Robinson, *On Being the Church in the World* (London: SCM Press, 1964), pp. 64–65.

70. Rosemary Ruether, *New Woman, New Earth* (New York: Seabury Press, 1975).

71. Murray Bookchin, "Deep Ecology Versus Social Ecology" (Speech to National Gathering of U.S. Greens, Amherst, Mass., 1987), cited in Jonathon Porritt and David Winner, *The Coming of the Greens* (London: Fontana, 1988), p. 239.

72. Charles Birch et al., eds., *Liberating Life: Contemporary Approaches to Ecological Theology* (Maryknoll, NY: Orbis, 1990), p. 1.

73. Thomas Aquinas, *Summa Theologica*, 2a, 2ae, q 964; Emmanuel Mounier, *L'engagement de la foi*, vol. 1 (Paris: 1933), p. 388.

74. Peruvian Bishops' Commission for Social Action, *Between Honesty and Hope* (Maryknoll, NY: Orbis, 1970), pp. 81 ff.

75. See Michael Howard, *War in European History* (Oxford: Oxford Univ. Press, 1976), pp. 4–5.

76. Alan Wilkinson, *Dissent or Conform? War, Peace and the English Churches 1900–1945* (London: SCM Press, 1945; Philadelphia: Trinity Press International, 1986), p. 45.

77. Donald Kennedy (Stanford University) at Conference on the World After Nuclear War, October 1983, cited in *Bulletin of the Atomic Scientists* 40:4 (April 1984).

78. Magnus Clarke, *The Nuclear Destruction of Britain* (London: Croom Helm, 1981), pp. 198–99.

79. Michael Howard, *The Causes of Wars* (London: Maurice Temple Smith, 1983; Cambridge, MA: Harvard Univ. Press, 1983), p. 144.

80. Royal Commission on Environmental Pollution, *Nuclear Power and the Environment* (London: HMSO, September 1976).

81. Richard C. Bell and Rory O'Connor, *Nukespeak: Nuclear Language, Visions and Mindset* (San Francisco: Sierra Club Books, 1982), p. xiii.

82. Dietrich Bonhoeffer, *Prisoner for God: Letters and Papers from Prison* (New York: Macmillan, 1958), p. 27.

83. Celsus, cited in Thomas Merton, *Seeds of Destruction* (New York: Farrar, Straus and Giroux, 1961), pp. 135–36.

84. Simone Weil, cited in *Walking on the Water*, ed. Sara Maitland and Jo Garcia (London: Virago, 1983), p. 7.

85. Martin Luther King, "Letter from Birmingham Jail," April 1963, reprinted in *Sojourners* 12:5 (May 1983), p. 19.

86. Stanley Hauerwas, *The Peaceable Kingdom* (Notre Dame, IN: Univ. of Notre Dame Press, 1983), pp. xvi–xvii.

87. Sara Evans, *Personal Politics: The Roots of Women's Liberation in the Civil Rights Movement and the New Left* (New York: Knopf, 1980).

88. See Don Cupitt, *Radicals and the Future of the Church* (London: SCM Press, 1989; New York: Trinity Press International, 1989).

89. Sheila Rowbotham, Lynne Segal, and Hilary Wainwright, *Beyond the Fragments: Feminism and the Making of Socialism* (London: Merlin Press, 1979), p. 40.

90. Beverly Wildung Harrison, *Making the Connections* (Boston: Beacon Press, 1985), p. 21.

91. See Sheila Rowbotham, *The Past Is Before Us: Feminism in Action Since the 1960s* (Harmondsworth: Penguin, 1989).

92. Bonnie Zimmerman, "The Politics of Transliteration: Lesbian Personal Narratives," in *The Lesbian Issue*, ed. Estelle B. Freedman (Chicago: Univ. of Chicago Press, 1985), p. 268.

93. "Mental Health and Violence Against Women: A Femimist Ex-inmate Analysis," *Phoenix Rising* 3:3 (Winter 1983), pp. 43–47.

94. Rowbotham et al., *Beyond the Fragments*, p. 58.

95. Ruth E. Hall, *Ask Any Woman: A London Inquiry into Rape and Sexual Assault* (Bristol: Falling Wall Press, 1985); Amina Mama, *The Hidden Struggle: Statutory and Voluntary Sector Responses to Violence Against Black Women in the Home* (London: London Race and Housing Research Unit/Runnymede Trust, 1989).

96. Harrison, *Making the Connections*, p. 216.

97. Sister Albertus Magnus McGrath, *What a Modern Catholic Believes About Women* (Chicago: Thomas More Press, 1972), p. 5.

98. See the works of Mary Daly since *The Church and the Second Sex* (New York: Harper Colophon, 1975).

99. Valerie Saiving Goldstein, *Journal of Religion* (April 1960), reprinted as "The Human Situation: A Feminist View," in *Womanspirit Rising: A Feminist Reader in Religion*, ed. Carol P. Christ and Judith Plaskow (San Francisco: Harper & Row, 1979).

100. Sharon D. Welch, *A Feminist Ethic of Risk* (Minneapolis: Fortress Press, 1990), p. 169.

101. Beverly Wildung Harrison, "The Power of Anger in the Work of Love," *Union Seminary Quarterly Review* 36 (1981), p. 49. Cf. Lorde, *Sister Outsider* (see note 44), pp. 129–30.

102. Carter Heyward, "The Power of God-with-us," *Christian Century*, 14 March 1990, pp. 275–78.

103. See, e.g., the writings of Kathleen Fischer, Janet Morley, Gail Ramshaw-Schmidt, and others.

104. Ruether, *New Woman, New Earth* (see note 70), p. xiii.

105. Carolyn Osiek, *Beyond Anger: On Being a Feminist in the Church* (New York: Paulist Press, 1986), p. 23.

106. Alice Walker, *In Search of Our Mothers' Gardens: Womanist Prose* (New York: Harcourt Brace Jovanovich, 1983), pp. 341–42.

107. Heyward, "The Power of God-with-us."

108. Colin E. Gunton, *The Actuality of Atonement* (Edinburgh: T. and T. Clark, 1988; Grand Rapids: Eerdmans, 1989), pp. 7–8.

109. Sharon D. Welch, *Communities of Liberation and Solidarity* (Maryknoll, NY: Orbis, 1985), p. 54.

110. The absence of references to Marx and to Marxist theory in most liberation theologians is as striking as is the insistence of many Western writers that this tradition is no more than Marxism in theological dress. Sobrino makes only nine references to Marx, and none to other Marxist writers, in the eight hundred pages of his two major works. Gutierrez refers to Marx in his first book but has not done so subsequently. Boff, in over thirty books, provides no instances of Marxist thinking. Even Miranda's study *Marx and the Bible* (Maryknoll, NY: Orbis, 1974) contains far more biblical exegesis and theology than sociopolitical analysis (270 pages of the former contrasted with 42 pages of the latter). See J. Emmette Weir, "The Bible and Marx: A Discussion of the Hermeneutics of Liberation Theology," *Scottish Journal of Theology* 35 (1982),

pp. 337–50; and Alistair Kee, *Marx and the Failure of Liberation Theology* (London: SCM Press, and Philadelphia, Trinity Press International, 1990).

111. Gutierrez, *A Theology of Liberation* (see note for chapter epigraph), p. 136.

112. Gutierrez, *We Drink from Our Own Wells: The Spiritual Journey of a People* (London: SCM Press, 1984; Maryknoll, NY: Orbis, 1984), p. 22.

113. Gutierrez, *On Job: God-talk and the Suffering of the Innocent* (Maryknoll, NY: Orbis, 1988), p. xiii.

114. Segundo Galilea, "Liberation as an Encounter with Politics and Contemplation," in *The Mystical and Political Dimensions of the Christian Faith*, ed. C. Geffre and G. Gutierrez (New York: Concilium, 1974).

115. Segundo Galilea, *The Future of Our Past: The Spanish Mystics Speak to Contemporary Spirituality* (Notre Dame, IN: Ave Maria Press, 1985), p. 9.

116. Rowbotham et al., *Beyond the Fragments* (see note 89), pp. 68–69.

117. Alasdair MacIntyre, *After Virtue* (Notre Dame, IN: Univ. of Notre Dame Press; London: Duckworth, 1981), p. 245.

118. Nicholas Lash, *Theology on the Way to Emmaus* (London: SCM Press, 1986; Philadelphia: Trinity Press International, 1986), pp. 197–200.

119. *English Hymnal*, no. 495.

Chapter 3. Stepping Out of Babylon

Chapter epigraphs: C. E. Raven, cited in Alan Wilkinson, *Dissent or Conform? War, Peace and the English Churches 1900–1945* (London: SCM Press, 1986; Philadelphia: Trinity Press International, 1986), p. 105.

James Joyce to his brother Stanislaus, in Stanislaus Joyce, *My Brother's Keeper* (London: Faber and Faber, 1958; Winchester, MA: Faber and Faber, 1982), p. 23.

Fredric Jameson, *Marxism and Form* (Princeton, NJ: Princeton Univ. Press, 1971), p. 204.

1. Enoch Powell, *No Easy Answers* (London: SPCK, 1973), p. 26.

2. Richard J. Neuhaus, *The Naked Public Square* (Grand Rapids: Eerdmans, 1984), p. 115.

3. Richard Hooker, *On The Laws of Ecclesiastical Polity*, vol. 3, books 6, 7, 8, ed. P. G. Stanwood (Cambridge, MA: Harvard Univ. Press, Belknap Press,

1981), pp. 334–35; T. S. Eliot, *The Idea of a Christian Society* (London: Faber, 1940). See Roger Kojecky, *T. S. Eliot's Social Criticism* (London: Faber, 1971).

4. A. P. Wadsworth, "The First Manchester Sunday Schools," *Bulletin of the John Rylands Library* 3 (1950–51), pp. 300, 305.

5. Robin Gill, *Prophecy and Praxis* (London: Marshall, Morgan and Scott, 1981), p. 59.

6. Karl Rahner, *The Practice of Faith* (London: SCM Press, 1985; New York: Crossroad, 1986), p. 16.

7. The Reverend Dick York (Unpublished manuscript of address at city-wide meeting, Berkeley Community Theater, 25 May 1968).

8. Douglas Hurd (Address to the General Synod, 10 February 1988). See report in *The Guardian*, 11 February 1988, and Hurd's article in *Church Times*, 9 September 1988.

9. Fred Catherwood, *The Christian in Industrial Society* (London: Inter-Varsity Press, 1964), p. 32.

10. Brian Griffiths, *Morality and the Market Place* (London: Hodder and Stoughton, 1982).

11. William Temple, *Christianity and Social Order* (Harmondsworth: Penguin 1942), pp. 35–36.

12. Robert Runcie, *The Times*, 8 October 1984.

13. John Atherton, *Faith in the Nation* (London: SPCK, 1988), p. 79.

14. The bishop of Saint Albans, cited in *The Guardian*, 10 July 1990.

15. E. Genovese, *From Rebellion to Revolution* (Baton Rouge, LA: Louisiana State Univ. Press, 1979); Philip Berryman, *The Religious Roots of Rebellion* (Maryknoll, NY: Orbis, 1984). For the earlier period, see William Dale Morris, *The Christian Origins of Social Revolt* (London: Allen and Unwin, 1949; reprint Westport, CT: Hyperion Press, 1979).

16. See Stanley Hauerwas, *Vision and Virtue* (Notre Dame, IN: Fides/Claretian, 1974); *A Community of Character* (Notre Dame, IN: Univ. of Notre Dame Press, 1991); *The Peaceable Kingdom* (Notre Dame, IN: Univ. of Notre Dame Press, 1983); and other works.

17. Hauerwas, *A Community of Character*, p. 74.

18. Hauerwas, "Work as Co-creation: A Remarkably Bad Idea," *This World* 3 (Fall 1982), pp. 89–102.

19. J. H. Yoder, *The Politics of Jesus* (Grand Rapids: Eerdmans, 1972).

20. Stanley Hauerwas and William H. Willimon, *Resident Aliens: Life in the Christian Colony* (Nashville: Abingdon Press, 1989), pp. 30, 38.

21. Martin Buber, cited by Colin Ward in *New Statesman and Society*, 25 May 1990, p. 27.

22. On Aristotle and the Greek political tradition, see Jonathan Barnes, ed., *The Complete Works of Aristotle*, 2 vols. (Princeton, NJ: Princeton Univ. Press, 1984); J. Peter Euben, *The Tragedy of Political Theory* (Princeton, NJ: Princeton Univ. Press, 1990); Alasdair MacIntyre, *Whose Justice? Which Rationality?* (Notre Dame, IN: Univ. of Notre Dame Press; London: Duckworth, 1988); William J. Prior, *Virtue and Knowledge* (London and New York: Macmillan, 1991); Brian Redhead, *Political Thought from Plato to NATO* (London: Ariel Books/BBC, 1984; Pacific Grove, CA: Brooks-Cole, 1988); Andrew Ross, ed., *Pericles of Athens and the Birth of Democracy* (London: Secker and Warburg, 1990).

23. Douglas Jay, cited in Raphael Samuel, "The Cult of Planning," *New Socialist* (January 1986), pp. 25–29.

24. C. Wright Mills, "Liberal Values in the Modern World," in *Power, Politics and People: The Collected Essays of C. Wright Mills*, ed. Irving Horowitz (New York: Oxford Univ. Press, 1963), pp. 189, 191.

25. Francis Fukuyama in *The National Interest*, Summer 1989. See also articles in *The Independent*, 21 September 1989, and *The Guardian*, 4 November 1989.

26. Max Horkheimer, "The End of Reason," 1941. Cf. John C. Bennett, "After liberalism—What?" *Christian Century* 50 (1933), p. 1403.

27. *The Times*, 13 July 1988. Cf. the report "British Social Attitudes" (Gower, 1988) in *The Independent*, 3 November 1988, headed "Thatcherite Values Rejected" and the report of a poll headed "Thatcherite Gospel Leaves Masses Unmoved," *The Independent*, 4 May 1989.

28. David Butler and Richard Rose, *The British General Election of 1959* (London: Macmillan, 1960), p. 19; David Butler and Anthony King, *The British General Election of 1964* (London: Macmillan, 1965), p. 115.

29. James E. Thorold Rogers, *Six Centuries of Work and Wages*, vol. 1 (1884), p. 14.

30. Frances Fox Piven and Richard A. Cloward, *Why Americans Don't Vote* (New York: Pantheon, 1988).

31. Moyra Grant, "You Wouldn't Want to Know," *New Statesman*, 30 May 1986, p. 12.

32. Alasdair MacIntyre, *After Virtue* (Notre Dame, IN: Univ. of Notre Dame Press; London: Duckworth, 1981), p. 253.

33. For the current debates on modernity and postmodernity, see David Harvey, *The Condition of Postmodernity* (Cambridge, MA, and Oxford:

Blackwell, 1989); E. Ann Kaplan, ed., *Postmodernism and Its Discontents* (London and New York: Verso, 1988); Andrew Ross, ed., *Universal Abandon? The Politics of Postmodernism* (Minneapolis: Univ. of Minnesota Press, 1988; Edinburgh: Edinburgh Univ. Press, 1989).

34. Ernest Mandel, introduction to *Capital*, vol. 1 (Harmondsworth: Penguin Marx Library, 1976), p. 85.

35. Martin Jacques (editor of *Marxism Today*), cited in *The Guardian*, 13 January 1990.

36. Eric Hobsbawm, cited in *The Guardian*, 13 January 1990.

37. Eric Hobsbawm, "Goodbye to All That," *Marxism Today* (October 1990), pp. 18–23.

38. P. Glotz, *Manifest fur eine Neue Europaische Linke* (Siedler Verlag, 1986).

39. Michael Howard, "Structure and Process in History," *Times Literary Supplement*, 23–29 June 1989, pp. 687–89.

40. See Louis Dupre, *Marx's Social Critique of Culture* (New Haven, CT: Yale Univ. Press, 1983).

41. David Selbourne, "The Intellectual Poverty of Today's Labourism," *Independent*, 6 February 1987.

42. G. K. A. Bell, *Christianity and World Order* (Harmondsworth: Penguin, 1940), p. 15.

43. G. K. A. Bell, in *Christian Newsletter* 13, cited in Bentley, *Between Marx and Christ* (see chap. 1, note 39), p. 9.

44. Hans-Jurgen Syberberg, *Vom Gluck und Ungluck der Kunst in Deutschland nach den Letzten Kriege* (Matthes and Seitz, 1990); Gerd Borgfleth in *Konkret*, 10 October 1990.

45. A. Dru, ed., *The Letters of Jacob Burkhardt* (New York: Greenwood, 1975).

46. On Hamsun, see John Carey, "Revolted by the Masses," *Times Literary Supplement*, 12–18 January 1990, p. 34.

47. See Edward Timms, *Karl Kraus, Apocalyptic Satirist: Culture and Catastrophe in Habsburg Vienna* (New Haven, CT: Yale Univ. Press, 1986).

48. Oswald Spengler, cited in Paul M. Hayes, *Fascism* (London: Allen and Unwin, 1973; New York: Free Press, 1973), p. 39.

49. See Paul Weindling, *Health, Race and German Politics Between National Unification and Nazism 1870–1945* (Cambridge: Cambridge Univ. Press, 1990); Robert N. Proctor, *Racial Hygiene: Medicine Under the Nazis* Cambridge, MA: Harvard Univ. Press, 1988).

50. See Richard C. Thurlow, "Fascism and Nazism—No Siamese Twins," *Patterns of Prejudice* 14:1 (January 1980), pp. 6–15.

51. Adolf Hitler, in Hermann Rauschning, *Hitler Speaks* (London: Thornton Butterworth, 1939), p. 232.

52. Sir Arnold Wilson, "Walks and Talks," *Nineteenth Century and After,* October 1936, pp. 506–11. On Wilson and other sympathizers with Nazism, see Richard Griffiths, *Fellow Travellers of the Right: British Enthusiasts for Nazi Germany 1933–39* (Oxford: Oxford Univ. Press, 1983).

53. See Claudia Koonz, *Mothers in the Fatherland* (London: Methuen, 1988; New York: St. Martin, 1987). For a curiously inadequate but interesting attempt to examine the links between Nazism and the dread of women, see Klaus Theweleit, *Male Fantasies* (Cambridge: Polity Press, 1987; Minneapolis: Univ. of Minnesota Press, 1987).

54. See Dusty Sklor, *Gods and Beasts: The Nazis and the Occult* (New York: Harper & Row, 1979).

55. See Thurlow, "Fascism and Nazism."

56. Christoper Dawson, *Religion and the Modern State* (London: Sheed and Ward, 1936), pp. 135–36.

57. John F. Pollard, *The Vatican and Italian Fascism 1922–1929* (Cambridge: Cambridge Univ. Press, 1985); Douglas Hyde, "Catholics and the National Front," *The Month,* April 1978, pp. 111–14.

58. *The Tablet,* 11 February 1939.

59. Telegram from the Ecclesiastical Council of the German Evangelical Church to the Fuhrer, *Kirchliches Jahrbuch 1933–34* (Gütersloh: 1948), pp. 478–79.

60. See Robert P. Erickson, *Theologians Under Hitler* (New Haven, CT: Yale Univ. Press, 1985).

61. Gilmer W. Blackburn, "The Portrayal of Christianity in the History Textbooks of Nazi Germany," *Church History* 49:4 (December 1980), pp. 433–45.

62. On Headlam, see Griffiths, *Fellow Travellers of the Right.*

63. *The Cicestrian,* Advent 1936.

64. See Alice Gallin, *Midwives to Nazism: University Professors in Weimar Germany 1925–1933* (Macon, GA: Mercer Univ. Press, 1986).

65. See Proctor, *Racial Hygiene.*

66. *The Collected Essays, Journalism and Letters of George Orwell,* vol. 2 (Harmondsworth: Penguin, 1970; San Diego, CA: Harcourt Brace Jovanovich, 1968), p. 29.

67. See the Runnymede Trust Bulletins for 1972 and 1973, esp. its Europe Supplement (January–December 1973).

68. Margaret Thatcher (Speech at Bruges, September 1988). On the background, see Paul Gordon, *Fortress Europe? The Meaning of 1992* (London: Runnymede Trust, 1989).

69. Ralf Dahrendorf, "Europe's Vale of Tears," *Marxism Today*, May 1990, pp. 18–23.

70. See Gunter Wallraf, *Ganz Unten*, 1988; English translation, *The Lowest of the Low* (London: Methuen, 1988).

71. See articles in *Le Monde*, 10 and 15 November 1988, and *Liberation*, 2 November 1988; *New Expressions of Racism: Growing Areas of Conflict in Europe* (Utrecht: Netherlands Institute of Human Rights, 1988); John Palmer, "Europe's Fascist Renaissance," *The Guardian*, 24 August 1977; A. Sivanandan, "The New Racism," *New Statesman and Society*, 4 November 1988, pp. 8–9. For the "holocaust denial" movement, see Gill Seidel, *The Holocaust Denial* (Leeds: Beyond the Pale Collective, 1986).

72. Alan Ecclestone, *The Night Sky of the Lord* (London: Darton, Longman and Todd, 1980), p. 51.

73. Karl Jaspers, *The Spiritual Situation of the Age* (1931); Jurgen Habermas, ed., *Observations on the Spiritual Situation of the Age* (Cambridge, MA: MIT Press, 1984).

74. See Kenneth Medhurst and George Moyser, *Church and Politics in a Secular Age*, (Oxford: Clarendon Press, 1988; New York: Oxford Univ. Press, 1988), p. 33.

75. *The Times*, 17 April 1978; *New Society*, 24 October 1986.

76. *The Right Road for Britain* (London: Conservative and Unionist Central Office, 1949), p. 65.

77. *The Independent*, 27 October 1987.

78. Margaret Thatcher, cited in *Sunday Times Magazine*, 4 March 1984, p. 49.

79. Peregrine Worsthorne, in *Conservative Essays*, ed. Maurice Cowling (London: Cassell, 1978), p. 149.

80. *The Times*, 18 October 1983.

81. Margaret Thatcher, interviewed by Peter Jenkins, *The Independent*, 14 September 1987.

82. Margaret Thatcher, 27 March 1982.

83. Mrs. Thatcher's statement was made in an interview with *Woman's Own* in November 1987. Cf. Epicurus: "There is no such thing as human society," cited in A. D. Lindsey, *Encyclopaedia of the Social Sciences*, 1932 ed., p. 675.

84. Margaret Thatcher (Address at St. Lawrence Jewry, London, 4 March 1981).

85. Ian Gilmour, *Inside Right* (London: Hutchinson, 1977), p. 158.

86. *The Times*, 10 May 1978; *Financial Times*, 31 March 1979; "Jimmy Young Show," BBC radio, 5 June 1987; *Independent*, 6 June 1987.

87. Brian Walden in *The Standard*, 4 June 1985.

88. *Daily Express*, 17 August 1982.

89. Margaret Thatcher (Address at St. Lawrence Jewry, London, 30 March 1978).

90. Norman Tebbit, correspondence with the Reverend Peter Sutcliffe, cited in *The Guardian*, 8 September 1984.

91. *The Guardian*, 16 October 1984.

92. Margaret Thatcher (Address to the Church of Scotland, 21 May 1988). The address was printed in *The Observer* on 22 May and in *The Guardian* and other daily papers on 23 May 1988.

93. Margaret Thatcher, interview with Gordon Burns, Granada Television, 30 January 1978. On the National Front, see C. T. Husbands, *Racial Exclusionism and the City: The Urban Support of the National Front* (London: Allen and Unwin, 1983; New York: Unwin Hyman, 1983).

94. *Sunday Times*, 12 June 1983.

95. Nicholas Boyle, "Thatcher's Dead Souls," *New Statesman and Society*, 14 October 1988, pp. 29–30.

96. F. H. Smyth Allocution of the Father Superior to the General Council of the Society of the Catholic Commonwealth, 31 August 1950.

97. F. H. Smyth, *Manhood into God* (New York: Round Table Press, 1940).

98. A. M. Ramsey, *From Gore to Temple* (London: Longmans, 1960), p. 14.

99. David Nicholls and Rowan Williams, *Politics and Theological Identity* (London: Jubilee Group, 1984), p. 20.

100. George Orwell, *Inside the Whale* (Harmondsworth: Penguin, 1979), p. 35; *Daily Worker*, 23 August 1932.

101. See Kenneth Leech, "Beyond Gin and Lace: Homosexuality and the Anglo-Catholic Subculture," in *Speaking Love's Name: Homosexuality: Some Catholic and Socialist Reflections*, ed. Ashley Beck and Ros Hunt (London: Jubilee Group, 1988), pp. 16–27.

102. Valerie Pitt, in *Essays Catholic and Radical*, ed. Kenneth Leech and Rowan Williams (London: Bowerdean Press, 1983), p. 223.

103. Cornel West, *Prophesy Deliverance! An Afro-American Revolutionary Christianity* (Philadelphia: Westminster Press, 1982), p. 95.

104. John A. T. Robinson, *On Being the Church in the World* (London: SCM Press, 1964), p. 70.

105. John Davies in *Essays Catholic and Radical*, pp. 188–89.

106. S. D. Headlam, *The Laws of Eternal Life* (London: Frederick Verinder, 1888), p. 52.

107. F. H. Smyth, *Discerning the Lord's Body* (Louisville, KY: Cloister Press, 1946), pp. 84–85.

108. Robinson, *On Being the Church in the World*, pp. 64–65.

109. Michael Reynolds, *Martyr of Ritualism: Father Mackonochie of St. Alban's, Holborn* (London: Faber and Faber, 1965), pp. 190–91.

110. James Adderley, "Christian Socialism, Past and Present," *The Commonwealth*, December 1926, cited in M. B. Reckitt, *Faith and Society* (London: Longmans, 1932), p. 86.

111. P. E. T. Widdrington, in *The Return of Christendom* (London: Allen and Unwin, 1922), p. 102. For the whole essay, see pp. 91–113.

112. S. G. Evans, ed., *The Return to Reality* (London: Zeno, 1954); *Religion and the People*, January 1957.

113. M. B. Reckitt, *P. E. T. Widdrington* (London: SPCK, 1961), p. 57.

114. Tony Benn (Address at Alliance for Socialism Weekend 1985), printed in *Socialist Action*, 22 November 1985.

115. Roger Haight, *The Experience and Language of Grace* (Dublin: Gill and Macmillan, 1979), p. 182.

116. The term *communities of resistance* was used by Jim Forest at a conference in 1973. See Alistair Kee, ed. *Seeds of Liberation: Spiritual Dimensions to Political Struggle* (London: SCM Press, 1973), pp. 29–36. It has recently been used by black activists in Britain. Cf. A. Sivanandan, *Communities of Resistance* (London: Routledge Chapman & Hall, 1990; London: Verso, 1991).

117. V. I. Lenin, "Left Wing Communism, an Infantile Disorder," in *Collected Works*, vol. 31 (Moscow: Progress Press, 1966), p. 31.

118. A. H. Hanson, letter in *The Listener*, 21 January 1960.

119. Sheila Rowbotham, Lynne Segal, and Hilary Wainwright, *Beyond the Fragments: Feminism and the Making of Socialism* (London: Merlin Press, 1979), pp. 37, 118–19.

120. Sheila Rowbotham, *Dreams and Dilemmas: Collected Writings* (London: Virago, 1983), p. 66.

121. Rowbotham, in *Beyond the Fragments*, p. 23.

122. C. Wright Mills, "The Powerless People: The Role of the Intellectual in Society," in *Power, Politics and People* (see note 24), p. 299.

123. Orwell, *Inside the Whale* (Harmondsworth: Penguin, 1979) and *The Road to Wigan Pier* (London: Gollancz, 1932; San Diego, CA: Harcourt Brace Jovanovich, 1972).

124. Ralph Miliband, cited by Stuart Hall, *The Guardian*, 12 December 1988.

Chapter 4. The Desert in the City

Chapter epigraphs: Lewis Mumford, *The City in History* (New York: Harcourt Brace and World, 1961), p. 247.

Paul Moore, *The Church Reclaims the City* (New York: Seabury Press, 1964), p. 10.

1. Spitalfields Vestry, March 1807, cited in *The Survey of London*, vol. 27, *Spitalfields and Mile End New Town* (London: Athlone Press for the London County Council, 1957), p. 8; Ian Nairn, *Daily Telegraph*, 19 August 1963.

2. Elizabeth Burney, *Housing on Trial* (Oxford: Oxford Univ. Press, 1967), p. 88.

3. Sophie Hyndman, "Housing Dampness and Respiratory Illness in Part of East London" (Ph.D. thesis, Queen Mary College, Univ. of London, 1989). See *Tower Hamlets People*, no. 2, Tower Hamlets Health Authority, September 1989.

4. *Tower Hamlets Health Inquiry Report*, Tower Hamlets Community Health Council, May 1987.

5. See *The Mental Health of East London* (London: Psychiatric Rehabilitation Association, 1966), and *Mental Health in City and Suburb* (London: Psychiatric Rehabilitation Association, 1970).

6. Patrick O'Donovan, "The Challenge of Cable Street," *The Listener*, 16 February 1950, pp. 287–88.

7. O'Donovan, "Challenge of Cable Street," pp. 287–88.

8. Roi Ottley, *No Green Pastures* (London: John Murray, 1952), p. 29.

9. Ashley Smith, *The East Enders* (London: Secker and Warburg, 1961), p. 75; George Foulser, "Cablestrasse," *The Observer,* 28 August 1960.

10. *Catholic Social Teaching and the U.S. Economy,* December 1984, par. 54.

11. See Gustavo Gutierrez, *The Power of the Poor in History* (Maryknoll, NY: Orbis, 1983); Julio de Santa Ana, ed., *Towards a Church of the Poor* (Geneva: World Council of Churches, 1978); David Sheppard, *Bias to the Poor* (London: Hodder and Stoughton, 1983). See also Donal Dorr, *Option for the Poor: A Hundred Years of Vatican Social Teaching* (Maryknoll, NY: Orbis, 1983).

12. R. H. Tawney, *Poverty as an Industrial Problem* (London: William Morris Press, 1913.

13. Frank Weston, *Our Present Duty,* Golden Jubilee edition (London: Church Literature Association, 1973).

14. Gustavo Gutierrez, *We Drink from Our Own Wells: The Spiritual Journey of a People* (London: SCM Press, 1984), p. 29; trans. Matthew O'Connell (Maryknoll, NY: Orbis, 1984).

15. See chap. 1, note 82.

16. Kenneth Leech, *The Social God* (London: Sheldon Press, 1981).

17. Austin Farrer, *A Celebration of Faith* (London: Hodde and Stoughton, 1970), p. 10.

18. The phrase "a long road to Canaan" occurs in Paul Simon's song "Bleecker Street" on his album *Wednesday Morning 3 AM,* CBS, 1966.

19. See Kenneth Leech, "The Junkies' Doctors and the London Drug Scene in the 1960s: Some Remembered Fragments," in *Policing and Prescribing,* ed. Philip Bean and David Whynes (London: Macmillan, 1991).

20. The phrase in the title of this section is from *Blood on the Streets,* a report on racial violence published by Bethnal Green and Stepney Trades Council in September 1978.

21. Hugh McLeod, *Class and Religion in the Late Victorian City* (London: Croom Helm, 1974), pp. 104–5.

22. *Bangladeshis in Britain,* First Report from the Home Affairs Committee, Session 1986–87, 3 vols. (London: Her Majesty's Stationery Office, 10 December 1986), vol. 1, p. iv.

23. Derek Cox, *A Community Approach to Youth Work in East London* (London: YWCA, 1970), pp. 117–18.

24. See C. T. Husbands, *Racial Exclusionism and the City: The Urban Support of the National Front* (London: Allen and Unwin, 1983); Kenneth Leech,

The Social God, pp. 116–26; Martin Walker, *The National Front* (London: Fontana, 1977).

25. Rodney Hilton, *Bond Men Made Free: Medieval Peasant Movements and the English Rising of 1381* (London: Methuen, 1977; New York: Routledge, 1979), p. 210.

26. Geoffrey Curtis, "Two Kinds of Marriage," unpublished paper, Julian 600th Anniversary Consultation, Norwich, England, May 1973.

27. A. M. Ramsey, *Sacred and Secular* (London: Longmans, 1965), p. 45.

28. Thomas Merton, *Mystics and Zen Masters* (New York: Delta, 1967), p. 142.

29. Julian of Norwich, *Revelations of Divine Love*, chaps. 63, 53.

30. Julian of Norwich, *Revelations of Divine Love*, chap. 31.

31. J. Huizinga, *The Waning of the Middle Ages* (Harmondsworth: Penguin, 1955; New York: Doubleday Anchor, 1954), p. 31.

32. Julian of Norwich, *Revelations of Divine Love*, chap. 57.

33. John R. Orens, "The Mass, the Masses and the Music Hall: Stewart Headlam's Radical Anglicanism" (Ph.D. diss., Columbia University, 1972), p. 1. Orens's study is by far the most thorough discussion of Headlam ever produced.

34. Edward Norman, *The Victorian Christian Socialists* (Cambridge: Cambridge Univ. Press, 1987), p. 103.

35. James Adderley, "Christian Socialism, Past and Present," *The Commonwealth*, December 1926, cited in M. B. Reckitt, *Faith and Society* (London: Longmans, 1932), p. 86.

36. *Church Reformer* 5:7 (July 1886), p. 146.

37. Stewart Headlam, *The Meaning of the Mass* (London: S. C. Brown, Langham, 1905), pp. 21–22.

38. Stewart Headlam, *The Laws of Eternal Life* (London: Frederick Verinder, 1888), p. 52.

39. Stewart Headlam, "The Sure Foundation" (Address to the Guild of Saint Matthew at the Annual Meeting, 1883).

40. Stewart Headlam in *Church Reformer* 4:10 (15 October 1885), p. 236.

41. Stewart Headlam, *The Service of Humanity* (London: John Hodges, 1882), p. 59.

42. Kenneth Leech, "Stewart Headlam 1847–1924 and the Guild of St. Matthew," in *For Christ and the People*, ed. M. B. Reckitt (London: SPCK, 1968), pp. 61–88.

43. Stewart Headlam, *The Meaning of the Mass* (London: S. C. Brown, Langham, 1905), pp. 122, 113.

44. Headlam, *Service of Humanity*, p. 16.

45. Headlam, "Sure Foundation," p. 13.

46. See Peter Coleman, *Christian Attitudes to Homosexuality* (London: SPCK, 1980), pp. 148–50.

47. Stewart Headlam, *The Church Catechism and the Emancipation of Labour* (London: G. J. Palmer, n.d.), p. 3.

48. Stewart Headlam, *The Service of Humanity and Other Sermons* (London: John Hodges, 1882), p. 37.

49. Headlam, *Service of Humanity*, p. 11.

50. Headlam, *Meaning of the Mass*, p. 122.

51. M. B. Reckitt, *Faith and Society* (London: Longmans, 1932), p. 87.

52. Clifford Stevens, "Thomas Merton 1968: A Profile in Memoriam," *American Benedictine Review*, March 1969, p. 7.

53. Thomas Merton, cited in George Woodcock, *Thomas Merton, Monk and Poet* (Edinburgh: Canongate, 1978; New York: Farrar, Straus & Giroux, 1978), pp. 41–42.

54. Thomas Merton, *Conjectures of a Guilty Bystander* (New York: Doubleday, 1968), p. 71.

55. Thomas Merton, *Seeds of Contemplation* (Notre Dame, IN: Univ. of Notre Dame Press, 1949), p. 65.

56. Thomas Merton, *Contemplation in a World of Action* (London: Unwin Paperbacks, 1980), p. 164.

57. *The Asian Journal of Thomas Merton* (London: Sheldon Press, 1974), p. 305; Naomi B. Stone et al., eds. (New York: New Directions, 1973).

58. Merton, *Conjectures of a Guilty Bystander*, p. 156.

59. Thomas Merton, *Raids on the Unspeakable* (London: Burns Oates, 1977; New York: New Directions, 1970), pp. 51–52.

60. Merton, *Raids on the Unspeakable*, p. 14.

61. Merton, *Raids on the Unspeakable*, pp. 29–33.

62. See David W. Givey, *The Social Thought of Thomas Merton* (Chicago: Franciscan Herald Press, 1983), p. 12.

63. This is a recurring theme in Merton's writing. See esp. his *The Climate of Monastic Prayer* (Spencer, MA: Cistercian Publications, 1969).

64. Henri Nouwen, *Pray to Live* (Notre Dame, IN: Fides, 1972), p. 54.

65. Merton, *Conjectures of a Guilty Bystander*, p. 142.

66. F. J. Kelly, *Man Before God: Thomas Merton on Social Responsibility* (New York: Doubleday, 1974), p. xix.

67. Thomas Merton, *The Sign of Jonas* (London: Burns Oates, 1953; San Diego, CA: Harcourt Brace Jovanovich, 1979), p. 41.

68. "Catholic Worker Positions," *Catholic Worker*, May 1977, p. 6.

69. M. McIntyre and V. Druhe, "The Worker: A Tradition in Contradiction," *The Round Table*, Summer 1984, p. 11.

70. Dorothy Day, in *By Little and By Little: The Selected Writings of Dorothy Day*, ed. Robert Ellsberg (New York: Alfred A. Knopf, 1983), pp. 263–64.

71. Dorothy Day, *The Long Loneliness* (New York: Curtis Books, 1972), p. 231.

72. Nancy L. Roberts, in *A Revolution of the Heart: Essays on the Catholic Worker*, ed. Patrick G. Coy (Philadelphia: Temple Univ. Press, 1988), p. 126.

73. Letter from Ammon Hennacy House of Hospitality, Los Angeles, September 1972, cited in Coy, *Revolution of the Heart*, p. 245.

74. Peter Maurin, "Blowing the Dynamite," cited in Mel Piehl, *Breaking Bread: The Catholic Worker and the Origins of Catholic Radicalism in America* (Philadelphia: Temple Univ. Press, 1982), pp. 63–64.

75. Cf. Marion K. Sanders, "The Professional Radical: Conversations with Saul Alinsky," *Harper's Magazine*, June–July 1965: "My philosophy is rooted in an American radical tradition, not in a Marxist tradition"; P. David Finks, *The Radical Vision of Saul Alinsky* (New York: Paulist Press, 1984), p. 32: "His ideological mentors were not Marx and Lenin but Thomas Jefferson and James Madison."

76. "Plato on the Barricades," *The Economist*, 13–19 May 1967.

77. *Christian Century*, editorial, 12 February 1964.

78. *Christian Century*, editorial, 5 July 1967.

79. Stephen C. Rose, "Saul Alinsky and His Critics," *Christianity and Crisis*, 20 July 1964, pp. 143–52.

80. Alinsky's methods were described as "thinly papered over Marxism" as early as 1962 *(Christian Century*, 18 July 1962). More recently a report in the *Daily Telegraph* observed that "Alinsky . . . was a Marxist revolutionary" (29 January 1983).

81. "Saul Alinsky," *Current Biography* 29:10 (November 1968), pp. 3–6.

82. Bernard Doering, "The Philosopher and the Provocateur: Jacques Maritain and Saul Alinsky," *Commonweal*, 1 June 1990, pp. 345–48.

83. Jacques Maritain, cited in Saul D. Alinsky, "Of Means and Ends," *Union Seminary Quarterly Review* 22:2 (January 1967), pp. 107–24.

84. Saul Alinsky, cited in Lois Wille, *Chicago Daily News*, 26 January 1968.

85. Saul D. Alinsky, *Rules for Radicals* (New York: Random House, 1972), pp. 126–29.

86. Eric Norden, "Saul Alinsky Interview," *Playboy*, March 1972, p. 60.

87. Alinsky, *Rules for Radicals*.

88. "Saul Alinsky," *Current Biography*.

89. *Diocesan Bulletin of the Episcopal Church Diocese of West Missouri* 35:2 (November 1965), pp. 6–13.

90. Saul Alinsky, cited in Dan Dodson, "The Church, Power and Saul Alinsky," *Religion in Life*, Spring 1967.

91. Norden interview with Alinsky.

92. "Saul Alinsky," *Current Biography*.

93. "Saul Alinsky," *Current Biography*.

94. Sanders, "Professional Radical."

95. Sanders, "Professional Radical."

96. Doering, "Philosopher and the Provocateur," p. 345.

97. "Plato on the Barricades."

98. Letter from the Bishop of London to Stanley Evans, 23 December 1946. I have drawn on the Stanley Evans archives in the University of Hull for this and other material.

99. David Loshak, letter to Stanley Evans, 4 September 1953.

100. Tom Driberg, letter to Stanley Evans, 18 December 1953.

101. Stanley Evans in *Religion and the People*, January 1957.

102. Evans Archives.

103. Harold Legerton, cited in *Stoke Newington and Hackney Observer,* 15 August 1958.

104. Stanley Evans, Lecture at Southwark Cathedral, 29 November 1962.

105. Stanley Evans, *In Evening Dress to Calvary* (London: SCM Press, 1965), p. 6.

106. "The Trinity" (Address to London group of Society of Socialist Clergy and Ministers, June 1952, ms. in Evans Archives).

107. Stanley Evans in *Junction* 8 (October–December 1959), p. 3.

108. Leaflet for *Junction*, January 1958.

109. Stanley Evans, *The Faith We Teach* (London: Jubilee Group and Church Literature Association, 1975). This paper was the last Evans ever prepared; it was delivered after his death in 1965.

110. Stanley Evans, sermon at Southwark Cathedral, 29 October 1961.

111. Stanley Evans in *Return to Reality*, p. 9.

112. Evans in *Religion and the People*, January 1957.

113. Stanley Evans, *The Social Hope of the Christian Church* (London: Hodder and Stoughton, 1965), p. 250.

114. Ruth Glass, *Clichés of Urban Doom* (Oxford: Blackwell, 1989), p. 3.

115. Ruth Glass, letter in *The Times*, 21 December 1973.

116. Ruth Glass, *Newcomers* (London: Centre for Urban Studies and Allen and Unwin, 1960), p. xi; *London's Newcomers* (Cambridge, MA: Harvard Univ. Press, 1961).

117. Ruth Glass, letters in *The Times*, 12 October 1964, 9 August 1965, 5 August 1967, 26 February 1968, 4 May 1968, and 4 August 1969. For a summary of these letters, see Kenneth Leech, *The Birth of a Monster* (London: Runnymede Trust, 1990).

118. Ruth Glass, letter in *The Times*, 5 August 1967.

119. Ruth Glass, letter in *The Times*, 20 September 1970.

120. Ruth Glass and John Westergaard, *London's Housing Needs* (London: Centre for Urban Studies, 1965), p. 10.

121. Ruth Glass, unpublished letter to *The Times*, 19 August 1982.

122. Ruth Glass, letter in *The Times*, 20 July 1963.

123. The word was first used in print in *London: Aspects of Change* (London: Centre for Urban Studies, 1964), reprinted in Glass, *Clichés of Urban Doom*, pp. 133–58. But Ruth Glass was using the word as early as 1958.

124. Ruth Glass, lettter in *The Times*, 8 June 1976.

125. Ruth Glass, letter in *The Guardian*, 10 May 1969.

126. Glass and Westergaard, *London's Housing Needs*, p. xi.

127. Ruth Glass, "Stability and Strife," *New Scientist*, 16 July 1964, pp. 155–56.

128. Ruth Glass, in *Conflict in Society*, ed. Anthony de Reuck and Julie Knight (London: J. and A. Churchill, 1966), p. 162.

129. Saint Anthony, cited in Benedicta Ward, *The Wisdom of the Desert Fathers* (Oxford: SLG Press, 1981), p. xv.

130. Alan Ecclestone, *The Night Sky of the Lord* (London: Darton, Longman and Todd, 1980), p. 39.

131. William Stringfellow, *The Politics of Spirituality* (Philadelphia: Westminster Press, 1984), p. 20.

132. Grace M. Jantzen, *Julian of Norwich: Mystic and Theologian* (London: SPCK, 1987), p. 57. See also Jean Leclercq, *The Love of Learning and the Desire for God* (London: SPCK, 1961; New York: Fordham Univ. Press, 1961).

133. J. N. Grou, *Manual for Interior Souls* (London: 1913), p. 16.

134. Walter Brueggemann, "The Formfulness of Grief," *Interpretation* 31 (1977), pp. 263–75.

135. Toni Morrison, *The Bluest Eye* (New York: Holt, Rinehart and Winston, 1970), p. 160.

136. Saint Basil, *Longer Rules* 7.

137. Aelred of Rievaulx, *Spiritual Friendship* (Kalamazoo, MI: Cistercian Publications, 1977).

138. See Kenneth Leech, *Spirituality and Pastoral Care* (London: Sheldon Press, 1986; Cambridge, MA: Cowley Press, 1989), pp. 55–65.

139. R. D. Hacking, *Such a Long Journey* (London: Mowbray, 1988), pp. 37, 38.

140. Christopher Rowland and Mark Corner, *Liberating Exegesis* (London: SPCK, 1990; Louisville, KY: Westminster John Knox, 1989), p. 138.

Chapter 5. Beyond the New Dark Age

Chapter epigraphs: Elie Wiesel, *The Town Beyond the Wall*, cited in D. J. Hall, *Lighten Our Darkness* (Philadelphia: Westminster Press, 1976), p. 9.
William Stringfellow, *The Politics of Spirituality* (Philadelphia: Westminster Press, 1984), p. 69.
Alasdair MacIntyre, *After Virtue*, pp. 244–45.

1. See Theodore Roszak, *The Making of a Counter Culture* (London: Faber, 1969).

2. On the counterculture, see Roszak, *The Making of a Counter Culture;* and Kenneth Leech, *Youthquake: The Growth of a Counter-culture Through Two Decades* (London: Sheldon Press, 1973).

3. *The Fundamentals* were published by Testimony Publishing Company, Chicago, from 1909 onward. The word *fundamentalist* was not, however, used until about 1920 and seems to have been coined by Curtis Lee Laws, editor of the Baptist paper *The Watchman-Examiner.* See Douglas Johnson,

"The Word 'Fundamentalist,' " *Christian Graduate*, March 1955, p. 22; George M. Marsden, *Understanding Fundamentalism and Evangelicalism* (Grand Rapids: Eerdmans, 1991), p. 57.

4. See T. S. Eliot, *The Idea of a Christian Society* (London: Faber, 1940); and *Notes Towards the Definition of Culture* (London: Faber, 1967).

5. Michael Saward, cited in *The Independent on Sunday*, 13 January 1991.

6. See Kenneth Leech, *The Social God* (London: Sheldon Press, 1981), chap. 10: "Is there a new religious fascism?" pp. 97–115.

7. Allan Bloom, *The Closing of the American Mind* (New York: Simon and Schuster, 1987).

8. See Viktor E. Frankl, *La Psychotherapie et son image de l'image de l'homme* (Paris: 1970), p. 150.

9. Martin Luther King, *Strength to Love* (London: Fontana, 1969; Minneapolis: Augsburg Fortress, 1981), p. 24. See my forthcoming book *Subversive Orthodoxy* for further discussion of this theme.

10. Augustine, Sermon 34:1–3.

11. Bhikhu Parekh, "Between Holy Text and Moral Void," *New Statesman and Society*, 24 March 1989, pp. 29–33.

12. Emily Brontë, in Karen Armstrong, *Tongues of Fire* (Harmondsworth: Penguin, 1987), pp. 44–45.

13. See Kenneth Leech, *Experiencing God* (San Francisco: Harper & Row, 1987); British title *True God* (London: Sheldon Press, 1985), pp. 421–22.

14. See Thomas C. Oden, *Pastoral Theology: Essentials of Ministry* (San Francisco: Harper & Row, 1983).

15. Walter Brueggemann, *Finally Comes the Poet* (Minneapolis: Fortress Press, 1989), p. 102.

16. Robert Bryan Sloan, Jr, *The Favourable Year of the Lord: A Study of Jubilary Theology in the Gospel of Luke* (Austin, TX: Schola Press, 1977), p. 39.

17. Walter L. Owensby, in *Social Themes of the Christian Year*, ed. Dieter T. Hessel (Philadelphia: Geneva Press, 1983), p. 75.

18. J. Lindblom, *Prophecy in Ancient Israel* (Oxford: 1962), p. 121.

19. Nicholas Berdyayev, *Freedom and the Spirit* (New York: Charles Scribners' Sons, 1935), p. 360.

20. Walter Brueggemann, "The Prophet as a Destabilizing Presence," in *The Pastor as Prophet*, ed. Earl E. Shelp and Ronald H. Sunderland (New York: Pilgrim Press, 1985), pp. 49–77. See also Brueggemann's *The Prophetic Imagination* (Philadelphia: Fortress Press, 1978), and many other works.

21. Alan Ecclestone, *The Night Sky of the Lord* (London: Darton, Longman and Todd, 1980), p. 37.

22. P. E. T. Widdrington in *The Return of Christendom* (London: Allen and Unwin, 1922), pp. 91–113.

23. Henry Sloane Coffin at the Edinburgh Missionary Conference 1910, cited by Philip Potter in *Your Kingdom Come: Mission Perspectives,* Report of the World Conference on Mission and Evangelism, Melbourne, 12–25 May 1980 (Geneva: World Council of Churches, 1980), p. 12.

24. Walter Rauschenbusch, *A Theology for the Social Gospel* (New York: Macmillan, 1917), p. 135.

25. See Norman Perrin, *Jesus and the Language of the Kingdom* (London: SCM Press, 1976).

26. Albert Nolan, *Biblical Spirituality* (Springs, South Africa: Order of Preachers, 1982), p. 57.

27. John Howard Yoder, *The Politics of Jesus* (Grand Rapids: Eerdmans, 1972), pp. 88–89.

28. Christopher Rowland, *Radical Christianity: A Reading of Recovery* (Cambridge: Polity Press, 1988), p. 8.

29. John A. T. Robinson, *The Body* (London: SCM Press, 1961; Louisville, KY: Westminster John Knox, 1977), p. 9.

30. Robinson, *The Body,* p. 51.

31. Jacob Jervell, *Luke and the People of God* (Minneapolis: Augsburg, 1972), p. 15.

32. Eric Abbott et al., *Catholicity* (London: Dacre Press, 1947), p. 13.

33. John Chrysostom, *In Ephes. Hom.* 3; Augustine, *Evangelium Joannis Tract,* 21. 8, etc.

34. Simon Tugwell, *Ways of Imperfection* (London: Darton, Longman and Todd, 1984; Springfield, IL: Templegate, 1985), pp. 8–9.

35. Daniel Berrigan, *America Is Hard to Find* (London: SPCK, 1973), pp. 77–78.

36. Robinson, *The Body,* p. 80.

37. Irenaeus, *Adv. Haer.* 4: 17: 5, etc.

38. Robert J. Karris, *Luke: Artist and Theologian* (New York: Paulist Press, 1985), p. 47.

39. Norman Perrin, *Rediscovering the Teaching of Jesus* (New York: Harper & Row, 1967), p. 107.

40. Wolfhart Pannenberg, *Christian Spirituality* (Philadelphia: Westminster Press, 1983), pp. 31–49.

41. *The Catholic Crusade 1918–1936* (London: Archive One, 1970), p. 17.

42. Frederick Hastings Smyth, *Sacrifice: A Doctrinal Homily* (New York: Vantage Press, 1953), pp. 87, 134.

43. John A. T. Robinson, *On Being the Church in the World* (London: SCM Press, 1964), pp. 59–60.

44. Robinson, *On Being the Church in the World*, p. 71.

45. Nicholas Arseniev, *Russian Piety* (London: Faith Press, 1964), p. 46 (Crestwood, NY: St. Vladimir's Seminary Press, 1964); Alexander Schmemann, *For the Life of the World* (Crestwood, NY: St. Vladimir's Seminary Press, 1973), p. 42.

46. E. L. Mascall, *The Christian Universe* (London: Darton, Longman and Todd, 1966), p. 163.

47. Rosemary Ruether in *Expanding the View*, ed. Marc H. Ellis and Otto Maduro (Maryknoll, NY: Orbis, 1990), p. 76.

48. Martin Luther King, *The Trumpet of Conscience* (London: Hodder and Stoughton, 1968; San Francisco: Harper, 1989), p. 26.

49. Wes Seeliger, *Western Theology* (Atlanta: Forum House, 1973).

50. Augustine, *Sermon 256*, in *Patrologia Latina*, ed. J. P. Migne, 38:1191–93. The sermon is read at Matins on the Saturday of the Thirty-fourth Week of the Year in the Roman Breviary.

INDEX

P. à 26